The
Of DOCTRINE
PROSPERITY

The Doctrine of Prosperity

The Doctrine of Prosperity

Copyright © 2018 By Chidi Collins Oparaojiaku
The Doctrine Of Prosperity

ISBN 978-0-9964267-9-4

All Rights Reserved.

No part of this publication may be reproduced, stored in a retrieval system, or transmitted in any form or by any means – electronic, mechanical, photocopy, recording, or any other except for brief quotations in printed reviews, without the prior permission of the authors who are the copyright owners.

All Scripture quotations are taken from the Kings James Version of the Bible, unless otherwise indicated.

The opinions expressed by the author in this book are not those of Rehoboth House

Book Available Online
amazon.com
ingramcontent.com

Author's Contact:
chidioparaojiaku@yahoo.com

Edited By:
Dr. Innocent Kasarachi

Cover And Interior Designed By:
Emeka Joshua Emeruem (Rehoboth House, Chicago)

Prints Internationally By Permission
First Print, February 2018 By Rehoboth Publishing, Lagos
rehobothpublishing@gmail.com

Published in USA by Rehoboth House, Chicago
info@rehobothhouseonline.com
www.rehobothhouseonline.com

The Doctrine of Prosperity

Table Of Contents

Dedication..i

Acknowledgments..ii

Introduction...iv

Chapter 1
God The Owner, We Are Managers..1

Chapter 2
Philosophy Of Management..27

Chapter 3
Human Resources Planning..59

Chapter 4
10 Immutable Laws..85

Chapter 5
7 Principles Of Wealth Creation..105

Chapter 6
Promises And Warnings About Money..................................141

Chapter 7
Principles For Achieving Financial Freedom.........................159

Chapter 8
The Budget As A Regulator..225

Chapter 9
Personal Financial Management (PFM).........................249

Chapter 10
God Hates Waste...275

Chapter 11
Types Of Business Organizations..283

Chapter 12
Develop A Speculator's Mentality......................................311

Chapter 13
Preparing For Retirement..317

Chapter 14
Start There..339

Chapter 15
Develop A Zero Mentality Thinking.................................349

Chapter 16
Total Prosperity..355

Dedication

To the poor and wretched in thinking and creativity.

The Doctrine of Prosperity

Acknowledgments

As with any major undertaking, this book has been a team effort. I am indebted to those people, children of God, who laboured with me by making wonderful sacrifices and contributions to the success of this work.

I appreciate Kasarachi Innocent and Dame Gift Roman who meticulously spent time on this work. God will bless them and grant them their heart's desires, in Jesus name. The same goes for Mrs. Chioma Iwunze who took the pain to type the manuscript. May the Lord bless your efforts.

To my wife, Joy Obiageli Oparaojiaku and children: Adaukwu, Chukwuka, Chukwuebuka, and Chidi, I remain indebted, for their prayerful support and understanding.

All those whose materials and thoughts proved helpful in putting together this work, we have properly acknowledged.

Above all, eternity would not be long enough to express my gratitude to you, Lord Jesus. Thank you Lord for the inspiration and for making the publication of this book possible.

To all, I say God bless and remain rapturable!

His Bondservant
Chidi Oparaojiaku, PhD.

The Doctrine of Prosperity

Introduction

It is undoubtedly interesting teaching people how to serve God better with their finances, but it is much more interesting bringing people face to face with their ignorance about financial matters.

What you don't desire you will not get, no matter how many people who strive to force it on you. The issue here is the difference between what you want and what you need. There are laws and principles governing everything we do and everything we will become on this earth. Each time these natural laws and principles are obeyed, you are bound to be successful in your life pursuits. Otherwise, you are in for failure.

Every game has a principle and law governing the players. For instance, the game of football is usually played under specific rules and regulations, and a goal is deemed to be scored if the players play within the ambits of these prescribed rules and regulations. I once watched a football match between Nigeria and another nation in which this other country scored an otherwise winning goal against Nigeria, but it was disallowed because it was scored from an offside position.

A glaring lack of adequate understanding of the science of finance by both the educated and uneducated, rich and poor, the businessman and professional, student and lecturer, is what prompted the writing of this book. The practical aspect of the science of finance is something lacking in the curriculum of our higher institutions; our schools do not teach students how to create wealth and how to use the created wealth to recreate more wealth. Our schools today are like a master carpenter who only instructs his apprentices on structures and platforms without providing them superglues, nails, and wood to hold together such structures and platforms.

This is the main reason some people start well but end up poorly, while some begin very promisingly only to crumble mid-way – they were just instructed on how to use the structures and platforms but not how to build them. Thus, once the existing structures and platforms wear out or become obsolete, the users find themselves in the middle of the sea of confusion. Till now, in our nation, we have succeeded only in creating structure-and-platform users and not structure-and-platform builders.

As you plan to use your finances, you need to plan how to use the expected returns to generate more wealth. Each time I teach on this vexatious area of our Christian faith, I observe that we have more finance users than finance builders. Users attract public admiration while builders control the foundation of the nation and dictate who gets what. I have also seen slaves in coorporate outfits, struggling and working hard for another man who is relaxing somewhere, only to surface at the end of the month to pay his slaves peanuts out of the large incomes they have earned for him. It is slaves that cannot go on vacation without the permission of their bosses or behave the way they feel or even improve on the job. They rush out every morning and return home very late - worn out. They cannot think for themselves; instead, they think for others, so they are more of thinking machines programmed to think for others! They wear expensive clothes to cover up their imposed complex.

I have seen people who eat the whole of their seeds at harvest time, thereby having nothing to replant, yet expecting to reap during the next harvest period. This is just not possible. A farmer who does not have a seed to sow during planting season should not expect anything at harvest time. It is simple mathematics. There is power in the seed to bring much more seeds, but that power is not unlocked until you put the seed in the soil. It could be in the soil of business – in form of investment – or preservation for future use. When no seed is planted, no harvest is possible.

Bayless Conley puts it this way-

- *When it is sown, it grows! Contained in a tiny mustard seed is the entire blueprint for the plant. Its shape, colour, and fragrance are all locked inside the seed. But when its sown, that power is unleashed. As it begins to grow, it even pushes out of the way, stones that may stand between it and the light of the day. It pushes towards the sky, stretches out its branches, and says: 'Here I am'".*

There is usually seed in all the money that come your way; no matter how much it is, there is a seed in it. Each time the seed is sown, the power in that seed is sparked into action, and it pushes every trace of poverty that may hinder it, out of the way.

An unplanned life usually ends up in regrets and frustration. Start today to reflect on your past mistakes and take necessary steps to correct them, and you will see a new life dawn for you.

The Bible is not silent about Biblical economics and financial management. The earliest economics were centered on the family and household (Oikos) which included, not only the nuclear family but also the clan and tribe. This extended family was the primary center of production, distribution, and consumption. With time, this center of economic activity shifted to the state from the family and clan (polis). Joseph taking control of Egypt's grain supplies during the seven years of plenty to sell back during the seven lean years is a typical example of the (polis) controlling the economy. This progressed to new model forms of economy, hence introduction of laziness and lack of creativity. People's needs were supplied centrally, and ownership of property and self-controlled wealth disappeared from the economic well-being of the people and the hunger to work reduced. This affected the church's financial lifestyle, and her economic model gradually became secularized, developing into other collectives.

Many of us have not taken seriously the Biblical principles that support economics. Principles such as hard work, property ownership, investment, savings, trading, wealth creation, rest and management as explained in the scriptures, yet very few church leaders are interested in these principles. Economic hardship and arguments concerning finances and its holder are the number one immediate cause of trouble, both in marriages and families. Yet very few couples give it the attention it requires but will spend more time and resources planning a three-week vacation after wedding and leaving the most essential aspect of their personal and socio-economic responsibility. A significant aspect of our spiritual growth as Christians is the need to think economically and biblically. God owns everything, and it is His will to do whatever He wants to do with it. As God's creation, we do not own anything, even our own bodies, and resources. But having been made in God's image and likeness, we have a delegated authority or ownership. This privilege gives us the opportunity to plan our economic and financial life under God's perfect will. This single opportunity given to us by God is the reason for this book.

The book is divided into sixteen chapters with each chapter dealing with an aspect of our human needs. Chapter one states that God is the owner of all resources while we are managers. Chapter two discusses the philosophy of management which states that every management success derives its management principles from Biblical principles. Chapter 3 handles human resources planning, which is the process that links the human resources needs of an organization to its strategic plan to ensure that staffing is sufficient, qualified, and competent enough to achieve the organization's objectives. Chapter 4 outlines ten (10) immutable laws, which explain that whatever dream you have, it is in all in your hand to accomplish. Chapter 5 deals with the seven (7) principles of wealth creation, which revolve around the ability to create wealth. Chapter 6 enumerates the promises of money and its warnings. Chapter 7 talks of principles for achieving financial freedom while Chapter 8 teaches us about the budget as the regulator of our finances. Chapter 9 discusses personal financial management while Chapter 10 informs us that God hates waste and teaches how to handle our wasteful attitudes and behaviour. Chapter 11 describes types of business organizations while Chapter 12 deliberates on how to develop a speculator's mentality. Chapter 13 reveals how to prepare for retirement while Chapter 14 says: start here. That is, start wherever you are now without regrets. Chapter 15 asks us to develop zero mentality thinking, that is, to overcome your previous mistakes without allowing it to distort your present strength while the last Chapter of the book summarizes with the topic, total prosperity, and states that true prosperity has four dimensions namely: spiritual, mental, physical and financial.

This book is put together to stir your heart and set you on the journey to where you rightly belong. This is a seed in your hand, and it is ready to be sown in any willing heart today for a better tomorrow.

CHAPTER ONE

God The Owner, We Are Managers

God owns all what we think we own; we are only managers of God's business. Whether it is company you struggled to establish, or marriage, or children you raised up, or career/profession you built, or leadership you merited, etc., you are only a manager. You don't own instead you manage. Managers take responsibility while owners decide what to do with the manager's responsibility. The best you can become in all of this is to prepare to give account when the owner requests for it. Managers work on assigned duty; it is their responsibility to see to the actualization of the owner's vision and expectation.

Who is a Manager?

Some definitions will build up a collective position for us here. A manager is:

- An individual who is in charge of a certain group of tasks, or a particular subject of a company. A manager often has a staff of people who report to him or her.

Henri Fayol, a French management theorist, defines manager

as a person who manages or is in charge of something. A manager can control departments in companies, or guide the people who work for them. Managers must be able to do the following:

- Plan Organize
- Lead
- Coordinate
- Control

On his part, Peter Drucker defines a manager by describing his tasks. He stated that managers do the following:

They Set Objectives: The manager sets goals for the group and decides what work needs to be done to meet those goals.

They Organize: The manager divides the work into manageable activities, and designates people to accomplish the tasks that need to be done.

They Motivate and Communicate: The manager creates a team out of his people, through decisions on pay, placement, promotion and his communications with the team. Peter Drucker also calls it the integrating function of the manager.

They Measure: Managers establish appropriate targets and yardsticks and analyse, appraise and interpret performance.

They Develop People: People are company's most valuable assets, and managers develop this valuable and important asset.

After Henry Mintzberg's study of five executives in 1960s

to determine the role of managers, he concluded with a role definition of managers as follows:

INTERPERSONAL ROLES: Managers should endeavor to develop a rapport with their employees and look into their relationship with others. This is necessary to maintain a friendly climate in the organization. They do this through the following:

Representative: The manager is seen as an icon of status and authority, as a representative of the department or the organization to others.

Leader: A leader is one who can protect the organization during crisis, motivate and direct employees, recruit and assign appropriate jobs to encourage self-development, provide training if necessary and appraise regularly.

Networking Chief: He is the link between different levels of the organization, enhancing, sharing of information, maintenance of goodwill and efficient networking.

INFORMATIONAL ROLES: This is very important because it deals with information sharing and handling.

Overseer: This involves assessment of internal operations, analyzing their success ratio, problems, and objective opportunities.

The Supplier And The Distributor: This has to do with the procurement of relevant information required by the company people from the external environment and then distributing it wherever necessary.

Brand Ambassador (Image maker): He must be capable enough to represent the organization before any external body regarding the company's plans, profits, policies, results, decisions, vision, and mission. He projects the image of the organization.

DECISIONAL ROLES: Managerial roles rotate around decision-making; there are four major decisional roles every manager should make.

Entrepreneur: They initiate many of the new projects and assignments for improving the performance and the image of their organization. They practically predict unforeseen circumstances, should be able to face risks, take sound decisions, acquire and utilize resources in an optimum manner.

Disturbance Handler: They are responsible for maintaining the culture of the organization, analyzing conflicts and resolving such conflicts and producing a fair judgment on each occasion.

Resource Allocator: They are responsible for the allocation of organizational resources - physical, monetary or human. This function is carried out through a schedule of measuring task requirement in each department, finding supplies, budget preparation, and implementation.

Negotiator: They act as negotiators when they enter into discussions with other bodies/groups of organizations.

From the various definitions, we discover that there are some definitions that place the manager as "all-in-all" while some place him as a link between employees and employers, yet there are those that see him as an Entrepreneur. Usually, managers are not owners; they are rather employees of a high status who manage the organization on behalf of the owners. Some owners are called Chief Executive Officer (CEO), some are called shareholders while others are called co-managers. Ordinarily, managers do not own any organization instead they manage the organizations within the roles we stated earlier.

Having defined and established the roles of managers in organizations, let us look at the Bible to establish if there were managers mentioned or discussed in the Word of God. The reason we need to do this is first, to redirect our focus to Biblical Economics. Secondly, to prove that every organization and profession draws its policies, vision, and mission from the Bible. Lastly, to affirm that there is no profession, organization or even theory that does not draw its foundation from the Bible.

Managers In The Bible

ADAM and his wife **EVE** were given the authority and responsibility as the first managers of the earth. God appointed them to manage His world for Him, setting their boundaries, limitations and provisional security for their duty. Every manager has his assignment outlined at the point of employment. Likewise, they were given the details of their assignment on day one of their appointment. God blessed them and said to them;

> *"Be fruitful and increase in number, fill the earth and subdue it. Rule over the fish of the sea and the birds of the air and over every living creature that moves on the*

ground" (Genesis 1^{28}).

By this, Adam became God's representative, set-man, point-man, manager, administrator and coordinator of his economy. The charge above should form Adam's Mission statement, the expectation of the owner of the world. Adam was not created without a defined purpose. The mission statement given to Adam includes the following:

- Be fruitful and increase in number
- Fill the earth and subdue it
- Rule over the fish of the sea and birds of the air and over every living creature.

This mission statement is all-encompassing. The mission statement of Adam forms the domain of his assignment, which is captured in two broad statements:

- **To work it**
- **Take care of it.**

> *"The Lord God took the man and put him in the garden of Eden to work it and take care of it" (Genesis 2^{15}).*

The man did not establish the Garden of Eden; rather he was "put" in there by the owner of the Garden with two major assignments that included to work it and take care of it. We will look at this manager again in a broad perspective later.

The next manager recorded in the Bible is Mr. **Noah**. When the earth became corrupt that God could no more tolerate it, He called for total destruction, with exception of Noah and his family. He appointed Noah to manage His estate for Him.

> *"The Lord saw how great man's wickedness on the earth had become and that every inclination of the thoughts of his heart was evil all the time" (Genesis 6^5).*

Now the earth was corrupt in God's sight and was full of violence. God saw how corrupt the earth had become for all the people on it had corrupted their ways. So God said to Noah, I am …" (Genesis 6 $^{11\text{-}7:6}$). Through the scripture above, we can observe the owner's role and instructions to his manager. He informed Noah of his pains, intentions, and conclusions. In Genesis 6:18, He appointed Noah His manager. Noah was to supervise and build an ark according to the specifications given to him, according to the dimensions detailed to him. He was not to initiate any change at all; he was to work according to the owner's directions. Remember before then, there was no ark or boat or ship built anywhere in the whole world, so the ark built was first designed by God and every other ship or boat builders got their technology from God's masterpiece of Noah's ark. The technology is from God. When we read verses 15-16, we will observe the specifications. God is the owner; we are mere managers. We will return to this point shortly.

Another manager in the Bible is **Jacob**. He was appointed to manage his mother's brother's business, whose name was Laban.

> *"Laban said to him, just because you are a relative of*

mine should you work for me for nothing? Tell me what your wages should be" (Genesis 29^{15}).

Managers receive wages while owners keep and manage the wealth of the organization. Managers can grow to become partners. Jacob grew in the business of Laban to become a partner (Genesis 30$^{31-36}$). For twenty years, Jacob acted as Laban's manager (Genesis 31^{35}). We will also return to this later.

The next is **Joseph,** the Apostle of Management. First, Joseph was appointed the manager of Potiphar's household even as a slave.

> *"The Lord was with Joseph and he prospered and he lived in the house of his Egyptian master. When his master saw that the Lord was with him and that the Lord gave him success in everything he did, Joseph found favour in his eyes and became his attendant. Potiphar put him in charge of his household, and he entrusted to his care everything he owned" (Genesis 39 $^{2-4}$).*

Potiphar owned the household, but he needed a man who carried God's divine presence to manage it for him, and he found that person in Joseph. The Bible did record that everything in Potiphar's house prospered from that day. So managers can bring business empires down or top list depending on whose presence they are carrying.

> *"....The Lord was with him, he showed him kindness and granted him favour in the eyes of the prison warden. So the warden put Joseph in charge of all those held in the prison, and he was made responsible for all that was done*

> *there. The warden paid no attention to anything under Joseph's care because the Lord was with Joseph and gave him success in whatever he did" (Genesis 39$^{21-23}$).*

Joseph was once again given an opportunity in the prison to manage other inmates and all the goings-on in the environment. Furthermore, Joseph was entrusted with National leadership in Egypt, after the king had his dreams and none of the wise men among his experts could give meaning to the dreams. Their failure introduced Joseph who was as at then in prison. When the information got to Pharaoh as concerning the capacity of Joseph to interpret dreams, he ordered for his release. He interpreted the dream by the grace of God, and the king appointed him next in command in Egypt. His terms of reference to Joseph included managing the first seven years of abundance and the second part of the seven years of famine.

> *"Then Pharaoh said to Joseph, 'since God has made all this known to you, there is no one so discerning and wise as you. You shall be in charge of my palace, and all my people are to submit to your orders. Only with respect to the throne will I be greater than you" (Genesis 41$^{39-40}$).*

We have kings, Presidents, and leaders who have dreams and burdens for their nation or kingdom but lack interpreters of these kings', presidents' and leaders' dreams. The wise men of Pharaoh's time could not offer meaning to the vision/dreams of the king and if Joseph was not sourced for, maybe, the wise men would have given their own interpretations. This is the major challenge of world leadership. Wise men who may act as representatives, persons trained in special areas, special assistants and personal assistants, may not have the capacity or knowledge of the leader's vision and as such, cannot give interpretation. Thank God for the wise men of Pharaoh's time who owned up to their inability to interpret the dreams. The confusion is everywhere in the world where men are appointed into political offices not on merit but on grounds of political compensation. Such people will definitely produce policies that are anti-people, not by intention but out of ignorance. The king understood the implications of proper interpretation of his dreams/vision to his nation. Again he also knew that wrong interpretation of the dreams would surely spread down to the nation and he did not want to be superstar. He acknowledged his limitation; hence he called for people to help him champion and interpret the dreams. This was why he was worried about the dreams (Genesis 41:8).

MOSES: Moses was appointed by God to bring about the deliverance and leadership of Israel to the Promised Land. When the people of Israel were suffering in the land of Egypt, they cried out to God in their pain and torture, God heard their cries and mandated Moses to go and deliver them from the hands of Pharaoh the king, "And now the cry of the Israelites has reached me, and I have seen the way the Egyptians are oppressing them. So now go. I am sending you to Pharaoh to bring my people the Israelites out of Egypt" (Exodus 3:9-10). His schedule mandate is to **"GO AND BRING GOD'S PEOPLE, THE ISRAELITES**

OUT OF EGYPT." He was sent or entrusted, put in charge, by those statements, he wasn't the owner rather a manager of God's people. Throughout that project of deliverance and taking the people to the Promised Land, Moses was always going back to God to seek clarifications on issues beyond his capacity. Few examples include the following:

> *Exodus 5$^{22-23}$, "Moses returned to the Lord and said, O Lord, why have you brought trouble upon this people? Is this why you sent me? Ever since I went to Pharaoh to speak in your name, he has brought trouble upon this people and you have not rescued your people at all."*

God mandated Moses to speak as His manager, and he obeyed but the aftermath reaction of the demand of Moses was more labour and very stressful conditions than before. God seemed to be quiet about the development and of a truth, Moses had no answer to the congregants' questions of the cause of their present predicament. However he had to go back to God. Managers are not owners rather managers are limited by their terms of employment. God is the owner of every business both in the church and outside the church. Managers should borrow a leaf from Moses, who did not manufacture excuses for failure but rather went to the owner of the business. And the owner of the business, responded in a very powerful way when He said **"Now you will see what I will do to Pharaoh" (Exodus 6^{1a}).** The displaying power and awesomeness of God prevailed over Pharaoh who drove them out from his country and the same invisible hand or power beyond the veil brought the end of Pharaoh.

After the death of Moses the servant of God, **Joshua** was appointed by God to lead the people to the Promised Land. Joshua became God's manager of His people. "Be strong and courageous, because you will lead these people to inherit the land I swore to their fathers to give them", and in order to have a very successful managerial tenure, the Lord went further to give him the principles to succeed in his new assignment: "Be strong and very courageous. Be careful to obey all the law my servant Moses gave you; do not turn from it to the right or to the left, that you may be successful wherever you go. Do not let this book of the law depart from your mouth, meditate on it day and night, so that you may be careful to do everything written in it. Then you will be prosperous and successful (Joshua 1^{7-8}).

Church leaders, Bishops, Archdeacons, Presbyters, Overseers, Apostles, Presidents and Founders, etc., are mere managers with a mandate. It is absolutely wrong when we claim or declare ourselves owners. We don't have the capacity to answer or be allowed to be addressed as such. We are ordinary servants, who by the mercies of God, are called to manage God's empire. We are to be responsible for the assignment but not sit as owners of the assignment. The description of ownership has created idol personalities and moulded mortal gods who assume God's glory. King Herod assumed the honour and glory due God and we read that worms ate him up before his subjects (Acts 12 $^{21-31}$). To avoid being eaten up by worms, give God his dues and stop where He has kept you. Man over time, has proved lack in this relationship. He has claimed what he has not, and right from creation he has remained a victim of ignorance. Man, you are not in control rather you are under control. The little power or authority granted to you does not put you in control but under control by the owner. Jay O'keefe refers to man's misunderstanding of this truth as "**OUR LUST FOR AUTONOMY.**"

Quest For Autonomy

God created man with the burning desire for autonomy, to do whatever he wants to do and the way he wants to do it, without question outside of him. Man has refused to acknowledge his position as a manager or steward rather he wants to be addressed as owner. Walter stated in his thoughts from the *Diary of Desperate Man*, when God created Adam and Eve, He placed them in a perfect environment, no sin, pollution, opposition, and no prohibitions, with the exception of eating of the tree of the knowledge of good and evil. Genesis records no other command given to our first parents. The issue of the tree was who gets to determine what is good and evil: what is in my best interest and what is not? This issue focused man's struggle with God. Satan said that if they were able to decide what was good and evil for themselves, they would be like God. You can see why taking of the fruit was such a temptation. Note that Adam and Eve's thirst for autonomy came before the fall. It brought about the fall. God created them with a desire to be autonomous or have autonomy, and then asked that they limit this appetite by allowing God alone to determine what was or was not in their interest. This same struggle remains with us today.

It will interest you to know that this suggestion is still on. This reflects in the number of churches we have in our world. Men could not bear staying under any authority in which they are not in control. Even among the mainland churches, there have been inner wrangles and infightings, sabotage and blackmail, all emanating from the quest for autonomy. Autonomy has virtually destroyed brotherhood; autonomy has abolished respect and honour. Dignity and courtesy have been thrown to the winds because of autonomy. Lovely relationships have been broken because of the hunger for autonomy. The desire for self-rule and self-design which is part of the man being created in God's image, has also demeaned the decorum of God's intentions. So, the origin of our desire for independence is creation, but like Adam and Eve, we are unwilling to surrender that desire and submit to God, to let Him decide what is best for us and what is not. This is exactly what Jesus came to correct when He yielded Himself to God in carrying out his mandate. He taught us in Philippians that even if we are created with the desire for autonomy, we can still surrender it to God who knows the best for us all.

> *"Your attitude should be the same as that of Christ Jesus; who being in the very nature of God, did not consider equality with God something to be grasped, but made himself nothing, taking the very nature of a servant, being made in human likeness. And being found in appearance*

> *as a man, he humbled himself and became obedient to death, even death on a cross" (Philippians 2$^{5-8}$).*

We are admonished to allow the attitude of self-sacrificing humility to dot our way of life as believers. If there is anybody who needs to insist on autonomy, it is our Lord Jesus Christ, who was in the very nature God, but chose otherwise to humbly accept a disposition of emptied life and the life of commoner. We are called today to choose that way of life and shun the quest for autonomy. In Mathew 4:1-10, Satan tempted Jesus with this lust for autonomy, he (Satan), wanted him to choose his own way, he wanted him to live in disobedience to God's mandate, he wanted him to think that He is also God, he wanted him to revolt at his father's instruction, but Jesus understood him and in all attempts he made through three classic temptations, Jesus defeated him unlike Adam and Eve who yielded to his tricks. Jesus showed us by example that it is possible to humbly accept God's choice, because he knows the best for us. He makes choices for our good, even when it seems to us to be negative. Romans 8^{28}, "And we know that in **all things** God works for the good of those who love him, who have been called according to his purpose." "All things" is a package, whether it is perceived as a good or bad, it is "all things." God knows the best for us. He has our best interest at heart, we cannot wish ourselves better than God's wishes; anything short of this is quest for autonomy which negates God's authority and ownership over our lives, turning stone into bread, being like God and assuming ownership. Adam and Eve did the same thing when they disobeyed the instruction barring them from eating from the tree in the middle of the garden. The tower of Babel initiators had autonomy in mind when they chose to erect a tower to meet God in heaven, thereby making a monument for themselves. Then they said, "come, let us build for ourselves a city, with a tower that reaches to the heavens so that we may make a name for ourselves and not be scattered over the face of the whole earth" (Genesis 11[4]). Autonomy has been the bane of our collective existence.

The tribal, kindred and village wars all over the place is the outcome of the spirit of autonomy. You own nothing; rather whatever you have is given to you in trust to hold for the owner. Even when Bishops are elected and consecrated, they are elected for a vacant 'See' and enthroned on behalf of the church, not to boss her but to manage or administer her. The lust for autonomy has created a mixture of inferior and superior blunders.

My dear Bishop, you own no Diocese or church, rather you are an employee of the Diocese whose paramount head is saddled with the responsibility of organizing and managing inputs and outputs.

The plague of man is the desire to want to be in control, be in charge, be able to elect, to detect how everything around him moves, wanting to take decisions without being supervised and coordinating his environment without interference from God. For him, God should continue to be in heaven but should not determine or detect how things work out here. Some have called it human rights, others freedom of speech and action, still some others call it development and civilization. Even animals, birds and reptiles have their rights of protection and their self-acclaimed lawyers who defend their rights in the court of law. Women have initiated women liberation, questioning why they should be described with prepositions like she or her, some others have adopted their father's name even when they are properly married. It is the consequences of lust for autonomy.

This quest for autonomy reveals our discontentment. Why must we not be like God, do things in our way and choose our principles and priorities, do things differently, bring to bear our ingenuity and strategic thinking? Lack of contentment is as a result of lust for autonomy. That is the same sin that dethroned Adam and Eve from the empire of authority to mere cowards; from control, dominion, subdue and multiplication, to fearful agents or managers; from stately status to just tenants at the Garden of Eden.

We Were Not Given Rather Entrusted

The earlier we understand that in the things of life, we are not given, rather we are entrusted, the better for us, the faster our struggles will cease, the faster our pains and regret will be over. Then, we will be able to submit and surrender to the owner who knows what best fits us. First, it must be established that God brought you to this earth and it is His will for you to take your humble place of honour as a manager, and do His biddings. Everything on earth belongs to God and as such, we must develop the attitude of our Lord Jesus Christ, who considered nothing to insist on His Godness with His father, rather He adopted the attitude of a servant, when actually He is God himself. The Lord Jesus Christ confirmed to us by this attitude that God owns all our possessions. He created all things for his good pleasure, and He never transferred or relinquished the ownership of His creation to man. So recognizing God's ownership is crucial in allowing Jesus Christ to be the Lord of all we do. Deuteronomy 10[1] says, "

> *To the Lord your God belong the heavens, even the highest heavens, the earth and everything in it." The scripture announces the real owner of the whole heavens and earth and those who are managers. Psalm 50[10-12] confirms who is in-charge, "For every animal of the forest is mine and the cattle on a thousand hills. I know every bird in the mountains and the creatures of the field are mine. If I were hungry I would not tell you, for the world is mine, and all that is in it. So for those who rear animals and make money from it, remember that they all belong to God.*

God wants us to acknowledge our dependence on him by accepting our position as managers, not owners, and giving Him thanks offerings for his mercies, and also by praying to him in times of need. Those who acknowledge Him, expect His mercies and gracious answers to their prayers. In the scripture passage above, God says the following belong to Him; every beast of the forest, the cattle upon the thousand hills, every bird of the mountain and creatures of the field. The whole world belongs to God, but is under the control of His servants who will give Him account at the close of the age. The only way to be on the safe side and to be counted worthy is to transfer ownership of all our perceived possessions to the Lord. We must give up claim to ownership and autonomy of all that we have. We are mere stewards or better put, managers. A steward is a manager of someone else's possessions or business. The Lord has mandated and commissioned us to be stewards or managers and our collective responsibility as stewards is summed up in the word: 'faithfulness', regardless of how much He has entrusted to us.

One graphic scripture that illustrates ownership and servant relationship is recorded in the Gospel of St. Mathew 25[14-30]. Jesus, while describing the nature of the kingdom of God, gave a parable about a man or an owner of a Business Empire, who had on the whole, eight talents which he shared to his servants according to their abilities. In the parable, the king or owner wanted to travel to a far country. He decided to put both his business and servants to work. So he gave five talents to one of the three servants, two to the second one while to the third one, he gave one talent, and told them to invest and multiply them during his absence or trip. On his return, he summoned them to give account of the business or investment. They were not the owners; rather they were stewards to manage the talents. The first two who received five talents and two talents respectively were commended by their master while the third who could not multiply his talent received the rebuke of his life. This parable simply reveals to us that we shall give account to the owner of our life someday; since He is the source of everything according to scriptures (Phil. 4[19]; Proverbs 8[20]).

It will be wonderful to state here as we close this chapter that God owns everything. As creator of the universe, God owns His creation. The Bible is replete with this truth. Since He created the universe and everything in it, it is His to do with it as He pleases and for His good pleasure. This includes the wealth of individuals and nations. As God's creation and servants, we do not own or control anything in its real sense, not even our own lives or bodies. However, having been made in God's image and after His likeness, we have and operate what is called delegated ownership. Haggai 2[8] confirms this position, **"The silver is mine and the gold is mine declares the Lord Almighty."** Psalm 24[1], further agrees with the idea of God owning everything when it states, **"the earth and the fullness thereof belong to the Lord and all those who live within."** So whatever we possess does not really belong to us rather to God, we are simply entrusted with our possession. Therefore, we are trustees, not owners. God owns while we are appointed managers. This is why we must be careful how we live our lives, because we were given this life to manage on behalf of the giver and it is required of all stewards, trustees, and all God's administrators, to prepare for account day. The Bible says we shall be called upon to give account on the Account Day, how we lived and managed this God-given opportunity.

As we observed from the talents given to the three stewards

according to their abilities, nobody will be called upon to give account of what has not been entrusted to him, rather we will be required to give account of assigned duties and assignments commissioned. The reward for good managers is same, no matter the volume of success. The reward remains a commendation. On the other hand, the punishment for bad managers is also equal in measure. Whatever you are given by the author of life, be it ability, capacity, resources, skill, creativity, management expertise - you will be required to give account to the ideal owner. We are also expected to give our earthly delegated owners account if we are charged with any assignment. Responsibility goes with accountability. We cannot afford to be carefree with our mandate and assignment given to us. If we know that one day we will be called upon to render stewardship account, we will be serious with our divine assignment as a people.

Without God many of us were nobody, we were abandoned, forsaken and despised by our friends, family members, pals and peer group when God picked us up and cleansed us from the guilt of sins, rewrote our story and appointed us to join in the management of His estate and kingdom resources. It is therefore astonishing how we forget so soon. We have gone our ways thinking we are smart, clever and well-connected to have merited our current positions. The Lord in Ezekiel 17[24] while letting us know the awesome power did say,

> *"All the trees of the field will know that I the Lord bring*

down the tall tree and make the low tree grow tall, I dry up the green tree and make the dry tree flourish. I the Lord have spoken, and will do it."

This represents the vanity and emptiness of man, especially those who hold authority. God has introduced here that the kings and rulers of the whole world hold the authority for God's pleasure. He can decide to bring any of them down and raise the other without consultation, because they hold the authority for Him. The economy of various nations cannot survive without God's approval, it does not matter the economic policies of such nations. Before our very eyes and time, we have seen sophisticated economies collapse in their numbers and minor economies rise in the world market. Before the economy of nations like United States of America and United Kingdom were incontestably superb, but today they literally depend on China for almost all their economic demands. China has been pointed out as one of the biggest economies in the world today, but it is the Lord who decides who goes down and when and who goes up and when. None of these decisions resides with man.

Few years ago it was announced that Nigeria is an investment destination and biggest economy in Africa. Meanwhile, her people are hungry each day and struggle to receive salaries worked for upward of twelve months in some cases. Her people struggle to have a good square meal a day while her per capital income index is about the lowest in the world. All these point to the fact that God is in perfect control of His world.

We were not given but entrusted. The earlier we realize this fact and drop our autonomy mentality the better for our good. You don't own anything rather you are a steward who will be required to give account at the appropriate time.

In concluding this chapter, it will be noteworthy to consider few questions God asked Job during his ordeal.

Who is this that darkens my counsel with words without knowledge? Brace yourself like a man; I will question you and you shall answer me.

> *Where were you when I laid the earth's foundation? Tell me, if you understand who marked off its dimensions. Surely you know: who stretched a measuring line across it? On what were its footing set, or who laid its cornerstone (Job 38$^{2-5}$)?*

> *Who shuts up the sea behind doors when it burst forth from the womb, when I made the clouds, its garment and wrapped it in thick darkness, when I fixed limits for it and set its doors and bars in place, when I said, this far you may come and no further, here is where your proud waves halt? (Job 38 $^{8-11}$).*

> *What is the way to the abode of light? And where does darkness reside? Can you take them to their places? Do you know the paths to their dwellings? (Job 38 $^{19-20}$)*

> *Have you entered the storehouse of the snow or seen*

storehouses of the hail which I reserve for times of trouble, for days of war and battle? What is the way to the place where the lightning is dispersed or the place where the east winds are scattered over the earth? Who cuts a channel for the torrents of rain and a path for the thunderstorm, to water a land where no man lives, a desert with no one in it, to satisfy a desolate wasteland and make it sprout with grass? Does the rain have a father? Who fathers the drops of dew? From whose womb comes the ice? Who gives birth to the frost from the heavens when the waters become hard as stone, when the surface of the deep is frozen? (Job 38 $^{22-30}$).

Will the one who contends with the Almighty correct him? Let him who accuses God answer him (Job 40^2).

No one is fierce enough to rouse him, who then is able to stand against me? Who has a claim against me that I must pay? Everything under heaven belongs to me (Job 41$^{10-11}$).

This is what God the Lord says – he who created the heavens and stretched them out, who spread out the earth and all that comes out of it, who gives breath to its people, and life to those who walk on it. I, the Lord here called you in righteousness; I will take hold of your hand, I will keep you and will make you to be a covenant for the people and a light for the Gentiles, to open eyes that are blind, to free captives from prison and to release from the dungeon those who sit in darkness. I am the Lord, that is my name! I will not give my glory to another or my praise to idols (Isaiah 42$^{5-8}$).

God The Owner, We Are Managers

The Doctrine of Prosperity

Reflection On Chapter 16

Personal Notes:

===== Guided Action Plan =====

CHAPTER 2

Philosophy Of Management

Every management success derives its principles from Biblical principles. Regrettably, most clergy or ministers of the gospel have not acquired the capacity to manage large, sophisticated and dynamic organizations. The Church is an organization and should be seen as such. Organizational managers must realize that management principles are not derived outside the biblical truth. The world belongs to its creator who is God, He alone has the whole principles to manage its people and resources and develop producers of the resources. All knowledge and wisdom belong to the source. We are the workman of God, with commissioned mandates to do His will all the time. Whatever happens in this world manifests God's ultimate intention. He does not make mistakes neither does He owe anyone an apology. These principles for great successful management skill are all found in the bible. Every economy, both super and lean, have confirmed their sources to derive from Biblical foundations and principles.

In other professions or organizations, most managers and leaders grow through the ranks and files, but it is not so in Christian organizations, especially in Africa. Leaders are groomed to fit into future leadership roles in organizations, but in Africa people can get up and claim they are called, and the following day, they start preaching and leading thousands to a destination they have no principle of driving. Many ministers feel capable of providing spiritual leadership and direction to their followers but unfortunately not very many feels adequately prepared to provide leadership for faith-based organizations.

Many seminaries and Bible Colleges are reviewing their curriculum to meet the desired goal of present-day organizational management. Before now, the church was not seen as an organization instead a spiritual body that does not need high capacity trained personnel. However, all that has changed, hence the need for well-trained, highly qualified and balanced leaders in Christian organizations is becoming a frequent topic of discussion in various Christian gatherings.

One major mistake is: this quest has led to adopting secular management philosophy and principles to run Christian organizations. Secular management philosophies and principles are often humanistic and materialistic. They use authority and power to run business. Such management philosophies "lord it over" the people and control them by intimidation and fierce and cruel approaches to achieve their goals. This approach is common and appeals to our human nature. By our nature, we demand to be worshipped by others who we feel are inferior to us. We demand honour and worship from our subordinates. That is the secular method of management philosophy and principles: using subordinates to achieve our desired goals or purpose which comes to us as reward or profit.

Regrettably, Christian organizations and indeed ministers of the gospel, have adopted and accepted this capitalist tendency to manage her organizations and as such attempt to accomplish God's works through the instrumentality of force and intimidation. Frankly speaking, there is a thin line between the secular management philosophy and principles that derive from Biblical management philosophy and principles. This difference manifests on how we use the authority and power. Each body of management philosophy and principles has elements of authority and power. A level of control is required in any organization. The Bible never left one in doubt of the requisite demand for leadership authority and power, but the authority and power embedded in the leadership is a controlled one.

A passage in the Bible will elucidate the point above. In the gospel of Saint Matthew $20^{20\text{-}28}$, "Then the mother of Zebedee's sons came to Jesus with her sons and kneeling, asked a favour of him, what is it you want? He asked. She said, "grant that one of these two sons of mine may sit at your right and the other at your left in your kingdom. You don't know what you are asking, Jesus said to them, "can you drink the cup I am going to drink? "We can, they answered. Jesus said to them, "you will indeed drink from my cup ….." The lesson in this passage is obvious and indeed free from ambiguity of interpretation. Jesus simply was handling the proper use of authority and power by those who have it. His position is that we are not supposed to use our position today to "lord it over" the people under us, a prevalent and acceptable way of administering organizations like the church today.

The Bible, through the Lord of life, states that leadership is for the people, when he says, "instead, whoever wants to become great among you must be your servant, and whoever wants to be first must be your slave." By this scripture, Christian leaders are to serve those they lead and those under them by helping them to develop their maximum capacity. In contrast to what Jesus advocated above, secular management philosophy is getting work done through others and sees people as tools to use to get a job done irrespective of the persons' or employees' condition or circumstance. The leader of the management is interested in my back, profit but not my brain; they pay to work, not to think. This management philosophy was condemned by the scripture above: "they lord it over." The biblical management philosophy should see employees as people who ought to work together to achieve the expected result and be interested in developing their brain, rather than what they will accomplish. They should inspire the people to think and be creative, as opposed to bullying them to get results at the detriment of cordial relationships that ought to exist between the employer and employee. Jesus typified this kind of relationship of employers and employees rather than boss-servant relationship.

This is not against authority and power. Without controlled authority and power, organizations will become beasts because anything that has two heads is a beast. Jesus did not in any way criticize authority and power; He even exercised it when He sent his disciples two by two to go out for evangelism. When they came back, they gave him account of their outreach. Apostle Peter was appointed the leader of the Apostles, and throughout scripture, he played that role of a leader of Apostles. We were not told, or at least we have not read throughout the scripture, where Peter was talking, and the other apostles interrupted him. It never happened. None of them spoke on behalf of the Apostles without express permission of Peter. Moses exhibited authority and power when he appointed leaders to manage smaller units of leadership in Israel while the problematic cases were brought to him. Joseph, as Prime Minister of Egypt, did appoint minor leaders who took instructions from him, but he never lorded it over them.

Jesus modeled his leadership management skill according to boss-servant relationship and recommended it to us. Lee Brase, a Christian leader on the West Coast, stated "Those of us in leadership positions frequently have difficulty with the ideas of serving others. We tend to assume that since we have worked our way to the top, we are the ones who should be served. I guess we get to thinking we have earned that right." He said, "I have discovered that if you train a man, he will become what you are; but if you serve him, the sky is the limit as to what he can become: 'When I learned this, it freed me to serve men who have greater capacity than I have'". Serving is one of the most powerful Kingdom principles demonstrated by our Lord Jesus in Matthew 20:28;

> *"Just as the Son of Man did not come to be served, but to serve, and to give his life as a ransom for many."*

From the definition of management as a process of planning, organizing, staffing, directing and controlling, we will continue to explore the concept and Biblical management philosophy and principle.

Planning

Planning is one of the five major management functions. Under this function, we have the following:

- Imagination
- Ideation
- Creativity
- Goal-setting
- Making a set of long-term and short-term goals
- Scheduling

Imagination: This has been defined as the act or power of forming a mental image of something not present to the senses or never been wholly perceived. It is a creation of the mind and the ability to confront and deal with a problem. It is the ability to form new images and sensations in the mind that are not perceived through senses such as sight, hearing or other senses. It helps make knowledge applicable in solving problems and is fundamental to integrating experience and the learned process. This principle is coined from the scripture as quoted in Hebrew 11^1, "Now faith is being sure of what we hope for, and certain of what we do not see." The author of Hebrew no doubt, narrowed faith in chapter eleven verse one, to what might be described as the future reference and present function of Christian faith. In the first instance, it anticipates the future. It does not place its reliance on that which is merely visible to our physical sight. It is the assurance of things hoped for. The "fruitful" characters arrayed in the whole of the chapter did not simply live for the passing moment; they realized that there was far more to life than the immediate and temporary scene.

They understood that there were better opportunities ahead because, in one way or another, God had told them so. God said, **"I am the Alpha and the Omega, says the Lord God, 'who is, and who was and who is to come; the Almighty"** (Rev 1^8). Alpha and Omega represent the first and end letters of the Greek alphabet. God says He is the beginning and the end (Rev. 2^{16}). His sovereignty rules over all human history, seen and unseen. He imagined the earth, and it came into being. He imagined the separation of lights and spoke it into being. He imagined the separation of waters from the land, and it came into being too. Jacob used imagination when he was bargaining his wages with Laban. The Bible records that Jacob would take freshly cut branches from poplar, almond and plane trees and make white stripes on them by peeling the bark and exposing the white inner wood of the branches. He placed the peeled branches in all the watering troughs so that they would be directly in front of the flocks when they come to drink. When the flocks were in heat and came to the stream to drink, they mated in front of the branches. And they bore young ones that were streaked or speckled or spotted. Imagination is one of the significant management philosophies and principles to get things accomplished. Without the power and ability to imagine, most ideas will continue to remain a mirage. Most business organizations have collapsed, not because of inadequate funding, but rather lack of imagination and innovative thinking. Hence, if any organization, secular or sacred, lacks the power and ability to imagine, its collapse is imminent. Imagination sustains the organization in times of difficulty and economic stagnation. Your imagination can recreate your world.

Ideation: Ideation is the capacity for or the act of forming or entertaining ideas. For instance, caregivers are trained to watch for signs of depression and suicidal ideation. Ideation is the creative process of generating, developing, and communicating new ideas where an idea is understood as an essential element of thought that can be visual, concrete or abstract. It involves all stages of a thought cycle from innovation through development to actualization. The Bible says, **"For as a man thinketh in his heart, so is he."** From this scripture, the idea a man generates under the influence of the Holy Spirit will keep him afloat.

Ideation involves basic elements of thought that can be visual, concrete or abstract, and embraces all stages of thinking in the process of management. Leaders should develop their ideation capacity and ability to enable them to remain relevant in their management positions. Every one of us is born with in-depth ideas, but just very few unbutton theirs, while very many die with their ideas untapped. Ideas rule the world. A man or leader with an idea will never remain leave this earth in obscurity. This is where the church leadership misses it. In most cases, the area of innovation is completely neglected, while the area of development is preaching service. Hence actualization becomes difficulty. However, if the whole idea can pass through the stages of innovation, development, and actualization, the church will not only grow but will be concretized.

Creativity: Creativity is the process of challenging accepted ideas and the usual ways of doing things to find new solutions or concepts. It involves becoming aware of the obstacles that stand in the way of the creative impulse and understanding the benefits that creative thinking can bring.

The authors of *Successful Managers' Handbook* have described being creative to mean seeing ideas or objects in a different context, either by recognizing their inherent potential to be used in a different way or by putting previously unconnected ideas together to create something completely new. All of us have the ability to be creative. However, we tend to be constrained by culture and circumstances and so, do things the way we have always done them. Instead of seeing problems as opportunities to find new ways of doing things, we tend to see them as "hurdles" to be jumped. We are supposed to use creative thinking to gain a new perspective on the world. Some of us are naturally creative, but most of us accept things the way they appear. Most of us are traditionally limited by our local beliefs in culture and norms. Challenges and unfriendly circumstances are real opportunities for greater success for creative minds. Failure is not bad on itself but what is bad is the inability to convert failure to greater success. Every success in mostly all inventions started with a great deal of failure and disappointment. All the original motor spare parts you see today started with less substandard ones before they improved to be where they are today. Creative minds are minds that are not ready to give up on projects simply because they failed at the first instance. The success ladder is saddled with ups and downs. Great minds are not ashamed of failure rather; they are ashamed of not conquering it.

According to *Successful Managers' Handbook*, great creative minds recognize and do the following:

- That everyone has the ability to be creative,
- The need to change your current patterns of thinking,
- That change begins with questioning,
- That you use your past experiences to find solutions,
- The need to understand how logical and creative thinking are integral to each other,

- That thinking creatively increases your opportunities,
- The need to explore possible options before making decisions,
- The Need to think of possible solutions to a problem and then evaluating them using logical thinking,
- The need to use your imagination to find different solutions,
- They must understand how conditioning forces you to think in a prescribed way and limits your potential,
- The need to aim to look at information in more productive, insightful ways,
- That creativity is driven by the desire to improve processes,
- The need to bypass your assumptions and think creatively,
- Believe that you can think of solutions,
- Try not to be constrained by rules,
- Accept that problems are the food of creativity,
- Understand your thinking processes so that you are able to adapt them,
- Identify the side of the brain that naturally influences you,
- Notice how you approach problems and think about whether you are naturally creative,
- Recognize the advantages and pitfalls of different thinking patterns,

- Structure your time to be more productive,

- Generate lots of ideas before making decisions,

- Be ready to question the accepted,

- View problems as an impetus to change,

- Ask questions even if they seem ridiculous,

- Recognize that developing creativity takes time and practice, but pays off afterwards,

- Think about the change you would like to make and how you could initiate it,

- Remove your self-imposed mental roadblocks by carrying out creative exercises,

- Ask a colleague you admire for advice on how to improve your creative skills,

- Use coaching to help you change your current thinking patterns,

- Form clear goals to work toward during a coaching session,

- Recognize that coaching is an effective means of changing your current patterns of behaviour,

- Do not set yourself goals that you cannot monitor. Make sure that you and your coach can assess your achievements,

- Pinpoint what you want so that you can set about achieving it,

- Think in terms of the results you want to achieve,

- Focus on questions rather than predicting answers,

- Learn to cross the natural barriers in your mind,

- Remember that problems are opportunities for change,

- Ask yourself why you perceive an issue as a problem,

- Question and challenge ideas, rather than just accepting them as the norm,

- Let your subconscious mind find solutions,

- Invest time in learning to do things differently, so that you can identify new opportunities,

- Consider whether a problem requires creative thinking or whether a solution is clear-cut,

- Use creative tools to help you think in more productive and strategic ways,

- Learn how to select the right tool to achieve the best result,

- Believe there are better ways of doing things and then find out what they are,

- Write down your ideas and start to evaluate them,

- Be clear and precise about your goals and ideas when you explain them to others.

- Recognize that ideas that are left unimplemented have no value at all, act on your ideas,

- Write out an action plan, so that you can begin to put your ideas into practice,

- Make sure that all your team members are clear about the goals of the project,

- Manage creative people by being open-minded and flexible,

- Evaluate creative ideas before you judge them,

- Avoid rejecting ideas without considering them,

- Always involve positive people in your decisions, as they often produce the best ideas,

- Acknowledge that everyone has something to offer,

- Remember that collective thinking can reap successful ideas,

- Make sure the composition of the team is appropriate for the problem to tackle,

- Just call ideas out rather than thinking about them first,

- Suspend judgment, encourage the generation of ideas and let other people's thoughts inspire you,

- Choose the easiest ideas to implement initially,

- Judge ideas on their achievability and their value, and rate them on a scale of one to ten,

- Empower people to generate solution,

- Use questions that challenge accepted thought,

- Set a good example to your team by being proactive,

- Be sensitive when asking questions, avoid making people feel as if they are being interrogated,

- Use closed questions to start a discussion, and then develop it by asking open questions,

- Analyze your current procedures to see how they can be improved on,

- Keep reviewing and questioning to stay ahead of the game,

- Avoid taking criticism personally,

- Remember that a team is only as strong as its leader.

Over the years, people who creatively think in the direction listed above have provided new solutions to the problems of their day. The ability of human beings to find creative solutions to problems is essential for the well-being of the human race. On a special level, collective creativity provides the opportunity to improve quality of life. In organizations, including faith-based organizations, creativity is essential to ensure a company's ongoing effectiveness in a changing world. Individually, creativity can help you break out of routines you dislike. The church in these times needs more of creative leaders to saddle leadership. The church has continued to build on obsolete, outdated and moribund strategies, especially the mainland churches. The principle is that the message of the gospel is the same, but methods can vary and can be creatively handled. Any manager of both people and resources must be a creative thinker in order to lead the people. Creative thinking involves opening up your mindset to find new solutions and new ways of doing things. Instead of getting stuck up in one's usual logical approach to problem-solving, learn to suspend your judgment. When you are faced with a problem, start to look for different, more inventive solutions.

Once you have generated as many ideas as possible, use a logical thinking process to refine your ideas, identifying the best solution. We are conditioned not to think the unthinkable, many of us prefer to remain where we are to asking questions that will make us look stupid or unintelligent. Let go of preconceived ideas and break the glass wall of conditioning in order to find your creative self. This limitation has kept many people at the primary level of their ideas perpetually. You are to avoid accepting procedures as they appear, just because they have always been that way. Learn to question these procedures and status quo, seek creative ways to provide fresh and inspiring ideas and techniques of solving problems in a modern world. Find a way of doing things differently.

There are stunning creative techniques, and all of them work on the basis of imposing a condition on your thinking and capacity, they encourage the use of your imagination. Imagination they say is the lifeblood of creativity. Use it to disrupt your natural thinking patterns and weak strategies. For instance, when you are not sure about what you want from your task, visualize your desired future or result, create a vision or expectation or target that you can work toward. Thereafter, apply your reasoning to work out how you can make this goal a reality.

The difference between failures and successful people is the capacity to become creative in the task. While a creative mind is worried on how to arrive at a desired goal, the procedural person is busy giving excuses why it is not the typical way to achieve the result. The two sides of the brain work differently, though for the same reason. The left part of the brain processes information in a logical way, while the right part of the brain focuses on the creative, initiative, part of your personality. Most people tend to be dominated by one or other side of their brains and the part of the brain that dominates determines the thinking style of the person. While very few can adopt the two modes, people who are governed by the right side of their brains are naturally creative, but this does not mean that people who are governed by the left side of their brains cannot be creative. Organized people are more influenced by the left side of the brain, which involves, being logical and analytical, objective and rational, and interested in focus and details. On the other hand, initiative people are influenced by the right side of the brain, which means they respond to situations initiatively. They are subjective and emotional and are more interested in the big picture.

Right dominance people do not find fulfillment in mere following instruction and principles to complete tasks. Instead, they want to know why they are doing it. They naturally want to see, hear and feel what is required of them in the whole task. They do not believe in giving them half information on any matter. From the onset, they want to be in the big picture of the whole task involved. They trust their feelings and answer questions initiatively. Whether you are a right brain-dominated or not, you can develop your approach.

Left dominance people typically processes information by taking it piece by piece, separately building up a 'big' picture from which they draw conclusions. People who are influenced by their left side of the brain work through problems logically. They are good at developing strategies and base their decisions on facts. They are articulate and good communicators. They conform to rules, but not neglecting adaptability. A critical example in the Bible of such a person is Joseph. He was able to manage both periods of abundance and scarcity. That was creativity in motion. Peradventure, King Pharaoh and his people would have doubled their wives and buildings during this period of abundance and suffer during scarcity. The same experience happened in our country Nigeria when we could not manage the oil boom for the rainy day. Joseph creatively made Egypt a distinction for all the nations of the then world.

> *"Joseph collected all the food produced in those seven years of abundance in Egypt and stored it in the cities. In each city, he put the food grown in the fields surrounding it. Joseph stored up huge quantities of grain like the*

sand of the sea; it was so much that he stopped keeping records because it was beyond measure" (Gen. 41[48-49]).

Goal Setting

Goal-setting involves making a set of long and short-term goals. Goal-setting is a robust process for thinking about your ideal future, and for motivating yourself to turn your vision of the future into reality. It helps you choose where you want to go in life. Goal-setting is a careful consideration of what you want to achieve and ends with a lot of hard work to actually do it. So in between what you want to accomplish ultimately are some well-defined steps of action that transcend the specifics of each goal. The proper understanding of these steps will enable you to formulate goals that you can achieve. *Successful Managers' Handbook* states that Mind Tools offer us five golden rules of goal setting and they include the following:

Set Goals That Motivate You: Goals are set for ourselves, and because of this, it is very important that they are capable to motivate you. This means making sure that they are very important to you, that they can take away sleep from you. Any goal that cannot interrupt your sleep is considered non-essential. Motivation is the key to achieving goals; any goal that attracts only little interest from you cannot produce an outstanding outcome. You are advised to set goals that relate to the high priorities in your life. Without this type of compassion and zeal, one can end up with far too many goals, leaving you too little time to devote to each one of them. To achieve your goal, you need unflinching commitment in order to maximize success; you need to feel a sense of urgency and have an "I must do this" attitude and approach. To make sure your goal is motivating, write down why it's valuable and important to you. Ask yourself, "if I were to share my goal with others, what would I tell them to convince them it was a worthwhile goal?"

Set SMART Goals: Your goal must conform to this acronym SMART. For goals to be compelling and accepted beyond self, it should be designed to be SMART. The SMART stated that goals should be:

- Specific
- Measurable
- Attainable
- Relevant
- Time Bound

Specific: States that your goal must be clear and well-defined. You need goals to show you the way you want to go. Make it as simple as possible to get where you tend to go by precisely defining where you want to end up. Clumsy goals are unhelpful and unattractive because they don't provide accurate and sufficient direction.

Measurable: States that it includes precise amounts, dates, etc., in your goals so you can measure your degree of performance or achievement. For instance, if your goal is simply defined as "to reduce expenses" how you will know when you have been successful? You must state categorically how and in what ways you want the reduction in expenses to occur so that within the specified date and time you will know by what percentage your spending have been reduced. Without a concrete way of measuring your success, you may likely miss out on the celebration that comes with knowing you actually achieved something.

Attainable: States that it must be possible to achieve the goals you set if you set a goal. If you know deep down in your mind that you have no power or muscle to accomplish a goal, you will only demoralize yourself and erode your confidence if you set it. A young man who by faith has set a goal to get married in the next one year, build a duplex in a choice city and buys a modern jeep and whose monthly take-home is not more than one hundred and fifty thousand naira only (N150,000), may have set a fantastic goal for himself, but it is not attainable. To procure a choice land in a choice city will not gulp less than thirty million naira (N30,000,000) and to build such a duplex will need a minimum of another thirty five million (N35,000,000). To finish everything about marriage will be within the neighbourhood of two million (N2,000,000). From the foregoing, he has set goal that is not attainable.

Relevant: States that every goal should be relevant to the direction you want your life and profession to take. Any goal that is not relevant will result in waste of energy and strength. When your goals align with your direction in life, you will develop the focus you need to get ahead and do what you want.

Time Bound: Means that your goals must have a deadline. Timeframe attached to any project or goals helps the person to be focused and tidy up any project at the targeted time or season. When goals are time-bound, they create a sense of urgency and curiosity and achievement will come much quicker.

Set Goals in Writing: The attitude of writing down your goal makes it real and tangible. It comes to man's world, not in the realm of the spirit. It creates in you an urgency and removes the excuse of forgetfulness far from you. In writing your goal, you are to use the language, "I will" instead of "I would like to." The latter creates room for excuses if you get distracted somewhere in pursuit of your goal. For instance, "I will reduce my feeding expenses by 15 percent this year", not "I will like to reduce my feeding expenses by 15 percent this year. The first instance goal statement has power. You can "see" or "imagine" yourself reducing expenses, while the second lacks passion and gives you ample excuses to slack if you get sidetracked. When you write your goals, please you are advised to paste them at strategic places in your room, office, bathroom, mirror, treadmill room, children's room or refrigerator as a constant reminder.

Make an Action plan: Action plan motivates us to take inventory of any accomplished assignment. This includes all the steps required and needed along the way to achieving your goal-setting targets. By writing out the action plans, that is, the individual steps, and then crossing each one off as you complete it, you will realize that you are making progress towards your ultimate goal. This is more so if your goal is big and demanding or long-term. Action plans are practical roadmaps that enable you to know when you are entering the next level of your goal. Action plans are concrete evidence that you really know where you are going. They get you focused to the real business without being distracted or derailed from the right track. Action plans help you to start business each day and moment with required expectation.

Stick With It: One of my senior friends told this story that a couple was once trekking together in the cool evening across the railway. While they were crossing the rail track, the wife's shoes stuck to the rail and while they were struggling to get the shoe out, they were jolted by blaring of oncoming train horns. The wife asked her husband to go, but the man refused and said we stick together in marriage, we shall stick together in death. In goal-setting, we are encouraged to stick with it whether it is favourable or not. Goal-setting is an ongoing exercise, not just a means to an end. Build in reminders to keep yourself on track, and make regular time slots available to review your goals. Your end destination; that is, your desired accomplishment may remain quite similar over the long term, but the action plan you set for yourself along the way can change significantly. Make sure the relevance, value, expectation, outcome, and necessity remain paramount and in sight all the time. Goal-setting goes beyond mere assumption without premise or you merely wanting something to happen; it is a precise a definition of what you want and an understanding why you want it. This knowledge will reduce your odds of success and achievement.

If you pursue these five golden rules of goal-setting, you can set goals with confidence and enjoy the satisfaction that comes along with knowing you achieved what you set out to do.

Scheduling

This is the process of arranging, controlling and optimizing work and workloads in a production or manufacturing process. It is used to allocate plant and machinery resources, plan human resources, plan production processes and purchase materials. It is the art of planning your activities so that you can achieve your goals.

It has also been defined as assigning appropriate number of workers to the jobs during each day of work, determining when an activity should start or end, depending on its duration, predecessor activity or activities, predecessor relationships, resource availability and target completion date of the project. The most primary sequence of scheduling is job scheduling. It means the process of allocating system resources to many different tasks by an operating system (OS). The system handles prioritized job queues that are awaiting CPU time, and it should determine which job is to be taken from which queue and the amount of time to be allocated for the job. The advantage is that it makes sure that all tasks are carried out fairly and on time. *Techopedia* explains job scheduling by stating that it is performed using job schedulers. Job schedulers are programs that enable scheduling and at times, track computer batch jobs, or units of work like the operation of a payroll program. Job schedulers have the ability to start and control jobs automatically by running prepared job control-language statements or by means of similar communication with a human operator. Generally, the present day job schedulers include a Graphical User Interface (GUI) along with a single point of control.

Organizations wishing to automate unrelated IT workload could also use more sophisticated attributes from a job scheduler, for example, real-time scheduling in accordance with eternal, unforeseen events, automated restart, and recovery in case of failing in notifying the operations personnel, generating reports of incidents and audit trails meant for regulatory compliance purposes. Though in-house developers can write these advanced capabilities, however, those are usually offered by providers who are experts in advanced systems management software.

In scheduling, different schemes are used to determine which specific job to run. Some parameters that may be considered are as follows:

- Job priority,

- Availability of computing resource,

- License key if the job is utilizing a licensed software,

- Execution time assigned to the user,

- Number of parallel jobs permitted for a user,
- Projected execution time,
- Elapsed execution time,
- Presence of peripheral devices,
- Number of cases of prescribed events.

Resource Scheduling: Resource scheduling is a collection of techniques used to calculate the resources required to deliver the work and when they will be required. There are two broad categories of resources – consumable and re-useable scheduling.

These resources ensure:

- Efficient and effective utilization,
- Confidence that the scheduling is realistic,
- Early identification of resource capacity bottlenecks and conflict.

The resource scheduling process has three major steps namely:

- Allocation
- Aggregation
- Scheduling

Allocation: Involves identifying what resources are needed to complete the work. In the case of consumable resources, it is simply the quantity required. In the case of reusable resources, it is the total effort required and the number of individual resources. Once time scheduling and resources allocation are complete, the resources can be aggregated on a daily, weekly or monthly basis as appropriate. The aggregate date is usually presented in a histogram that illustrates the fluctuating use of resources against time. In the case of consumable resources, a cumulative curve (which usually takes the form of an s-curve) is also used to show the total amount consumed at any point in time.

Organizing

The following functions are included in organizing and developing a system which God perfected in developing the solar system. When God was framing the principles of time, he listed it as seconds, minutes, hours, days, weeks, months, years, century and millennium. Countries may defer in their timing, but it is all listed in the above sequence. System design and development was first and foremost showcased by God when He arranged the creation procedure in their order of defining the components, modules, interferences, and dates for a system to satisfy specified requirement which we observe in the arrangement of creatures for the lateral coordinated relationships among the habitants of the earth.

System development is the process of creating or altering systems along with the procedures, practices, models, and methodologies used to develop them. God created and also altered the creation when He separated the greater light to govern the day while the lesser light ruled the night. God also designed an office for the entire universe including the planet and everything in it. So, office design in organizing is God's initiative. Man was assigned to coordinate every other creature and give them names. Delegation of authority was initiated by God when he asked Adam to name all creatures and told him to work and take care of the Garden of Eden.

The development of workflow chart was initiated by God during the creation period. In His first seven days of creation, God had a plan or a schedule to follow, from which each government or organizational structure especially an enduring one, must be dependent on. To plan or organize does not require crowds of nonexistent brains or a multitude of weak-willed policy persons. Two or three eggheads can put together an organization's pendulum. It is such innovative brains that shaped both the government, economy, and destiny of United States of America (USA), namely; Alexander Hamilton, James Madison and John Jay. They sat and wrote the 75 papers referred to as the Federalist papers that provided the fundamental ideas upon which the constitution of United States of America is built. So, it does not take a thousand persons or mending negotiations to put together a successful organization.

Staffing

Staffing is not man's making, rather God's. In the creation bid, God created different staff and their assignments. We are strongly advised to follow God's way in our staffing, and we will not fail. While we are enjoined to rule the entire earth and to replenish it, God has created man in his own image and likeness. He has created a wide range of living creatures of all kinds which might be impossible to list. Each of these creatures is assigned a definite role for the maintenance and sustenance of the world and environment. The solar and the lunar systems provide heat and light at their time and at the right degree. They do operate by chance but through the agencies and for the benefit of the various kinds of living creatures wherever they might be found. For example, crabs and shrimps carry out the task of maintaining the cleanliness of river beds and the lower parts of the sea, by consuming the dirt that accumulates at the lower part of the water, while certain kinds of eagles and vultures, as well as pigs and other kinds of animals, serve as scavengers at the surface of the earth they consume dead creatures. Other creatures (God's staff) are assigned specific roles in the organization. The plant kingdom supplies the needed oxygen and different kinds of gases, while some natural phenomena that operate in the atmosphere clean and maintain it through weather patterns or phenomena such as storms, lightning, thunder, and earthquakes. These are known as the acts of God, which are devastating and catastrophic but may yet provide a conducive atmosphere for living creatures to survive.

From our analogy above, we can observe that God is the sole initiator of staffing; we are borrowing from what His ideas. Like every staff in an organization is assigned a duty in administration, marketing, production, or commercial unit, God has also provided self-regulating measures for the welfare and renewal of the environment of the living creatures on the earth.

Staffing could be defined as 'the selection and training of individuals for specific job functions and charging them with the associated responsibilities. In Exodus 18$^{17\text{-}23}$, Jethro, Moses' father-in-law taught him how to recruit and deploy staff: "But select capable men from the people – men who fear God, trustworthy men who hate dishonest gain - and appoint them as officials over thousands, hundreds, fifties and tens. Have them serve as judges for the people at all times, but have them bring every difficult case to you, the simple cases they can decide themselves. That will make your load lighter because they will share it with you. If you do this as God so commands, you will be able to stand the strain, and all these people will go home satisfied." Staffing is a very essential part of any organization, especially the church. The capacity of the apex leader to identify the capabilities of other workers under him in order to assign them the work they have ability for is a tedious task. The personality or job task of the person designated to lead the 'thousand' group is quite different from the task of the man over 'hundred', likewise for the persons over 'fifties' and 'tens'. In staffing, you do not give the task of a thousand people to someone who has capacity just for ten people because you love such a person or have a relationship with him.

Moses was to meticulously select persons honestly to officiate over the people according to their abilities. In Matthew 25$^{14\text{-}}$

[15], a certain man was travelling and gave his servants talents for investment in his absence. He gave one of the servants five talents, to another he gave two while the third person go one all according to their abilities. In the same vein, staff in organisations have different capacities and must identify these in order to succeed.

Reflection On Chapter 2

Personal Notes:

===== Guided Action Plan =====

CHAPTER 3
Human Resources Planning

This is the process that links the human resources needs of an organization to its strategic plan to ensure that staffing is sufficient, qualified, and competent enough to achieve the organization's objectives. Human resources planning is becoming a vital organizational element for maintaining a competitive advantage and rescuing employee turnover."

Organizational Structure

This is defined as 'the typically hierarchical arrangement of lines of authority, communications, rights and duties of an organization. Organizational structure determines how the roles, power, and responsibilities are assigned, controlled, and coordinated, and how information flows between the different levels of management. A structure depends on the organization's objectives and strategy. In a centralized structure, the top layer of management has most of the decision-making power and divisions. In a decentralized structure, the decision-making power is distributed, and the departments and divisions may have different degrees of independence.

Pre-Bureaucratic Structure: The pre-bureaucratic structure or entrepreneurial structures lack standardization of tasks. This structure is most common in smaller organizations or new start-ups and is best used to solve simple tasks. It is totally centralized. The strategic leader makes all key decisions, and most communication is done on a one-on-one bases. It is particularly useful for new start-ups or entrepreneurial businesses as it enables the founder to control growth and development. It is usually based on traditional domination or charismatic domination in the sense of a Max Weber's tripartite classification of authority.

Bureaucratic Structures: Weber (1948) gives the analogy that, "the fully developed bureaucratic mechanism compares with other organizations exactly as does the machine with the non-mechanical modes of production. Precision, speed, un-ambiguity, strict subordination, reduction of friction and material and personnel costs are raised to the optimum point in the strictly bureaucratic structures and have a certain degree of standardization. They are better suited for more complex or large-scale organizations, usually adopting a tall structure. The conflict between bureaucratic and non-bureaucratic is echoed in Burns and Stalkers *The Management of innovation* where a distinction is made between mechanistic and organic structures.

Weber's characteristics of bureaucracy include the following:

- Clearly defined roles and responsibilities

- A hierarchical structure and

- Respect for merit

Bureaucratic structures have many levels of management ranging from senior executives to regional managers, all the way to department store managers. Since there are many levels, decision-making authority has to pass through more layers than flatter organizations. It has rigid and tight procedures, policies and constraints. It is reluctant to adopt or change what people are used to in the management of the organization. Organizational chart exists for every department, and everyone understands who is in charge and what their responsibilities are for every situation. Decisions are formulated through an organized process, and a strict command and control structure is present all the times. The authority is usually at the top and information is then flowed from top to bottom. This arrangement brings into existence, more rules and standards for the company which operational process is watched with close supervision.

Some advantages for bureaucratic structures for top-level managers are that they have a tremendous control over organizational structure decisions. This works best for managers who have a command and control style of managing. Strategic decision-making is also faster because there are only fewer people it has to go through to approve. Disadvantages may include: discouraging creativity, innovation, and self-development in the organization, which can make it hard for a company to adapt to changing conditions in the marketplace.

Post Bureaucratic Structure: The term 'post-bureaucratic' is used in two senses in the organizational literature review. The first is generic, while the second is much more specific. In generic sense, the term post bureaucratic is often used to describe a range of ideas developed since the 1980s that specifically contrast themselves with Weber's ideal type bureaucracy. This may include total quality management, culture management, and matrix management, amongst others. Still, hierarchies exist, authority is still Weber's rational, legal type, and the organization is still rule-bound. Heckscher and Donellon (1994), arguing along these lines, describes these hierarchies as clean up bureaucracies, rather than a fundamental shift away from bureaucracy.

An unknown source maintains that "the essence of bureaucratic control – the formalization, codification, and enforcement of rules and regulations – does not change in principle; it shifts focus from organizational structure to the organization's culture. Heckscher and Donellon (1994) have developed an ideal type of bureaucracy, the post-bureaucratic organization, in which decisions are based on dialogue and consensus rather than authority and command. The organization is a network rather than a hierarchy, open at the boundaries; there is an emphasis on meta-decision-making rules rather than decision-making rules. This sort of horizontal decision-making by consensus model is often used in housing cooperatives, other cooperatives and when running a non-profit or community organization. It is mostly used in order to encourage participation and help to empower people who usually experience oppression in groups.

Functional Structure: A functional organizational structure is a structure that consists of activities such as coordination, supervision and task allocation. The organizational structure determines how the organization performs or operates. The term organizational structure refers to how the people in an organization are grouped and to whom they report. One way to organize people is by their function. Most of these functions in an organization include production, marketing, human resources, and accounting.

The most typical challenge with a functional organizational structure is that communication within the company can be somewhat rigid, making the organization slow and inflexible. This results in lateral communication between functions becoming very important, so that information is disseminated not only vertically, but also horizontally within the organization. Communication in organizations with functional organizational structures can be rigid because of the standardized way of operation and the high degree of formalization.

In functional organizational structure, coordination and specialization of tasks are centralized in a functional structure, which makes producing a limited amount of products or services efficient and predictable. With this, efficiencies can further be realized as functional organizations integrate their activities vertically so that products are sold and distributed quickly and at low cost too. This high efficiency does not in any way prove that the level of cooperation of these organizations with each other is not sometimes compromised. They may have difficulty working well with each other as they may be territorial and unwilling to cooperate. This potential infighting among units may cause delays, reduced commitment due to competing interests, and wasted time, making projects fall behind schedule. This ultimately can bring down production levels overall, and company-wide employee commitment toward meeting organizational goals.

Divisional Organizational Structure: The divisional structure or product structure consists of self-contained decisions. A division is a collection of functions which produces a product. It also utilizes a plan to compete and operates as a separate business or profit center. According to Zainbooks.com, the divisional structure in America is seen as the second most common structure for organizations today. Employees who are responsible for specific market services or types of products are placed in divisional structures in order to increase their flexibility.

The advantages include:

- It uses delegated authority so the performance can be directly measured with each group. This results in managers performing better and high employee morale.
- It is more efficient in coordinating work between different divisions, and there is more flexibility to respond when there is a change in the market.
- A company will have a simpler process if they need to

change the size of the business by either adding or removing divisions.

- When divisional structure is utilized, more specializations can occur within the groups.

- When it is organized by product, the customers have their own advantages especially when only a few services or products are offered which differ significantly.

- It allows business decisions and activities coordinated locally.

The disadvantages include the following:

- It can encourage unhealthy rivalries among divisions.

- It has the capacity to increase costs by requiring more qualified managers for each division

- There is usually an over-emphasis on divisional more than organizational goals which results in duplication of resources and effort like staff services, facilities, and personnel.

Matrix Organizational Structure: It is a permanent organization designed to achieve specific results by using teams of specialists from different functional areas in the organization. The matrix organization structure superimposes a horizontal set of divisions It reports relationships into a hierarchical functional structure. It is often used when the firm has to be highly responsive to a rapidly changing external environment. In matrix structures, there are functional managers and product (project) managers.

Functional managers are in charge of specialized resources such as production quality control, inventories, scheduling and marketing while product or project managers are in charge of one or more products and are authorized to prepare product strategies or business group strategies and call on the various functional managers for the necessary resources. The major challenge with this structure is the negative effects of dual authority similar to that of project organization. The functional managers may lose some of their authority because product managers are given the budgets to purchase internal resources. In a matrix organization, the product or business group managers and functional managers have somewhat equal power. There is possibility of conflict and frustration but the opportunity for prompt and efficient accomplishment is quite high. There are advantages and disadvantages of matrix structure.

The advantages include:

- Decentralized decision-making
- Strong product/project coordination
- Improved environmental monitoring
- Fast response to change
- Flexible use of resources
- Efficient use of support systems

The disadvantages include:

- High administration cost
- Potential confusion over authority and responsibility
- High prospects of conflict
- Over-emphasis on group decision-making
- Excessive focus on internal relations.

Organizational Circle - Moving Back to Flat: This flat structure is common amongst small organizations. As organizations grow, they tend to become more complex and hierarchical in operations, which leads to an expanded structure, with more levels and departments. Definitely, unchecked growth will result in bureaucracy. Shell group of companies used to represent the typical bureaucracy, top-heavy and hierarchical. It featured multiple levels of command and duplicate service companies existing in different locations. This resulted in shell becoming apprehensive to market changes, leading to its incapacity to grow and develop beyond that limit. The failure of this cherished structure became the main reason for the organization's restructuring into a matrix organizational structure.

With the conquering power of Internet, and the associated access given all levels of an organization to information and communication via digital means, power structures have begun to align more as a hierarchy, enabling the flow of power and authority to be based, not on hierarchical levels, but on information, trust, credibility, and a focus on results. In general, over the last decade, it has become increasingly clear that through the forces of globalization, competition and more demanding customers, the structure of many companies has become flatter, less hierarchical, more fluid and even virtual.

Team Organizational Structure: This is the newest organizational structure developed in the 20th century. In a small business, the team can define the entire organization. Teams can be horizontal and vertical. While an organization is constituted as a set of people who synergize individual competencies to achieve newer dimensions, the quality of organizational structure revolves around the competencies of teams in totality.

Network Structure: The Network structure is the modern organizational structure. While business giants' risk is becoming clumsy to proact, act and react efficiently, the new network organizations contract out any business function that can be done better or more cheaply. In essence, managers in network structures spend most of their time coordinating and controlling the external relations, usually by electronic means. The potential management opportunities offered by recent advances in complex networks theory have been demonstrated including applications to product design and development and innovation problems in market and industries.

Strategic Leadership

This is the process of using well-considered tactics to communicate a vision for an organization or one of its parts. Strategic leadership typically manages, motivates and persuades staff to share that same vision, and can be an essential tool for implementing change or creating organizational structure within a business. Strategic leadership provides the vision and direction for the growth and success of an organization. A strategic leader institutionalizes a vision and helps the members of the organization to learn how to convert the objectives into action.

The business world is changing more rapidly and more dramatically than ever before: technology, globalization, competition, the rise of Asian business superpowers, have entirely changed the business environment and strategy. We are all involved in this toxic, and to deal with such a complex and dynamic situation, organizations need experienced people with well-developed leadership capacities, abilities, and acumen. Leadership they say permeates society but from a business perspective, it is the identification, development, and use of organizational leadership which is critical to organizational performance. It is generally accepted that leadership is a crucial determinant factor of organizational performances. Leaders make a difference. While leadership is highly vital, still there are few debates about the process and nature of leadership. This is not our primary focus, but then; Robbins and Judge (2007) define leadership as, "the ability to influence a group toward the achievement of a vision or a set of goals"; "the ability to influence people toward the attainment of organizational goals." Robbins distinguishes the leadership role from the managerial role, stating that managers merely use the authority inherent in formal positions to obtain compliance from organizational members.

Evolution Of Leadership Theories

We cannot possibly discuss strategic leadership without looking briefly on the evolution of leadership theories. So, let's attempt a brief highlight of the evolution of leadership theories.

Leadership Trait Theory: This is the early type of leadership; it tried to identify the personality traits associated with being a leader. The challenges with this theory is that there is no accepted set of traits that can be linked to effective leadership. The perspective is that everyone has varying levels of necessary leadership traits, and it is how one uses them that matters. The understanding of this trait today is that leaders can be developed, they are not just born. Kirkpatrick and Locke (1991) identified the following wider trait components of leadership: drive, leadership motivation, integrity, self-confidence and emotional maturity.

Leadership Behavioural Theory: This tries to understand better what effective leaders do, that is, their behaviours. This theory suggests two groups of leadership behaviour, namely; **Task-centered** which emphasizes roles and task, plans and scheduled work and sets performance standards and procedures, and ***people-centered*** which emphasizes friendly and supportive, employee relationship showing trust and confidence, and concern with employees' welfare.

Contingency Theories: This attempts to analyze the importance of the situation to the impact of the leader, and concludes that leadership effectiveness depends on the context in which the leader must operate.

Contemporary Theories or Perspective on Leadership including substitutes for leadership, "authentic" leadership, charismatic leadership and transformational leadership. For instance, in transformational and charismatic leadership, leaders empower and coach followers while the followers closely identify with the leader. This leads to a more motivated workforce that performs to a high level and embraces significant changes.

Hoskisson (2004) described strategic leadership as "the managerial ability to anticipate, envision, maintain flexibility, and empower others to create strategic change as necessary."

The Doctrine of Prosperity

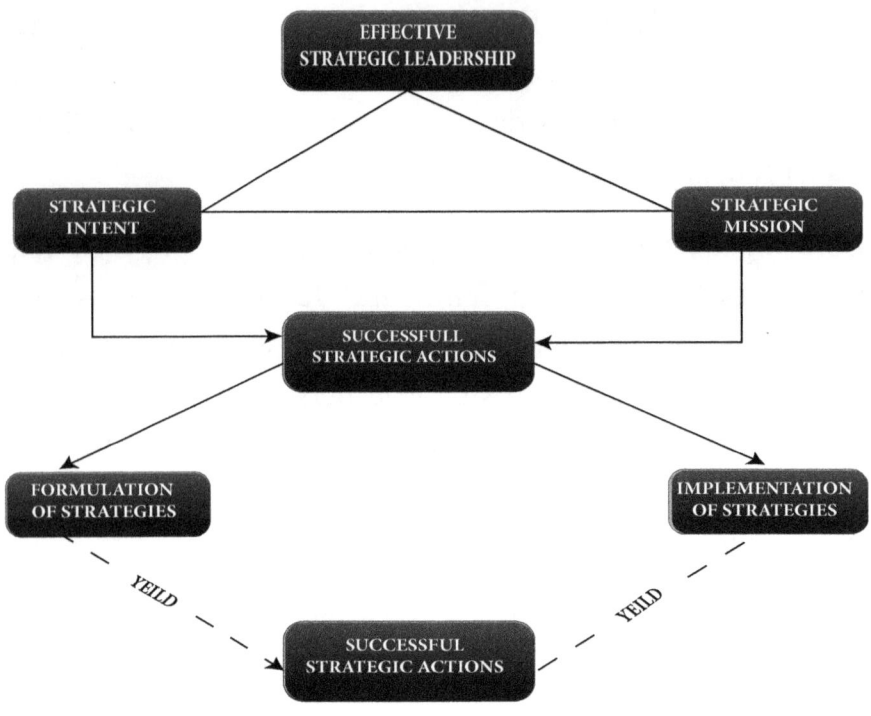

Key Strategic Leadership Actions
Source: Hoskisson P. 36

Hoskisson (2004) identified a number of actions that effective strategic leaders and top management teams focus on to contribute to the performance of the organization. They overlap and interlink more than they are isolated independent activities.

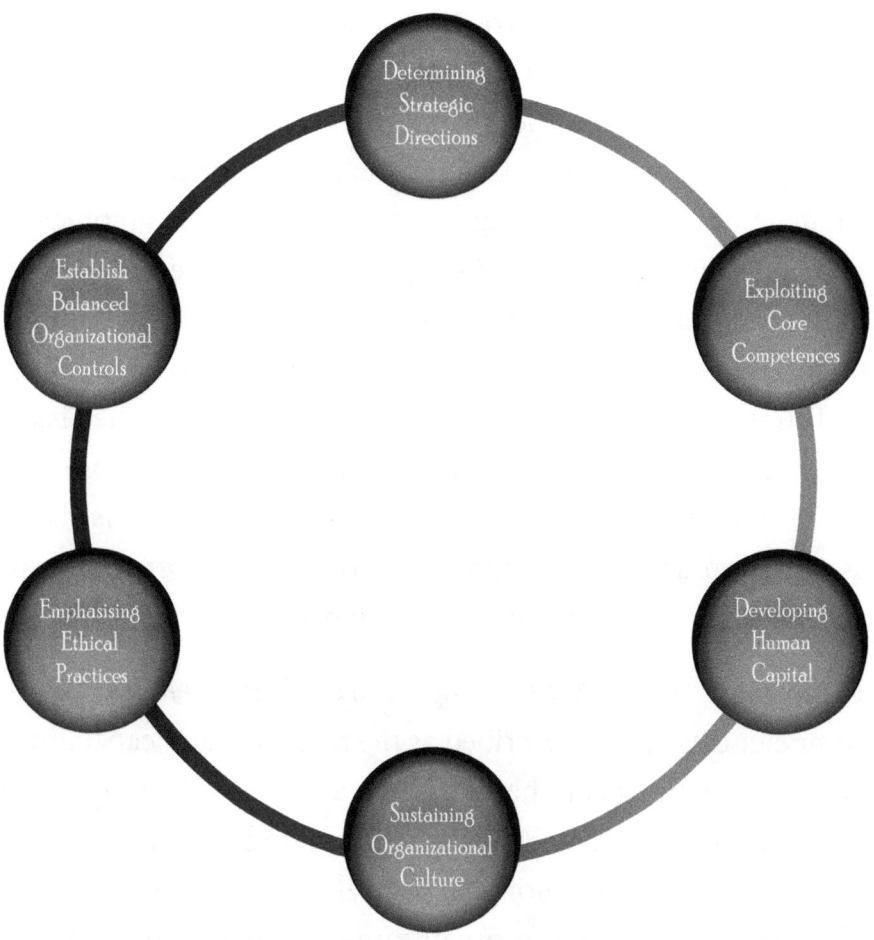

Key strategic leadership Actions:
Source Hoskisson (2004)

Determining Strategic Direction: The top management team must develop a clear vision for the organization. The body of top managers in the management must articulate and communicate on exciting vision which is the critical task of the strategic leadership of the organization. They need to graphically position a picture of where the organization is expected to be in five to ten years and motivate workers to buy into and commit themselves to this expectation. This vision is expected to push and stretch staff beyond their current expectations. The vision serves as a destination for the organization and therefore as a guide for strategy formulation and implementation. This vision as well should be able to outline the core values, norms, culture and ideology that will govern the organization.

Exploiting And Maintaining Core Competencies: Core competencies can be described as the resources and capabilities available to the firm that serve as a source of competitive advantage over its rivals; they are those things the organization (firm) has or does that allow it to set itself apart from competitors. The management of the organization must ensure that this source of competitive advantages over its rivals is maintained, invested in and developed over time to ensure relevance and continuity over a long time. They are the advantages, strength and secret source of the organization.

Developing Human Capital: In developing human capital, the major capital is staff. They are capital resource that requires enormous investment attention. There is no gainsaying that in the globalized and dynamic competitive environment, people are perhaps the only truly sustainable source of competitive advantage. Building human capital requires investment in training and development, and requires that top management provide the support and budget necessary to make this happen. HRM (Human Resource Management) activities have central roles in all of this, but without the blessings of the top management in the organization, such activities will neither have the impetus nor budget to be effective.

Sustaining An Effective Organizational Culture: Peter Drucker (2002) states, "culture eats strategy for breakfast" This illustrates the importance of organizational culture. In some sense, organizational culture is the personality of the organization. Thompson (2007) sees culture as "the character of a company's internal work climate and personality – as shaped by its core values, beliefs, business principles, traditions, ingrained behaviours, work practices, and styles of operating". Organizational culture can be a source of competitive advantage. It creates the context in which the organization develops and implements its strategy, and helps to regulate employees' actions and attitudes. There are a number of influences on the nature of an organization's culture, and the top management team are perhaps the most important. This group of people called senior management set the tone for the organization, through the values they espouse, the behaviours they reward, and possibly most importantly, through the recurring communication of the type of culture they desire to evolve in the organization. For them to achieve this desired behaviour, the top management will create the selection and promotional policies and criteria that can encourage the desired behaviours.

Emphasizing Ethical Practices: The effectiveness of the implementation of a firm's strategies improves when based on reliable and uncompromising ethical behaviours. In the absence of the above, an ethical culture employee and management may act opportunistically, taking advantage of their positions to benefit themselves. Hence, to create and ensure a strong ethical ethos in the organization, top management must themselves set an excellent ethical example and build a compliance and enforcement process around ethical behaviour. For instance, this will include developing and communicating a code of ethics, providing ethics training to staff, forming an ethics committee to give guidance on ethics matters and openly encouraging employees to report possible infractions.

Establishing balanced Organizational Controls: Organizational controls are a critical aspect of effective strategy implementation processes. Hoskisson (2004) puts it this way; they are "Formal information-based procedures used by managers to maintain or alter patterns in organizational activities." Organizational controls facilitate making reactive and proactive corrective adjustments to strategies as they are implemented. Organizational controls allow top management to determine when adjustments are needed and what type of adjustments to make.

Strategic Leadership Style

The style of leadership determines a lot in the sphere of strategic leadership. Rowe (2001) defines strategic leadership as, "the ability to influence others to voluntarily make day-to-day decisions that enhance the long-term viability of the organization while maintaining its short-term financial stability.

Rowe, quoting Steven Ross, former CEO of *Time Warner* states, that "there are three categories of people – the person who goes into the office, puts his feet up on his desk and dreams for twelve hours, the person who arrives at 5am and works for 15 hours, never once stopping to dream, and the person who puts his feet up, dreams for one hour, then does something about those dreams."

The Three Leadership Styles In Top Management
Source: Rowe (2001)

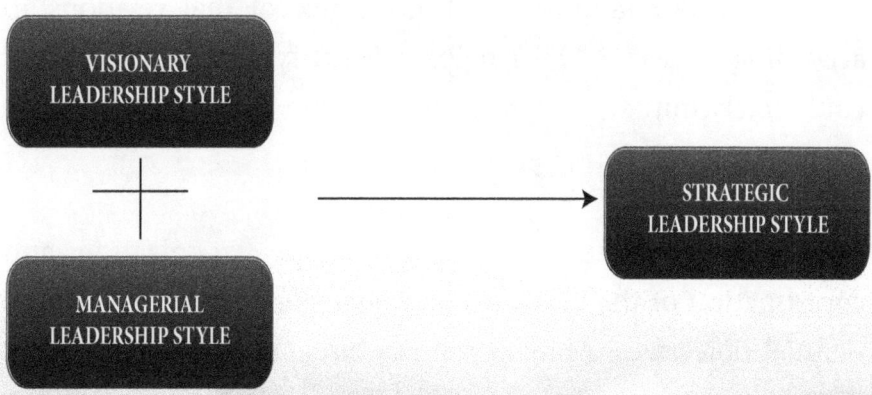

The visionary leader dreams; the managerial leader has no time for dreams while the strategic leader is synergistic; combining what is best about the visionary leader and the managerial leader.

Colder and Tellis (2005) state that purpose and focused leadership with committed top management is an incentive for achieving, exploring for what is possible than exploiting what is currently available. Billy (2006), Johnson (2006), Carnegie (2007) have also argued that the leaders' vision is what is needed to give the organization the strategic focus that rail-road other stakeholders in order to achieve predetermined goals.

Quinn (2005) notes that strategic and visionary leaders influence corporate efforts on goals. The management style of top managers according to him affects the level and performance of new corporate organizations. It gives support to entrepreneurial ideas and helps in building coalitions that will facilitate goals attainment. Visionary leadership according to Teece *et al.* (1997) creates an organizational climate that empowers all work members to behave and function entrepreneurially through a one-on-one relationship. The essence of that relationship according to Teece (2000), helps to identify skill deficiency and could likely initiate an update programme.

Management

Management has been defined as; 'the organization and coordination of the activities of a business in order to achieve defined objectives. Management is often included as a factor of production along with machines, materials, and money. According to Peter Drucker (2002), the basic task of management includes both marketing and innovation. The practice of modern management originates from the 16th Century study of low efficiency and failure of certain enterprises, conducted by the English statesman Sir Thomas More (1478-1535). Management consists of the interlocking functions of creating corporate policy and organizing, planning, controlling, and directing an organization's resources in order to achieve the objectives of that policy. The size of management can range from one person in a small organization to hundreds or thousands of managers in multinational companies.

Directing

Directing has been defined as a basic management function that includes building an effective work climate and creating opportunity for motivating, supervising, scheduling, and disciplining. It also includes assigning jobs to the staff members or team members and appointing supervisors to train and direct staff. It involves guiding and leading members of staff. In the Biblical context, this is not lacking at all. There are series of instances in the Bible that reveal this matter of directing and assigning specific roles to specific persons. Few of the examples include, the appointment of fivefold ministry in the Epistle of Paul to Ephesians church. These gifts were given by the Lord Jesus Christ Himself after resurrection, to perfect the saints for ministry work, beyond the four walls of the church.

> *"It was he who gave some to be apostles, some to be prophets, some to be evangelists, and some to be pastors and teachers to prepare God's people for works of service, so that the body of Christ may be built up" (Eph. 4$^{11\text{-}12}$).*

This scripture obviously reveals directing under a fivefold plan and design, assigned and given to the church. It defines and lists clear demarcation of authority flow to accomplish the intended task of equipping the saints to fulfill the task of making disciples of all nations and nurturing and guiding them to the kingdom of God. Again in Daniel chapter six (6), the king Darius appointed 120 satraps to rule throughout the kingdom, with three administrators over them to direct and guide the people. The king assigned jobs to members of leadership teams and appointed three supervisors to train and direct them. The king made sure that there were no osses. Hence he made the 120 satraps to be accountable to the three administrators. The three administrators were like the principal managers of the whole kingdom. Every organization has the five-fold ministry administrators – *Apostles representing entrepreneurs, prophets representing the policymakers of the organization, evangelists representing the image makers of the organization, pastors representing the managers of the organization and teachers representing the artisans of the organization.*

The Jethro Counsel to Moses on delegation still stands top in management principles. In Exodus, Jethro rebuked Moses' thoughts of infallibility and indispensability. In his sole counsel, he asked him to select capable men from all the people –men who fear God, trustworthy men who hate dishonest gain and appoint (assign) them as officials over thousands, hundreds, fifties, and tens. Have them serve as judges for the people at all times, but have them bring every difficult case to you; the simple cases they can decide themselves. That will make your load lighter because they will share it with you (Exodus 18$^{21-22}$). In Moses' mandate to the people he appointed, we see assignment of jobs to the staff; some were to handle thousands, some others to handle hundreds, while some others were to handle fifties and tens. Supervisors were appointed for them to hear their cases and possibly give rulings, depending on the critical position of the matter (case). The most difficult cases were naturally sent to him (Moses).

Joseph, in the land of Egypt, did direct the whole country both during seven years of abundance and the seven years of scarcity. He appointed supervisors who were in charge in various cities. In each city, he put the food grown in the fields surrounding it. He did all of this in preparation for the seven years of severe famine. During the famine, he brought the foods saved or invested for sale. He created employment from this act of management of resources; he saved lives, not only that of Egyptians but the whole world. Even his own people came all the way from Israel to buy food from the land of Egypt. In short, through the ingenuity of Joseph, Egypt became the world investment destination. In verse 25 of chapter 42, Joseph gave orders to fill his brothers' bags with grain, meaning there were those appointed to oversee the distribution of the goods and those responsible for finances. All of these were to make sure nobody cheated the king.

The command and commissioning of all believers by our Lord and Saviour Jesus Christ to go into all the world and preach the gospel to every creature, heal the sick, cast out demons, bring succour to the broken-hearted, including other commissions and mandate given by Him including sending disciples to all nations, are typical comparisons to the assignment; Job details and guiding given to various Heads of Departments working in any organizations or government agencies. Among the apostles that worked with our Lord Jesus, were some who had designated offices to supervise other ones. Paul says he was an Apostle sent to the Gentiles while Peter was an Apostle sent to the Jews.

Controlling

Controlling is defined as the basic management function of establishing benchmarks or standards, comparing actual performance against them, and taking corrective actions if required. It involves ensuring that the goals set in the organization by the management are achieved at the set time and period. It is making sure the deadlines of various decisions are met and delivering budgetary policies within the approved limits and ensuring that quality control is consistently maintained. The Bible is replete with God's supremacy over nature; He is in control of everything. He has fixed all the reward and punishment system in place. God has given the

Ten Commandments, the Sermon on the Mount and over hundreds of biblical principles both in the time of Moses, and our time, to maintain peace, order, and righteousness. The Biblical principles if adhered to, lead to success, healthy living, good lifestyle, joy, peace, strength, prosperity, abundance and more, while disobedience to these Biblical principles lead to failure, sickness, sorrow, worry, anxiety, weakness, poverty, lack and more. Every biblical principle is to make us prosperous, whether it is a family, individual, business organization, nation, economy, etc. If we apply these principles, success is granted.

The management principles in churches and Christian organizations reveal the creator of the universe in a very orderly pattern and systematic way, with checks and balances. It explains beyond any shadow of doubt, or questioning, that we can draw ideas, concepts, strategies, patterns, policies, or principles from the Bible, to manage whatever responsibilities we have been assigned, in a systematic and successful way.

Reflection On Chapter 3

Personal Notes:_____

Guided Action Plan

CHAPTER 4
10 Immutable Laws

"Financial Freedom starts with the first coin, but Financial Liberty is the end product of profitable use of the first coin."

1. The Law of Belief

Whatever dream you passionately believe in eventually becomes a reality. What you believe determines your action and prejudice. The man who acts out his beliefs is simply a rational human being. Your belief can constitute a barrier to your expectations in life. Brian Tracy once said in his book, *"The 100 Absolutely Unbreakable Laws of Business Success*: "...For you to progress, to move onward and upward in your life and business, you must continually challenge your self-limiting beliefs. You must reject any thought or suggestions that are limited in any way. You must accept as a basic principle that you are a **no-limit** person and that what others have done you can do as well."

The law of belief is the key to all the laws. It is the nucleus of all the ideas for success and prosperity. A reflection on the biblical concept of Moses and the twelve spies reveals a lot about this law.

The twelve men sent to spy the Promised Land left as a team but returned as two teams, with one as majority and the other minority. The majority was the ten that gave an evil report that caused an uproar in the camp. A close examination of their report will reveal the Law of Belief as the basis for action.

The report from the spies:

> *"We went into the land to which you sent us, and it does flow with milk and honey, here is its fruits: but the people who live there are powerful, and the cities are fortified, very large, ... and the descendants of Anak are there. ... The land we explored devours those living in it. All the people we saw there are of great sizes... we seem jinxed"? (Numbers 13:$^{27\text{-}33}$)*

They believed they could not make it due to the size of the inhabitants, the fortified cities, the strength of the people (who were descendants of Anak), but these obstacles were factors that should have brought out the best in them. It is at such times you take your ability to the next level. If you continue to restrict yourself to your usual level without reaching out for greater heights, you will stagnate in life.

2. The Law of Responsibility

You are entirely responsible for everything you are or eventually become in life. This law states that you are in charge of your life; as such, you are responsible for every decision you take; no one interferes with your choice. You are where you are because of yourself, and no one else. You choose the kind of wife to marry, the kind of career to pursue, the kind of house to live in, the type of association to keep; nobody else does these things for you; it is your personal responsibility. Hence, when choosing, you must be ready and courageous enough to accept the attendant consequences, for every choice has a consequence attached to it. The consequences of any action could be positive or negative; but whatever it may be, you are responsible for it.

A typical scriptural example is Moses and the Promised Land. Moses was given the mandate to take the people of Israel to the Promised Land, but he never got there because of his temperament. For lack of water to drink, the people murmured against and even gathered to oppose Moses and Aaron. God told Moses what to do, but he could not control his temper and so angrily said:

> *"Listen, you rebels; must we bring you water out of the rock? Then, Moses raised his hand and struck the rock twice with his staff. Water gushed out, and the community and their livestock drank. The Lord said to Moses and Aaron, Because you did not trust in me enough to honour me as holy in the sight of the Israelites, you will not bring this community into the land I gave them" (Num. 20:10-12).*

3. The Law of Creativity

Each advancement in human life begins as an idea in the mind of a single person. More than anything else, it is the idea that you generate that will enable you to solve your problems, overcome your obstacles and achieve your goals. Ideas are the keys to the future; they are a new mode of transportation, a vehicle you can use to take yourself wherever you desire to go. Your ability to generate constructive ideas is, to all intents and purposes, unlimited. Therefore, your potential is limitless.

Napoleon Hill said,

- *"Whatever the mind of man can conceive and believe, it can achieve."* Brian Tracy also said, *"The very existence of an idea in your conscious mind means that you have within you and around you the capacity to turn it into reality."*

In my book *Anointing for Creativity*, I posited that *"A man without the spirit of creativity and excellence can hardly succeed in life."*

Creativity makes the difference in all things; it distinguishes between two persons on the same salary grade, two managers, course mates, professionals, authors, vocations, companies, businessmen, and even students. The very nature of creativity comes from the idea inside a man, which is converted into information and action.

"Then the Lord said unto Moses, See, I have called by name Bezaleel the son of Uri, the son of Hur, of the tribe of Judah: and I have filled him with the spirit of God, in wisdom, and in understanding, and in knowledge, and in all manner of workmanship, to devise all cunning works, to work in gold and in silver, and in brass, and in cutting of stones, to set them, and in carving of timber, to work in all manner of workmanship" (Exodus 31:1-5).

4. The Law of Compensation

The Ziglar Law says:

- *"You can have anything you want in life if you just help other people get what they want."*

To quote Brian Tracy again:

- *"You are always fully compensated for whatever you do, positive or negative."*

Commenting on compensation, Ralph W.E. says:

- *"The longer you put in without getting out, the greater will be your return when it finally comes."*

For me,

- *"Your involvement with anything you do provides exactly your expectations in multiples of hundred."*

The following definitions of compensation reveal that this law is closely associated with the law of sowing and reaping, which the Scripture confirms in Galatians 6:6-10:

> *"Anyone who receives instruction in the word must share all good things with his instructor. Do not be deceived; God cannot be mocked, a man reaps what he sows. The one who sows to please his sinful nature, from that nature will reap destruction; the one who sows to please the spirit, from the spirit will reap eternal life. Let us not become weary in doing good, for at the proper time we will reap a harvest if we do not give up. Therefore, as we have opportunity let us do good to all people, especially to those people who belong to the family of believers."*

5. The Law f Reproduction

Reading through the Five Laws of Gold as written by Georges Clason in his book, *The Richest Man in Babylon*, we find:

Gold cometh gladly and in increasing quantity to any man who will put but not less than one-tenth of his earnings to create an estate for his future and that of his family.

Gold laboureth diligently and contentedly, so the wise owner who finds for it profitable employment, multiplying even as the flocks of the field.

This law is the multiplying effect. Whoever desires a guaranteed future must know how to multiply his income. According to the first law of Georges Clason, the setting apart of not less than one-tenth of one's earning, for paying one's tithe is not enough, investing or creating an estate for its future use is most desirable. Setting apart one-tenth of your income can reproduce itself several times over if diligently and adequately invested. This brings us to the second law of Georges Clason that Gold, which I refer to as money, laboureth diligently and contentedly for the wise owner who gives it appropriate employment or investment. On its own, it will multiply in multiples of thousands of what was invested. The law of reproduction is a process of geometric multiplication. It can produce beyond the expectation of the owner. The biblical support for this law is found in the gospel of John 12^{24}:

> *"I tell you the truth unless a kernel of wheat falls to the ground and dies, it remains only a single seed. But if it dies, it produces many seed."*

The law of reproduction demands an initial death of the single seed for many more seeds to emerge, but if the seed, which represents the one-tenth, remains intact, be sure that it abides alone and remains only a seed and just one-tenth. Hence the need for the death of your single seed or one-tenth, for many seeds and many 'one-tenths' to emerge, or it will remain and possibly die as a single seed and one-tenth.

6. The Law of Faith

Faith begins where the will of God is known. What constitutes faith today will become reality tomorrow. While vision sees it, faith believes it. Men of faith have defined faith in varying terms. Hebrews 11:1 gives us the scriptural definition of faith:

> *"Now, faith is being sure of what we hope for and certain of what we do not see."*

The mystery of faith is that it suspends the laws of nature. Faith honours God and His ability and goes beyond our human limits and ability. Faith respects no barrier or blockage; it dislodges and destroys spiritual encumbrances. Faith can confound all proven calculations, and mesmerize all proven scientific laws and theories.

Faith is the hope booster that conjures up our expectations to manifest in the physical realm. It is the spiritual fuel that surges through to produce or bring the word of God to manifestation.

Kenneth Copeland says that faith is the parent force of all that exists; the natural world must respond to faith. Faith is the dominant force for the five sensory organs, and it is set in motion when we act upon the word of God. The word of God is the trigger of faith while faith is the force of discharge.

Faith and risk are twin brothers; the level of faith or risk you are ready to take determines the level of success you will have in anything you do; less risk, therefore, means less success.

Faith can be defined as spiritual risk. Our world is full of risks, and only the people who are ready to take risks will succeed. Few years ago, in a particular semi-urban part of the state where we lived, a plot of land was going for Thirty Thousand Naira (N30,000), because of its location (it was entirely inside the bush and nobody expected development there in the next ten to fifteen years). However, land speculators went in to purchase as many plots as they could, while 'cautious' others like me were busy calculating how many years it would take for development to commence there, and so did not bother to invest. Shortly after that, the government of Rivers State decided to locate one government agency at the place. Consequently, this necessitated the building of state roads and other amenities. Immediately, the asking price of land rose from Thirty Thousand Naira (N30,000) to Five Hundred Thousand Naira (N500,000) within thirty (30) months.

The people who invested in the land acted according to the law of faith. Remember that faith is what we believe and the certainty of what we do not see. The scriptural support of this law is contained in Ecclesiastes 11:4[6];

> *"Whoever watches the wind will not plant, whoever looks at the plant will not reap. As you do not know the path of the wind or how the baby is formed in a mother's womb, so you cannot understand the work of God the maker of all things. Sow your seed in the morning and at evening let not your hands be idle, for you do not know which will succeed, whether this or that or both will do equally well."*

7. The Law of Passion

The law of passion talks of your preoccupation, your desire – your longings. Your destiny is connected to your passion. Until you have a burning passion for something, that thing cannot become a vision. Without a vision, the people perish, as popularly known from the Bible.

You can never grow beyond your passion, as your passion is what fires you into action. If your passion is below average, your success will automatically come under the breakeven point. If your passion is at the average level, automatically your success will, at best, be at break-even point. If your passion is above average, your success line will definitely be above break-even point, and can even go far above this with time.

Many people with humble backgrounds find it very difficult to aspire beyond their limit. In fact, any effort to push them beyond their limit is usually met with: "Please, I don't want trouble. Let me remain here, meant for people like us." For such people, their desire to remain where they believe they belong to has put a limit to their achievement. For some, their willingness to remain where they feel they are experts and are revered has limited to their growth, while others see no reason to improve on what their father did or died for. Such people are complacent to advance beyond where they are. While the rest of the world keep moving forward, they refuse to change, preferring to go to the village to settle for unskilled jobs with no risks involved. There are people who distaste wealth and disdain those who are wealthy. These people have no aspiration for wealth and success. They are not motivated by wealth, neither do they desire nor long to be wealthy. Instead, they prefer to put up with the status quo.

No one attracts what he hates with a passion. Such people need a change of attitude towards wealth and to realize that wealth comes from God. The fact that some people cheat and engage in all sorts of dishonest and unethical practices to get wealth does not mean that there are not people who honestly get their wealth.

Lack of passion for wealth because of the way some people go after it cannot be overlooked, but that should not make anyone detest wealth. Only those who get theirs dishonestly deserve our condemnation. In the Bible, Elijah once told God to take him away for he was the only righteous person around, but God refuted his claim and told him that He had about seven thousand prophets who had not bowed their knees to Baal. Indeed, we still have people who made their wealth by thoughtful planning and investing wisely (1 Kings 19:18).

Detesting wealth will never attract wealth your way; instead, it will make you a cheap and ordinary fellow, thereby being a reproach to your God. The scripture that illustrates the law of passion is found in Hebrews 11^{10};

> *"For he was looking forward to the city with foundations whose architect and builder is God."*

This passion enabled Abraham to endure hardships; he obeyed God when He demanded for his only child. Even when he was told to leave his inheritance for an unknown country, Abraham obeyed. This passion made a whole lot of difference in Abraham's life that God called him a man of faith. Passion for your future is essential, and nobody but you can bear the intensity. Passion makes you not to accept everything for an answer.

8. The Law of Perception

Perception is the ability to understand or perceive, while to perceive is to be aware of something by any of the five senses. Some writers have defined perception as the power of imagination, while others say it is the supernatural ability to appreciate things beyond the common knowledge.

One writer said,

- *"What you know through natural understanding can be wrong, but anything you got by revelation lasts."*

From the latter standpoint, perception is a sort of revealed knowledge to guide anyone in anything he or she wishes to embark upon. The law of perception is an essential law for everybody as it rules out guesswork and minimizes risks.

Before our wedding, the Scripture Union and our churches set up committees to interview my wife and I, as tradition demands, to ascertain our convictions. During the interview, they asked my wife to state her convictions. She did. Then one of the brothers asked her to explain how God communicated the things she mentioned to her. She said, "By perception," and added that one of the ways that God speaks to her is through perception.

Anyone who desires to be successful must develop a keen sense of perception. It enables one to identify the problems and prospects inherent in whatever one is about to venture into.

As a minister, one gets posted from one station to another. As I prayed with my wife on the mind of God about one of such postings, she told me that she perceived that the Lord was about to do something new for us and that we should go. Another colleague of mine came to my house in the cathedral then and told me that he perceived that there was gold in that new church and I should look beyond the unattractive surface. He said that below the dirty surface was precious gold. And, indeed, there was gold there.

There are some people who would see, touch, taste, smell, and hear, but would not perceive. Before them lie tremendous business opportunities, yet they do not understand it. Some have great marriage and career opportunities before them, yet they would not perceive it. Some have open doors for business contracts, but they will not understand it. Some have great opportunities for promotion starring them in the face, but it would not get to them because of lack of perception. Consequently, many incredible opportunities have slipped off their hands without them knowing it.

These two Bible references validated this law of perception.

> *"He said, Go and tell this people: be ever hearing, but never understanding be ever seeing, but never perceiving" (Isaiah 6^9).*

> *"For this people's heart has become calloused, they hardly hear with their ears, and they have closed their eyes. Otherwise, they might see with their eyes, hear with their ears, understand with their hearts and turn, and I would heal them" (Acts 28^{27}).*

The law of perception, if properly interpreted and applied, does not fail. It is a principles that works, regardless of who applies it.

9. The Law of Sowing and Reaping

This is an indispensable law that guides all humans. No man is exempted from this law. Believers and unbelievers, Greeks and Gentiles, free born and slaves are governed by this law. The daily life we share with one another is being determined and controlled by this law. In the business world, this law is very active; in the marriage world, it is very effective; in the academic world, it is most excellent in function; in the farming world, it is the yardstick for the farmer; at the community level, it is the guiding principle; at the national level, it is appropriate.

It is what you give that you stand to get back. You are not expected to reap where you did not sow; neither are you supposed to reap above your sowing ability. Whenever this happens, it becomes abnormal.

Let's take a farmer as an example: if the farmer sows a small piece of yam tuber, he is expected to reap just a little above that size. There is a saying that a part of our country is more fertile than others. But, upon close observation and random interview, it was discovered that this part of the country actually plants big yam seedlings, while the other parts cut their yam seedlings into pieces. So at harvest time, since this law of sowing and reaping must take effect, the land gives back the corresponding size of yam seedlings planted. The same applies in the business world. For instance, if businessman 'A' invests N100,000 in a particular business, while businessman 'B' invests in the same business only N10,000, there is no way this law will allow businessman 'B' to reap the same size of profit as businessman 'A' if they exerted equal effort. Beyond this, the struggle between both of them will not be the same and their standards of living will never be the same. It is what you are able to commit into your relationship that you will reap. "It does not matter", should not in any way be spiritualized. The law is perfect in all situations and works in all circumstances.

Among academics or students, it works – it is what you sow that you will reap eventually. I have heard many lecturers complain of how qualified they are to become professors over years but have not been so honoured. After investigating their claims, I discovered that they have not met even the minimum requirement for the office of a professor. On the other hand, some have not published the required publications, yet they wish to be called professors.

Some students also have accused their lecturers of victimization in their marking while, in actual sense, they did not read for the exams and therefore had nothing to write. In short, they wrote nothing yet expected to pass their courses. Please, whatever a man sows, that shall he reap.

> *"Do not be deceived; God cannot be mocked: a man reaps what he sows" (Galatians 6^7).*

> *"The one who sows to please his sinful nature, from that nature will reap destruction, the one who sows to please the spirit, from the spirit will reap eternal life" (Gal. 6^8).*

> *"Let us not become weary in doing good, for at the proper time, we will reap a harvest if we do not give up" (Gal. 6^9).*

> *"Remember this Whosoever sows sparingly will also reap sparingly, and whosoever sows generously will also reap generously" (2 Cor. 9^6).*

10. The Law of Focus

This law helps you not to lose concentration or get distracted from the target, and to fix your sight on the most critical issues in your life. Many people today are lagging behind because of loss of initial focus. The law of focus helps you to multiply your likes and creates multiplicity. Focus locks you in and challenges you to think your way out. A friend of mine had planned to study Medicine, but when that year's JAMB result was released, like me, he scored below the cutoff point. He consequently lost focus and decided to change to statistics. Today, instead of being a Medical Doctor, he is a Statistician; instead of being in the hospital, he is in the Statistics office.

Another one had a dream of becoming a lawyer, but his JAMB result that year fell below the required mark. He quickly changed his mind for Political Science and has long finished his course. He has recently enrolled to study Law on part-time at the National Open University.

The law of focus thinks of posterity and determines to justify the end product. A focused person never misses out, irrespective of the circumstance (s). Reading through Hebrews 12^2, you will discover more about focus:

> *"Let us fix our eyes on Jesus, the author, and perfecter of our faith, who for the joy set before him endured the cross, scorning its shame and sat down at the right hand of God."*

A close study of this verse reveals that focus has to do with absolute concentration. Just as a runner concentrates on the finish line, so we need to focus on the finish line of our pursuits. To come to this level of concentration, we must first concentrate on Jesus Christ who enables us to focus on the finish line. In line with this law, the apostle Paul states in Philippians 3:13-14:

> *"Brothers, I do not consider myself yet to have taken hold of it. But one thing I do, forgetting what is behind and straining toward what is ahead, I press on towards the goal to win the prize for which God has called me heavenward in Christ Jesus."*

The ultimate aspiration of any individual, either in business or the professions or even in marital matters, is to get the best out of whatever he or she does. The ultimate aspiration of any businessman is to continue to be in business, in season and out of season, and this can only be possible if he is able to press on towards the goal of winning the prize of making profit far above his expenditure.

Likewise, the ultimate aspiration of any married couple is to press towards the goal to win the prize of a good relationship and a healthy marriage. Again, the life of Abraham explains the law of focus as we find in Hebrews 11:8-10:

> *"By faith Abraham, when called to go to a place he would later receive as his inheritance, obeyed and went, even though he did not know where he was going. By faith he made his home in the Promised Land like a stranger in a foreign country; he lived in tents, as did Isaac and Jacob, who were heirs with him in the same promise. For he was looking forward to the city with foundation, whose architect and builder is God."*

The law of focus rules out the spirit of fear and believes absolutely in faith. It considers nothing outside of faith and always believes things will definitely work out for good. When you stay focused, after some time, you will automatically get absorbed in your focus, and every symptom of pregnancy will come upon you. You would not realize when you slide into travailing, which will eventually give birth to your heart's desire. In keeping to his service in the household of Laban, Jacob adopted this strategy, and it worked out wonderful results for him. He agreed with his father-in-law on wages of coloured/streaked or speckled/spotted flocks:

> *"Jacob, however, took fresh-cut branches from poplar, almond, and plain trees and made white stripes on them by peeling the bark and exposing the white inner wood of the branches. Then he placed the peeled branches in all the watering troughs so that they will be directly in front of the flocks when they come to drink. When the flocks were in heat and came to drink, they mated in front of the branches. And they bore young that were streaked or speckled or spotted" (Genesis 30^{37}-^{39}).*

Reflection On Chapter 4

Personal Notes: _____

_____
_____
_____
_____
_____
_____
_____

Guided Action Plan

_____
_____
_____
_____
_____
_____
_____
_____

CHAPTER 5
7 Principles Of Wealth Creation

"The only thing that stands between a man and what he wants from life is often merely the will to try it and the faith to believe that it is possible" – **Richard D.**

The Ability to Create Wealth

The principle of wealth creation revolves around the ability to create wealth, which is inherent in every human being. While some may consciously develop their own, others may ignorantly neglect theirs.

Ability is defined as "the mental or physical capacity, power or skill required to do something." It could as well be defined as "the power and skill to make, to do and to think." Ability could also mean "the capacity to discipline oneself."

There are different kinds of ability. The ability to solve complex problems is different from the ability to solve simple problems. The ability to add one and one to equal two is the same ability to solve geometric progression, but it is not the same with the ability to solve calculation problems. There are elementary problems that do not require high level of ability, but every ability leads to the creation of wealth of some sort.

Abilities range from athletics, through artistic to ministerial, professional, literary, and martial arts.

The ability to create wealth requires a vigorous effort to develop it before the wealth can start rolling in. This ability has been given to every one of us, but the ability to put it to work is up to each individual to develop. There are many wealthy people who are in the grave as poor wretched fellows because they could not put into use the ability given to them while they were alive. Due to the inability to unlock the potentials in them, many died as beggars, while they were supposed to have lent to nations.

Brian Tracy has this to say from the book of *Tony Buzan*;

- *"The mental potential of the average person is largely untapped and virtually unlimited."*

The part of one's brain that controls thinking has approximately one hundred billion cells or neurons. Each of these cells bristles like a porcupine with as many as twenty thousand ganglia or fibers that connect it to other brain cells. These cells are in turn, connected and interconnected to thousands and millions of other cells, like an electric grid that lights up and powers a large city. Each cell and each connection contain an element of mental energy or information that is available to every other cell. This means that the complexity of your brain is therefore beyond belief or imagination.

According to Tony Buzan and other experts in brain development, the number of combinations and permutations of brain connections you have are greater than the number of molecules in the known universe. It would be the equivalent of the number 'one' followed by eight pages of zeros, row after row and page after page.

The statement above goes a long way to reveal the wisdom behind God's statement in Deut. 8:18;

> *"But remember the Lord your God for it is he who gives you the ability to produce wealth, and so confirms his covenant, which he swore to your forefathers, as it is today."*

The ability to create wealth is given, but the ability to develop this ability to reproduce or work out its full-blown result is for you to exercise. According to a research conducted by *Prof. Sergei Yeframor* in Russia some years ago, if you could use just 50 percent of your existing mental capacity, you could complete the doctoral requirement of a dozen universities, learn a dozen languages with ease and memorize the entire twenty-two volumes of the Encyclopedia Britannica.

If this is anything to believe, it does mean that everybody is only making use of less than one percent of our inherent abilities.

The art of creating wealth is the action of tasking your ability and your power of thinking. If you task your ability, your mental potential will definitely increase without struggle and of course your expectation, what the economist calls profit will definitely double or increase. If you refuse to create wealth with your God-given ability, be assured you will die as a poor man and in poverty. God cannot create wealth for you, but He can remind you that you have the ability to make a change in your situation today.

This truth is about to turn you around; it since turned me around. It turned Elisha, it turned Joseph and other people around, grasp it today and be on top tomorrow. The ability to create wealth is a powerful principle God did not hide from man. Instead, He gave it to man for his upkeep and welfare. There are lots of people who have missed it, and today, they are beggars. There are some who are using their ability to create wealth for others and every month; they collect salary. Each time they threaten that they want to go, the management will pacify them with an increase in pay and promotion and they will settle down. Why must they be appeased with salary increase and promotion? Simple: if they go, the creating ability of the company or the business will go down, which will, in turn, affect the income with a downward slope. This kind of reaction is common among people in different fields of businesses and professions. The man who succeeds in putting two percent of his mental potentials to action is usually regarded as a first-class student or worker. The ability functions more when challenged by constant bombardment; when you stop creating, your ability will become inert and blunt. Continuous creating sharpens your ability for reflective thoughts. So, your ability to create ideas must continuously be utilized to remain in excellent condition.

The difference between the poor and the rich is that the poor refuses to task his ability to create while the rich tasks his ability to create. The difference between the first class and third-class student is that the first-class student uses his ability to create wealth while the third-class student does not. The difference between a successful and unsuccessful medical doctor is that one decides to use his creative ability, while the other is just satisfied by having the title 'doctor' attached to his name. The critical news to every one of us is that the natural and typical ability has the capacity to create wealth of some sort. You must become highly restless about the present performance of your ability and struggle to increase the usage of your mental potential to at least three percent and I tell you, everything about you will shoot up: your finances will triple, your marriage will be provoked, your spiritual life will improve, your material well-being will be noticed by everybody around you, life will begin to ooze out of you that you and everybody around you will be amazed.

The Ability to Consider No Limitation

Merely thinking of or imagining a limitation is enough limitation to stop you from moving forward. The ability to consider that you have all it takes to have a breakthrough is a substantial advantage in a positive direction. But if you sit down to bemoan all the obstacles and hindrances that confronts you, you cannot advance further. The ability to think beyond your limitations brings confidence in your ability, talent, and belief.

A lot of people have excuses why they should not take the initial step to success. They will recount to you, the experiences of people who have attempted the same thing without result or success. They recount the stories of people they esteemed above themselves who did not make it, how much more themselves. Limitations are man-made and develop out of unbelief and doubt. Often times, they are not there in the real sense. They are mental constructs created by our imaginations. These paradigms can cripple your creativity and disable your ability to function and soar high in life.

There are people who are already defeated before they take the first step. There was a young man I talked with a few years ago about his business and how he could improve or change his line of business. When I wanted to proffer solutions to his problem, he began enumerating the number of people who had failed in that line of business and why he thinks that he would also fail. After his statement, I was not eager to give him my suggestions anymore, since he has made up his mind.

For you to make break barriers and accomplish remarkable success, you must deliberately refuse to imagine limitations or even consider its possibility. This ability carries surprise, because everybody who has failed in that business may be all out to see your failure, but once they see that you have and gradually scaled through and dismantled those supposed limitations, they will come back to you to narrate how they made several attempts that never worked out.

I was once constituted into a committee as the chairman. By the time we finished our feasibility study, reported our findings and made our recommendations to the body that set up the committee, one of the persons there got up and said, "This will not work, I have a better option." I struggled to cancel that limitation he placed, but nobody understood me. Unfortunately, that was the end of that project and also the end of his 'better opinion' as at the point of writing this book.

If there is anybody you should dread, it is a man who often sees or identifies why anything will not work out. If you can get rid of such persons, I tell you the truth; you have climbed the first step of success.

I was in a meeting with a group of people discussing how to register an organization with the Corporate Affairs Office, Abuja. Everyone in that meeting made their suggestions. Sadly, every suggestion ended with the impossibility of getting it registered if we didn't have anybody at Abuja. I told them that I had just registered one and that it was easy and straightforward but they almost said it was impossible. So, after the meeting, I asked the leader of the body to hand over to me every document relating to the registration in his possession. He did, and within six months, the certificate arrived safely to us. For them it was unbelievable. There have been cases where people will take time to educate you on the limitation rather than the possibilities, and if you are a feeble minded fellow, you will fall into the pit of uncountable limitations.

In Ecclesiastes 11^4, the writer drove his message home in style;

> *"Whosoever watches the wind will not plant; whoever looks at the clouds will not reap."*

The scripture above suggests that there should not be a room to consider a limitation whether they are known limitations or not. It does not matter how many people that have not succeeded before you, your case is a different one. Genesis 26$^{1-3}$, says;

> *"Now there was Famine in the land-besides the earlier famine of Abraham's time – and Isaac went to Abimelech king of the Philistines in Gerar. The Lord appeared to Isaac and said; 'Do not go down to Egypt, live in the land where I tell you to live. Stay in this land for a while, and I will be with you and will bless you. For to you and your descendants, I will give all these lands and will confirm the oath I swore to your father, Abraham."*

The Bible accounts that Isaac obeyed the word of the Lord without considering any limitations to the voice of the Lord. This was a man who had experienced famine in its detail and had seen more than four famines. He knew how disastrous famines were. Common sense told him that he should prepare and take his family to a nearby nation where there was food to eat, at least. He imagined a limitation, that was why he went to the king to ask for permission to go and settle in Egypt. But when God spoke to him and assured him of His presence, the Bible says that Isaac did not go down to Egypt anymore. Instead, he planted in the land of famine and reaped bountifully.

Join me to see the tremendous result of harvest in *verses 12-13* of the same chapter.

> ***"Isaac planted crops in that land and in the same year reaped a hundredfold, because God blessed him. The man became rich, and his wealth continued to grow until he became very wealthy."***

When the ability to disregard limitation is channeled correctly, I tell you, things happen beyond human imaginations. Who would have believed that a man who considered no limitation planted in the land of famine and reaped a hundredfold in the same year, while others reaped nothing. This was the land where people were going hungry, but a man suddenly began to grow rich, continued to be prosperous until he became very wealthy. He became an envy in Gerar and was asked to leave.

The ability to consider no limitation even in the face of problems is a rare ability. It is the ability that makes one businessman, minister or professional to have an edge over his colleagues. This ability considers everything possible without a minute consideration of being stopped by anything: The same land favoured one man and did not favour the rest of the people.

The Ability to Save

People have the notion that savings is only possible when you earn a high income or when your cash flow is high, but over the years it has been proved that if you cannot save from a low income of N10,000, you cannot save from an income of

N100,000. If you cannot set aside ten percent of your income, you are not saving. Your savings is what you pay yourself from your income.

George S. Clason said in his book, *The Richest Man in Babylon,* that;

- *"A part of all I earn is mine to keep."*

If ninety percent of your income cannot solve your problems, the extra ten percent cannot either. The ability to save is a disciplined ability. It is the ability to say no to anything that wants to force you to use up what you have set aside or what you have decided to safeguard from spending. If your expenditure is equal to your income, it means that you are not saving, and you have nothing to invest, nothing to yield revenue in the future, nothing to sow, and nothing to harvest during harvest time.

In the lesson of the saving process of Alhamish to Arkad recorded in George S. Clason's *The Richest Man in Babylon*:

- *"If you did keep for yourself one-tenth of all you earn, how much would you have in ten years? My knowledge of the numbers did not forsake me, and I answered; As much as I earn in one year. You speak but half the truth, he retorted. Every gold piece you save is a slave to work for you. Every copper it earns is its child that also earns for you. If you would become wealthy, then what you save must earn, and its children must earn, that all may help to give to you the abundance you crave."*

A part of all you earn is yours to keep. It should not be less than a tenth no matter how little you earn. It can be as much more as you can afford. Pay yourself first. Do not buy from the clothes makers and the sandals makers more than you can pay out of the remaining and still have enough for food, charity, and penance to God.

Wealth, like trees, grow from a tiny seed. The first copper you save is the seed from which your tree of wealth shall grow. The sooner you plant that seed, the sooner shall the tree grow and the more faithfully you nourish and water that tree with consistent savings, the sooner you may bask in contentment beneath its shade.

The initial saving is the tiny seed that eventually becomes a tree of wealth. It can grow to any size provided it is being taken care of and continuously put in use. If your savings is dormant, your tree of wealth cannot grow. But if there is constant addition and efficient use of your savings, the tree of your wealth will flourish. He said each savings when gainfully employed, will bring up baby-savings which are the children of the initial savings. While the mother-savings is producing children, the children are producing, the grandchildren are producing, and you cannot imagine how great a wealthy man you will become in the next few years.

He called them slaves, but I choose to say that slaves are being paid and taken care of, but this level of 'slavery' of your saving is expenses-free, it does not take out of you any kobo or leisure.

While you are sleeping, they are earning income for you; while you are resting or relaxing, they are yielding income for you. Even when you are retired, they do not retire, do not sleep nor rest, neither do they have time to relax. They work twenty-four hours a day. Their yield has no limitations. They have a recurring incoming earning system.

What is Savings?

This definition will only consider the personal disposable income, which entails the income households receive from firms or businesses, plus transfer payments received from government, dividends from investments, minus direct taxes paid to the government. This is the income that is available for spending or saving.

Savings is defined as the difference between income and current consumption. It is that part of income that is not spent on buying goods and services. It can further be explained by taking a personality 'A,' whose monthly income is N100,000. Personality A spends N80,000 buying goods and services and setting aside N20,000. The set-aside N20,000 becomes his savings for that month, but not yet an investment. It becomes an investment only when he employs that N20,000 in an investment or trades with it. It is at this point that it can begin to produce children and grandchildren 'who' will, in turn, produce their own children and grandchildren. Let us consider this quotation from the Bible which lends credence to this conclusion:

> *John 12* [24] *"I tell you the truth, unless a kernel of wheat falls to the ground and dies, it remains only a single seed, but if it dies, it produces many seeds."*

Your savings abides as a single seed except it is invested. When invested, it is referred to as falling and dying, after which it brings many more seeds (savings) your way.

George S. Clason in his book titled *The Richest Man in Babylon* described savings as the first step leading to the temple of wealth and no man may climb who cannot plant his feet on the first step."

Saving is a deliberate action by an individual or household. Since you cannot meet all your personal needs or household needs even if you spend all your given income and add borrowed resources, your action should be to watch or put an eye on your current consumption to make sure it does not take up all your income. Remember that you have the right to pay yourself first before spending your income and that part you pay yourself before spending is called your savings or seed. Don't just keep it floating because nature abhors floating cash, instead put it to work. Jesus Christ in the gospel of Matthew 25[14-30] talked about hidden talent that was supposed to be invested.

> *"His master replied, you wicked and lazy servant. So, you knew that I harvest where I have not sown and gather where I have not scattered seed? Well then, you should have put my money on deposit with the bankers,*

> *so that when I returned, I would have received it back with interest" (vs.* 26-27*).*

The lazy and wicked servant hid the talent where it did not bring additional funds. Instead, it remained exactly what it was, and the interest of Christ was not the accusation, but his inability to invest or engage the talent for possible increase in value. He said;

> "Well then, you should have put my money on deposit with the bankers." For what purpose? "So that when I come I would receive interest" (increase).

This is the difference between the wealthy man and the poor man. The wealthy man employs his excess inflows over outflows while the poor man digs hole and puts his own without future increase. What you sow is what you reap, as a result.

Red and Green Lights of Savings

George S. Clason says,

- *"I found the road to wealth when I decided that a part of all I earned was mine to keep."*
- *The following points illustrate our attitude towards savings and its overbearing influence:*
- *Trying to meet all your needs before you consider keeping a part of all you earn.*
- *Keep an eye on all your expenditure to meet only a few urgent ones at a time.*

- *Consider that your income is insufficient or too small to consider setting aside a part of it, continually look at your needs instead of at your seed.*

- *Without deliberate discipline to save, you cannot harvest tomorrow.*

- *Without investing your excess inflows over your outflows, your excess abides alone.*

- *Savings does not create wealth, but the employment of your savings does.*

- *It is only in contentment that savings are made possible.*

- *Without savings, there is no tomorrow expenses.*

- *The root of all wealth is savings properly employed and deployed.*

In summarizing this topic, I leave you with the principle of George S. Clason;

- *"Wealth, like a tree grows from a tiny seed. The first copper you save is the seed from which your tree of wealth shall grow. The sooner you plant your seed, the sooner shall the tree grow. And the more faithfully you nourish and water that tree with consistent saving, the sooner you will bask in contentment beneath its shades".*

The Ability to Put your Hand to Work

There are lots of people whose hands are idle. An idle hand does not create any wealth.

A young friend of mine graduated from school, and for six years he looked for employment without success. Few years ago, he came to my office to inform me of his intention to start something for himself. This was a paradigm shift.

The ability to commit your hand to work is the beginning of wealth creation. Wealth is created when our hands are engaged in meaningful ventures. Listen, anything your hands are laid upon creates that thing for you. The Lord did say; "I will bless the works of your hand…" not the certificate nor your profession, not the vocation you choose, not the career you pursue, rather the works of your hands. I once suggested to a friend who has obtained an MBA degree to look around for a small-scale business he can start for himself, but he said; "I cannot do that! Why did I go to school, won't I use my certificate to work?" There are many of us who have a misconception about schooling and obtaining a certificate. Education does not guarantee employment. There are lots of unemployed graduates roaming the streets, seeking for jobs. Education expands your mental faculty and improves your reasoning capacity. It accelerates your velocity of personal management and gives you a better understanding of interpersonal relationship, and how to employ the factors of production.

He has an MBA certificate, and I am meant to understand that MBA means Master of Business Administration. Still, a Master of Business Administration graduate has been looking for employment for almost three years when there are business opportunities and openings all around him. This reveals the harm of education or what education has not taught us. A man with Master of Business Administration cannot create a business for three years. Let your hands be put to work, stop lazing about and begging for food when you can produce food for every one of us.

I have seen young men full of life accepting between N5,000 to N10,000 as monthly salaries. Come to think of it; this is a symptom of laziness and idle hands. In line with Proverbs 10[4],

> **"Lazy hands make a man poor, but diligent hands bring wealth."**

When a man's hands are lazy, the result is poverty. But if a man is diligent, wealth naturally comes. Such a man needs not beg for what to eat. Today, you can change your financial position if only you will develop diligent hands. It did not say inherit wealth; instead, it brings wealth. Again, in Proverbs 12[24],

> **"Diligent hands will rule, but laziness ends in slave labour."**

When we observe the society, we will discover that all the lazy hands are slaves, including all civil servants and public servants. I see a lot of slaves in the society.

Who is a slave? By conventional definition, I define a slave as someone who cannot do what he wants to do because of constraints by the authority over him. In the scripture above, diligent hands will rule the lazy hands. How? By employing him to do jobs for him with little or no salary when compared to the market force(s). Proverb 13:4

> *"The sluggard craves and gets nothing, but the desires of the diligent are fully satisfied."*

The sluggard wants more of good things and pleasure, yet cannot work. He goes for free food, drinks at gatherings and quarrels over food and drinks, yet he cannot work. You find them everywhere: in the family front, in the community front, in the office front. You can identify them by these simple attitudinal traits. They quarrel over minors. They are also possessed with the spirit of greed and envy. In qualifying a wife of noble character, one of the essential traits used was the efficient use of her hands. Proverbs 31:13;

> *"She selects wool and flax and works with eager hands."*

Ecclesiastes 10:18, the Bible described a particular man by saying:

> *"If a man is lazy, the rafters sag, if his hands are idle, the house leaks."*

You can imagine all the 'rafters' of families that have sagged around you. All the 'rafters' of marriages, professions, businesses, the future, and ministry that have sagged due to the laziness of the man. You can as well imagine all the houses that are leaking due to idle hands. Join me in this prayer as said by the Psalmist in Psalm 90:17;

"May the favour of the Lord our God rest upon us, establish the work of our hands for us, yes establish the work of our hands."

The Ability to Conquer your Gentile Mentality

Gentile mentality is the short-term perspective actions seen exhibited everywhere. It does not see beyond 'now.' Everything around the Gentile is for immediate consumption. His emphasis is on three major areas of need:

- What to eat
- What to drink
- What to wear

Dr. Edward Banfield defined the opposite of short-term perspective thinkers when he said; long-term perspective is *"the ability to think several years into the future while making decisions in the present."*

The ability to redress the Gentile mentality is the beginning of wealth creation. Jesus while addressing the disciples at the mount in the gospel according to Saint Matthew 6^{31-32} says,

"Therefore, take no thoughts saying, what shall we eat? Or what shall we drink? Or wherewithal shall we be clothed? For after all these things do the Gentiles seek, for your heavenly Father knoweth that ye have need of all these things (KJV).

The whole human need centers on these three needs our Lord mentioned in the verse above: He started by warning the believers not to allow these things to bother them:

- What shall we eat
- What shall we drink
- Wherewithal shall we be clothed

These are the nuclei of our expenses. All our income is divided into these three significant items. People with Gentile mentality work, earn salaries and spend same on 'what shall we eat,' 'what shall we drink,' and 'what shall we be clothed with.' Various misunderstandings in our marriages are traceable to these three major areas of need. They do not think of what to keep behind from their earnings. Instead, they consider more of immediate satisfaction without a plan for the future.

Anything you invest in and still maintain is not an asset but rather, a liability. All the demands of the Gentiles are liabilities. Gentiles zero more into liabilities than into assets. Liabilities do not yield future income, but assets do. What shall we eat? Think of it, after you have eaten; give it few hours, it is gone. As you finish drinking, it is passed out as urine. Clothing does not last, at most you find a particular dress in vogue for two years, after which it becomes obsolete and out of fashion. Women will tell you better; that some wrappers only last but few months. Yet these are the major areas of our expenditure.

I once went to pray for a family. As I got there, the wife of the man was in her shoes and hats room. When she heard my voice, she screamed 'my pastor.' As she was stepping out from the room, I was stepping into the same room with her husband. Brethren, what I saw that day was better seen than told or narrated. Without exaggeration, I saw well over two thousand female shoes and over three thousand female hats, then bags of different sizes and shapes. I did not know when I shouted. Her husband said, "Pastor, there are many more in other rooms and especially in our bedroom." I mean a room of standard length and width was allocated to just shoes and hats. Your guess will be as good as mine in calculating how many boxes of wrappers she has since women naturally wear to match. I don't want to talk about jewelries and others that go with women's dressing. Our Lord Jesus Christ called such mentality 'Gentile mentality.' I told the woman that what she was doing was unnecessary and a waste of future investment and she replied, "but Pastor if I want money now, I will take some of these things to the market and sell them." I asked her "at what price?" Liabilities never return their worth. Instead, they are sold lower than their price, but assets appreciate in value and worth.

Paul in Ephesians 4$^{17-19}$ warned the brethren in Ephesus against the Gentile mentality when he wrote:

> *"So I tell you this, and insist on it in the Lord, that you must no longer live as the Gentiles do, in the futility of their thinking. They are darkened in their understanding*

and separated from the life of God because of the ignorance that is in them due to the hardening of their hearts. Having lost all sensitivity, they have given themselves over to sensuality so as to indulge in every kind of impurity, with a continual lust for more."

There is a particular way of life the Gentiles lead which Paul was referring to in the scriptures and warning us to desist from. How do they live?

- In the futility of their thinking,
- They are darkened in their understanding and separated from the life of God,
- In ignorance due to the hardening of their hearts,
- They have lost all sensitivity,
- They have given themselves over to sensuality so as to indulge in every kind of impurity,
- With a continual lust for more.

When you put these things together, you can assess yourself whether you are a Gentile in mentality or not. Gentiles think that acquiring more of liability materials; that is what to eat, drink or clothes to wear, makes them important. It's sad and pathetic. But they forget that those things will not stand the test of time. The 'Gentile mentality' kind of people do not consider tomorrow or posterity, all they know and understand is consumption. They belong to the 'consuming group' with nothing to set aside for the rainy day. They buy goods on credit, and they borrow a lot to satisfy their appetite. They lack contentment due to their desire and longing for more, just as Paul said; "… with a continual lust for more…" they compete with people and brag a lot. They tell lies to retain their 'status.' Mentally, they are illiterates. Before their monthly earning arrives, they have already spent it. Such people hardly maintain any savings, as there is nothing to set aside, as such, no seed to plant (invest) and nothing brings extra income to them. **"Life without Christ is intellectually frustrating, useless and meaningless."**

The Ability To Develop A Passion For What You Do

"Passion is power," they say. For me, passion is an intoxicating power capable of putting you always on the achiever's seat. There are seats meant for achievers; non-performers cannot sit on such seats. Not that they cannot, but they consciously despise the seat and believe that nature has set it aside for a particular group of people.

What you do will only produce results:

- If its love begins to consume you and draw you apart and away from the large crowd;

- If its love begins to take hold of your mind, such that your mind has no room for meanness;

- If its love captures your thoughts, such that you are not thinking about any other thing;

- If its motivational aspiration dominates your daily conversations, such that people identify you with that thought;

- If its claim begins to take charge of your schedules and if its relevance preoccupies your sleeping, dreams, and goals in life.

Mike Murdock says in one of his books, 'you will never have significant success with anything until it becomes an obsession with you.' (Obsession means, to fill the mind of somebody continually so that they can think of nothing else).

An obsession is when something consumes your thoughts and time. And until a businessman, minister, housewife, professional, student, etc., becomes obsessed with a thing, he will make little or no progress in that thing.

If people just want to do any available thing, whether it interests them or not or gives them time, they will crash out of that thing because of lack of interest and passion. I see a lot of people doing what ordinarily they wouldn't like to do but which they succumb to because of pressure. I have seen a lot of students who are in school studying courses or pursuing careers they don't have interest in at all. I have also seen women who are in marriages they never have interest in.

Symptoms of Persons who Lack Passion

- They complain about everything they do and the people around them.

- They give reasons for every failure recorded and dwell there without making progress.

- They hate competition and challenges that are capable of exposing them.

- They don't care whether the business is progressing or not, all they know is their salary or allowance, at the end of the month, or week as the case may be.

- They dearly desire closing hours to come up earlier than it's supposed to.

- They rejoice and jump at public holidays.

- They look out for other places and with their thoughts wandering out towards other places of work.

- They get involved in private practice.

- Their attitude to business is exactly the attitude of government workers and civil servants.

- They have no plans of improving the place they are in.

- They are 'eye service' people.

- They rejoice over the downfall of their present place of work.

These kinds of people are dangerous to the health of any business and should be shown the way out. If they are your business partners, you are in big trouble; if it is in marriage, that marriage will never see the light of the day. That is why many talented people are in the grave without their talents exploited.

Everybody who wants to create wealth must have passion for whatever he does. It does not matter what the business is, what matters is your passion; get obsessed with it and see it as the only opportunity you have to succeed. People who have 'other' opportunities hardly succeed in life pursuits. Alternatives are enemies of obsession and great enemies of passion. They reduce the velocity of your burden to pursue that business with total zeal. You can start small, but your passion for that small beginning will expand the small to a very outstanding success, that people who saw you when you started will be left with only the job of gossiping about you and blackmailing you. It does not matter how little your beginning is, whenever the love of it begins to consume your whole being, then you are in for extraordinary success and achievements. We have seen people who started from rags, but today they are the leading millionaires in various nations.

This scripture is in perfect line with the above. Colossians 3^{23} says **"Whatever you do, work at it with all your heart as working for the Lord, not for men."**

Paul was encouraging us in this scripture to work with passion when he says; "… work at it with all your heart…." Anything you commit your heart to must prosper, but most times, people work as unto men and not as unto the Lord.

It does not matter how small it is; if you work as unto the Lord, with all your heart, I tell you the truth, success must surely greet your efforts. Zechariah 4^{10}, says **"Who despises the day of small** *things"* and according to Isaiah 28[10], ***"For it is do and do, do and do, rule on rule, rule on rule a little here, a little there."***

Whatever you possess today is sufficient enough to create the wealth you will ever desire and imagine in future.

- *"Whatever you have been given is enough to create anything you have been promised."*

Success does not depend on large sums of money, but a little sum can achieve it. I have seen Mr. Success crying out aloud concerning the misconceptions people have about him and the wrong judgment they have given about him. Start today with the little oil or the small hand cake or slingshot and see your success great, tomorrow.

The Ability To Understand The Real Meaning And Whereabouts Of Money

The academic definition of money limits the real meaning of money. Let us consider some definitions of money and establish if they actually define the real meaning of money.

In the book titled *Economics Beyond Demand and supply, Edet B. Akpakpan* defines money to be:

- *"Anything which is generally acceptable and can, therefore, be used in a community as a medium of exchange."*

It is the standard object used in a community for effective exchange of goods and services. It is good to be aware that what may serve as money in one community may not be accepted as money in another community.

Another definition of money is:

- *"What you choose to receive in exchange for what you give out."*

Yet, another definition of money is:

- *"Anything of value."*

By the third definition, "money's definition includes; your time, your knowledge, your skills, your gifts, your talents and your valuables."

The functions of money include the following:

A Medium of Exchange: It is the means by which trade and other forms of exchange are affected in the community.

A Measure of Value: It is a common denominator of value in the community. That is, it is the thing in terms of which the value of every other thing in the community is expressed.

A Store of Value: It is the object into which people can convert their wealth and store for a long time to avoid losses.

A Standard for Deferred Payments: It is the unit by which accounts are kept so that they can be collected in future.

It is a common knowledge that money is not only what we carry around in our wallets; it is anything we possess that solves a problem for another person. Money is localized anywhere; different people have found money outside the confines of conventional employment or business. Kanu Nwankwo found money in football while Mary Onyeali found financial breakthrough in athletics. Different people have found financial success in different things. Some persons have found money in their professions and careers, some others in the deep ocean. Some persons have found money in politics, some in teaching, boxing, supply, palm oil produce, petroleum products or in media. For some others, it is in communication, some in technology, in publicity, in editing and proofreading other people's works, farming, etc. Money is everywhere you can think of. Don't limit your search for money to only one place or give up your search when it is not there. Search some other place. You must search because if you don't, there will be no medium of exchange for you.

Your talent is money; exchange it for the medium of exchange, transfer it to meaningful venture and your money will come. Stop living a beggarly kind of life. Convert your gift into money, convert your knowledge into money, convert your valuables into money, convert your time into money, and you will see money come your way. Many people are carrying money around but still for search it every day.

What do you like doing? That is where you will find your money. Interest cannot be divorced from the whereabouts of money. Interest creates the atmosphere for money generation. Start today to look for the money everywhere. It is not located in one place; instead, it is everywhere.

> *"Diligent hands will rule, but laziness ends in slave labour"* (Proverbs 12^{24}).

The Ability To Overcome Grasshopper Mentality

It does not matter how your father died, whether as a poor wretched man or not. It does not matter whether your lineage has been known for being poverty-stricken, it does not matter whether your family has been stigmatized as a poor family, or you have not inherited anything from your parents. You can prove to the whole world that you are not going that way at all by breaking the stigma. Hear this from 1 John 5[4],

> *"For everyone born of God overcomes the world. This is the victory that has overcome the world even our faith."*

Again, Galatians 4[7] says; "

> *So you are no longer a slave but a son, and since you are a son, God has made you also an heir."*

The foundation should not in any way influence you to succumb to its pressure. You don't need to die the way your father died, neither is it proper for you to fail where your father failed. You must learn how to say "No" to the contradictions of life especially when it is constantly presenting itself for a repeat. You are meant to overcome the world in marriage, profession, and business. It is a divine right to live above the reproach of poverty, the limits of servanthood, and the inhibitions of failure. Your status has changed from servant or slave to a son and heir. Stop disgracing God as if He who made a promise is unable to bring it to pass.

Jabez was quiet for a long time, but a day came when he realized his new position and status. Therefore, he called on God for complete change, both in status and material blessing. The Bible did record that Jabez became more honourable than his brethren who never bothered to ask for a change in their predicaments.

1Chronciles 4$^{9-10}$ says,

> *"Jabez was more honourable than his brothers. His mother had named him Jabez, saying; I gave birth to him in pain. Jabez cried out to the God of Israel; oh, that You would bless me, and enlarge my territory! Let your hand be with me, and keep me from harm so that I will be free from pain. And God granted his request."*

Jabez did not continue in that mentality of woe and sorrow; he sought for a change that was divine, and he knew where to get the solution and change for his terrible experience.

The grasshopper mentality is the mentality of fear, unworthiness, lack, limitations, and helplessness. These mentality indices can perpetually keep you as a slave. It is capable of holding you static and not allow you to take meaningful steps towards a positive change. It will scare you from making attempts. Above all, it will make you look down on your strength, ability, capability, and portray you as weak and helpless.

As long as you are focused on the opposing giants of life, you can hardly make progress in your efforts. Giants will always be there to deter you from making meaningful progress. Neglecting their existence is making a fool of yourself, but remember that you are a son and an heir and no more a servant. Remember, you can overcome your world by impartation and promise.

The twelve men Moses sent to spy the Promised Land were leaders of repute and men of war. They came back with the following findings:

The land was rich in honey, milk, grapes, and giants. Looking at their report, it is right to say they came back as two groups of spies and as such, had two variant reports. One group came back with an evil and negative report while the other came back with an encouraging and positive report. Both reported about the giants and the sons of Anak.

Mike Murdock, says in one of his books that;

- *Your conversation reveals whether you are a winner or a loser: Losers major on their problems, winners talk about the possibilities; Losers discuss their obstacles, winners talk about opportunities; Losers talk about disease, winners talk about health; Losers talk about the devil's achievements, winners talk about God's victories; Losers talk like victims, winners talk as victors. Losers generally have slaveship mentality, winners have sonship mentality."*

From the Israeli Spy story above, one group saw themselves as grasshoppers while the other saw themselves as giant killers. A group said, "In our opinion, we are like grasshoppers. Even the giants think we are like that." This is precisely where many of us belong. We judge ourselves by other people's opinion about us. At times, we even insinuate and presume people believe we are nothing. Who has sponsored this mentality in you? It is dangerous to slap yourself with such a neglect, abuse, and self-abasement. We are not talking about being self-absorbed, No, far from it! We are talking about self-development. In the world of business, marriage, profession, ministry, you are not a grasshopper, and so you should not be afraid of the giants. Instead, you see yourself as a giant killer.

> *In life, you can excel, whether you are formally educated or not. Excellence does not depend on one's level of education; it depends on the mentality. It does not depend on 'connection' either. It depends on your God-consciousness; it does not depend on the height of your father, it depends on the height you want; it does not depend on claiming it, it depends on the risk you are ready to take.*

Change your mentality; your world will begin to succumb to your pleasure. Develop the mindset of change and change will naturally come your way. Problems don't last, but solutions do. The problem you avoid tackling today will be your greatest enemy tomorrow. Each problem should be faced squarely for proper solutions to come. Remember, grasshoppers are not meant for the Promised Land; that is why all the grasshoppers were destroyed in the wilderness.

Perspective of Money

Money, in all of its ramifications, has been a controversial concept in Christian circles. While some persons believe that Christians don't need to struggle to make money, some others believe that Christians are the right people to own wealth. Another group believes that money has the capacity to influence Christians while yet another group believes that Christians should compete with unbelievers in possessing wealth. The varying beliefs about money have created different shades of opinion about the subject resulting in serious criticisms, negative and positive.

There are questions I may require you give answers to here:

- *Who created wealth (money)?*
- *For what purpose was it created?*
- *Who is supposed to manage it for the creator?*
- *Who finally controls it?*
- *When will it its usefulness end?*
- *Who was the first wealthiest man on earth and who made him wealthy?*
- *Which is evil: the love of money or money itself?*
- *Without money can I still live on this earth and fulfill my created desires?*
- *With money, am I any different?*

- *What about money and heaven, is it possible to go to heaven or hell without money?*

With these questions in our minds, can we look at the promises and warnings about money in the Bible?

Reflection On Chapter 5

Personal Notes:

=== Guided Action Plan ===

CHAPTER 6

Promises And Warnings About Money

"The love of money is the root of all evil, but it answers all things. Greediness and selfishness in the quest for money germinates evil tendencies. Drawing the thin line between the love and need for money will create a balance by meeting both ends of the purpose and the warnings of money."

Promises of Money

Before we look at the promises concerning money in the scriptures, I would want you to void yourself of any bias that is capable of depriving you of the insight God wants to bless you with. First, let us look at the purposes of money.

Deuteronomy 8[18] says,

> *"But remember the Lord God for it is he who gives you the ability to produce wealth and so confirms His covenant which he swore to your forefathers, as it is today."*

From the scripture above, part of the promise package to our forefathers includes to prosper through wealth creation. God gives the ability to create or produce wealth. Without doubt, you know that money represents wealth. In confirmation of the promises made to Abraham, Isaac, and Jacob, which by extension belong to us, we are wired to become wealthy people. God has given us this ability to create wealth in the society where we live. Genesis 26:1-3,12-13 says,

> *"Now there was a famine in the land besides the earlier famine of Abraham's time-and Isaac went to Abimelech king of the Philistines in Gerar. The Lord appeared to Isaac and said; do not go down to Egypt: live in the land where I tell you to live. Stay in this land for a while, and I will be with you and bless you. For to you and your descendants, I will give all these lands and will confirm the oath I swore to your father, Abraham.' Isaac planted crops in that land and the same year reaped a hundredfold because the Lord blessed him. The man became rich, and his wealth continued to grow until he became very wealthy."*

In the context of the scripture before us, we can see a state of abject poverty and the man Isaac could no longer cope with the level of poverty, so he decided to relocate, which is normal. But God resisted him by asking him not to leave the land promising to remember His oath with his father. In verses 12 and 13, God made up His promises of prosperity. The man planted in that land of abject poverty and reaped a hundredfold, that is, he had no loss of any kind. Instead, he got rich and continued to prosper to the extent that he became very wealthy. God made him to become rich, God made his riches to grow into wealth, and the same God caused him to become very wealthy to the extent that he was more prosperous than the nation of Gerar. God made one man's wealth more significant than the wealth of a whole nation! I Isaac wealthier than the country of Gerar.

> *"The Lord sends poverty and wealth, He humbles and exalt" (1 Samuel 2^7).*

Both poverty and wealth according to the scripture above come from God. Humility and exaltation also come from Him. I have the right to demand from my Father wealth and exaltation provided it is not for show.

In Psalm 25^{13} the Bible says,

> *"Will spend his days in prosperity and his descendants will inherit the land."*

This is a prophetic promise, and it is not wrong or sinful for me to appropriate it to my life and my descendants. You can also claim it and believe it will come to pass in your life. Spending my days in prosperity cannot be complete without money. From whatever dimension you want to look at it, it requires the use of money to spend your days in prosperity.

Psalm 112^3 says,

> *"Wealth and riches are in his house and his righteousness endures forever."*

If you accept this scriptural record that wealth and riches are in his house, I think it is meant for people who are in the house. It is intended for heirs-apparent and His adopted children, not for pagans, heathens or unbelievers. It is our divine right to inherit it by virtue of our conversion.

> *Proverbs 8:18 "With me are riches and honour, enduring wealth and prosperity."*

In Proverbs chapter 8, it is wisdom personified which talks about the personality of Christ. Christ is saying that with him are riches and honour, enduring wealth and prosperity. If riches and honour are with our Master and Saviour, it does belong to us, not to the heathens and unbelievers.

> *"The blessing of the Lord brings wealth, and He adds no sorrow to it" (Proverbs 10:22).*

The Lord's blessing is meant for us, and the Bible has informed us that this blessing of the Lord brings along with it, wealth. The kind of wealth it brings does not add sorrow or trouble to it. It is divine wealth which comes from the Lord, reserved for his children. Ecclesiastes 9:11 says,

> *"I have seen something else under the sun: The race is not to the swift or the battle to the strong, nor does food come to the wise or wealth to the brilliant or favour to the learned, but time and chance happens to them all."*

For the sole desire of man is to look upon God to allow the events you cannot control come positive to you. The worst thing that can happen to any man is to be passive over important matters. Success is guaranteed, but you must position yourself in order to occupy and experience it. Wealth is not meant for the brilliant or favour given to the learned. Many people have resigned to fate with the understanding that they are not qualified and as such will never make any attempt or even ask for a change. Ecclesiastes 7^{12} says,

> *"Wisdom is a shelter as money is a shelter, but the advantage of knowledge is this: that wisdom preserves the life of its possessor."*

Money is referred to here as shelter and shelter is capable of providing protection, covering and security. In the secular, or what I may call carnal language, any man who has money is protected from the things money can provide solution to. I want you to imagine all the reproaches you have suffered simply because you don't have money. Some live in shabby houses because there is no money to rent better apartments. Some don't have food to eat due to lack of money. Some others die in clinics and hospitals due to limited financial resources to deposit as requested by the hospital. For some, their property has been taken from them by their relations because there is no money to contest their rights. Some others have given up their birthrights due to lack of financial muscle to stand the pressure. Look around you today. You will see people who have given up their positions by force due to lack of financial capability. Money is a shelter.

> *"A feast is made for laughter, and wine makes life merry, but money is the answer for everything"* (Eccl. 10^{19}).

The preacher wrote from a practical experience. As a wealthy man who lived and died, one who touched and used wealth, his ideas would be ideal in the circumstances. He said;

- "Money is the answer for everything."

Looking at this statement carefully, one may want to ask, what are the things money can answer to? But he said; "all things" or "everything." I want you to imagine how many problems you would have solved if you had the money. Think about how many places you would have gone for crusades, outreaches, and planting of churches if you had the money. Think of how many people you would have sponsored to school if you had the money. What of the patients you would have paid their hospital bills, if you had the money. Just think of how many things you would have accomplished if you had the money. Money is the answer for everything on earth and the things of carnal nature.

There was a minister who contested this scripture one day, but not quite a few weeks after; he was looking for money to complete his church building. Many of us, while looking for money, have invited unbelievers, pagans and evil men to chair our church harvests or launching of church building funds and these men have donated large sums of money to our church treasury. Money is the answer for everything. Believers have been running after heathens and evil men – people we know have killed to retain their position of authority to sponsor our projects and buildings. Meanwhile, we are criticizing money. You cannot criticize money, because it answers for everything including your clothes, your food and upkeep, your children's school fees and maintenance, your movement from place to place, etc. You need it to ease your tension.

I went to a home one day for pastoral visitation, and everybody, from the husband and wife to all the children were looking worried, and you could see the anxiety on their faces. I reasoned, this is why I am here this evening; what do I do? Immediately, I realized there was nothing in that home that evening to eat. Though I did my best, but this story is just to let you know that the absence of money in a home may lead to sorrow, murmuring and anxiety. There are many Christian brothers who have scheduled their marriage plans over the years and are still in the planning stage because of lack of money. There are many people whose buildings have been abandoned for well over five years due to lack of money to complete the project. Again, there are many building projects, spiritual and physical, that have been forgotten because of lack of funds.

There are visions that have become moribund because of lack of money; businesses have collapsed due to lack of money to restock wares. There are marriages that have folded, and some ended in divorce due to lack of money to keep them going.

There was a case of a woman who packed out of her matrimonial home because her husband could no longer provide for the family. I have seen engagements broken because the money expected to carry out the marriage rites was not forthcoming and the lady could no longer wait. I have seen students drop out of school and from pursuing their intended careers, or who fail exams because of financial constraints. In Andrew's Foundation (my NGO), I have seen thousands of people applying for one financial aid or the other. Money is essential, and it gives answers to everything on this earth. Don't desire it, work for it appropriately, for it is necessary for your existence here on earth.

> *"But so that we may not offend them, go to the lake and throw out your line. Take the first fish you catch; open its mouth, and you will find a four-drachma coin. Take it and give it to them for my tax and yours"* (Mat. 17^{27}).

Our Lord Jesus knew the importance of money, so He advised Peter on where to get it in order to pay their temple tax. Who knows what would have happened that very day if Jesus didn't have money to pay for the temple tax. There was nothing to substitute it with; it has to be cash and not fish. It's either money or nothing else. No more trade by barter, the era is over. Imagine how many times you have evaded tax collectors because you didn't have the money to pay your tax.

Warning About Money

The Bible is a very balanced book that does not leave its reader in the blues. It has the capacity to help the reader develop a balanced mental fitness. In looking at the warnings about money in the scripture, I would want you to play down on every ignorance that manifests in narrow-mindedness formed from little biases.

We are warned by the scripture about money and our disposition towards it. Money is not meant to rule over man, but to serve man. It is not intended to be wasted or spent on satisfying our lusts and carnal desires. It is to be used primarily to promote the plan of God for the earth. Many people misplace priorities when they are financially buoyant. Some believe that having more money in their possession warrant them to acquire more possessions and properties for themselves. This is a flagrant misplace of priority.

> *"No one can serve two masters. Either he will hate the one and love the other, or he will be devoted to the one and despise the other. You cannot serve both God and money" (Matthew 6^{24}).*

This is one of the profound statements of the Lord Jesus Christ in the scriptures about money. Jesus tried to compare worship and service here. He pointed out the fact that God is to be worshipped while money is to serve us. We have God to be our master and to rule over us, but directly or indirectly, the spirit of money (mammon) also seeks worship and mastery over us. "You cannot serve both God and money," money is not meant to be worshipped. Instead, it is intended to serve us. Our attitude towards money determines the position it occupies in our lives. If money causes us to neglect God in any way, then we are servants of (mammon) money.

There are people, who because of money, cannot come to church programmes, attend revival programmes or even church services on Sundays. Such people are worshipping money; money is their lord and master. Some people in paid employment go to work on Sundays just for money. Worship is meant for God, while money must be treated as a servant. It is only given or entrusted into our hands to serve the purpose of God on earth. I Timothy 6:10 says,

> *"People who want to get rich fall into temptation and a trap and into many foolish and harmful desires that plunge men into ruin and destruction. For the love of money is the root of all kinds of evils. Some people, eager for money, have wandered from the faith and pierced themselves with many griefs."*

The scripture is not talking about money, but the attitude towards it. The wrong attitude towards money is what God is against. From the scripture above, we identify the following attitudes towards money:

The inordinate desire to get rich will lead one into temptation and traps, and into many foolish and harmful desires that plunge men into ruin and destruction.

The love of money is the root of all kinds of evil. Don't love money to the extent that its love influences and controls you.

The eagerness for money has led to various kinds of iniquity and atrocity. Some have killed, cheated, played *419 and 'OBT.'* These are different aspects of inordinate quest for money. It has caused sorrow and grief to the hearts of many, leading them to backsliding and piercing themselves with harm.

If we carefully avoid the above attitudes, money will come to us naturally. It is God's intention to bless us with wealth, but He expects us to turn our trust to Him first. Proverbs 23$^{4-5}$ says,

> *"Do not wear yourself out to get rich, have the wisdom to show restraint. Cast but a glance at riches and they are gone for they will surely sprout wings and fly out to the sky like an eagle."*

Our trust must be in God, not in money, because it is capable of bringing us to ruin, physically and spiritually. The warning in this scripture is explicit, "Do not wear yourself out to get riches." Riches is not something to kill oneself to get; it is always there and can easily be forgotten. As such it should be acquired with caution. Proverbs 11^4 says,

> *"Wealth is worthless in the day of wrath, but righteousness delivers from death."*

In the state of death, money does not deliver anybody, but righteousness does. Once a wealthy man was sick, they flew him abroad, and all kinds of medications were administered on him in order to preserve his life. However, after much spending to restore his deteriorating health, he gave up the ghost. At the very gate of heaven, wealth or money is not what matters but righteous living, which will play a significant role in our deliverance.

> ***Proverbs 11[28] says "Whoever trusts in his riches will fall, but the righteous will thrive like a green leaf."***

The desire to trust in your money is a wrong attitude towards money because it will definitely fail you. Trusting in riches is like building your house on sand, without a proper and solid foundation.

There is another warning that we should not put our trust in our money because money has an unstable future. Those who put their trust in money have always fallen. I invite you today to put your trust in the righteousness of God, which will thrive like a green leaf. Acts of Apostles 8[20] says,

> ***"Peter answered; may your money perish with you because you thought you could buy the gift of God with money."***

Though the scripture says that money provides answer for everything, this does not include the gifts from God. The gifts of God cannot be purchased with money, donations, philanthropic moves or good works. There are many wealthy people in the church today who believe that their gifts and donations to the church will help wipe their sins. You cannot buy the gift of God with money. There is a preacher in this nation who preaches that the amount of money you are able to pay determines the level of gifts you will obtain. Some who were looking for the fruit of the womb paid close to N200,000, some N150,000 and some N100,000, depending on the sex of baby they wanted. The ones who desired male and female twins paid higher, while the ones who could not afford the first option, paid for the second option which was a male child and the last option was for people who just wanted babies without specification. If children are gifts from God as Psalm 127[3] says, then they cannot be purchased with money.

> *"Lo, children are a heritage from the Lord; and the fruit of the womb is his reward" (KJV).*

No amount of money can buy children, even test-tube babies. Psalm 49[5-9] says,

> *"Why should I fear when evil days come, when wicked deceivers surround me – those who trust in their wealth and boast of their great riches? No man can redeem the life of another or give to God a ransom for him – the ransom for a life is costly, no payment is ever enough – that he should live on forever and not see decay."*

In verse six, we can see the mindset of people who put their trust in their wealth. Wealth cannot redeem a man, it can never buy escape from death, and not even one's kinsman redeemer can accomplish it. The possession of great riches is not enough to redeem another man from decay or give God ransom for another because the ransom for a life is costly to the extent that no payment is sufficient for it. It is only God Himself that can redeem a life from the grave. So, those who put their trust in money should begin to reconsider their stance and shift their focus from money to God. Proverbs 13:11 says,

> *"Dishonest money dwindles away, but he who gathers money little by little makes it grow."*

Any money you make through any form of dishonesty, extortion, and deceit dwindles away. But money honestly gathered little by little grows. Learn how to make money little by little and watch how it progressively becomes an enduring wealth. Proverbs 13:22 says,

> *"Goodman leaves an inheritance for his children's children, but a sinner's wealth is stored up for the righteous."*

Every good man is expected to leave money or an inheritance for his children and his grandchildren. But in our time, people invest in their children with the expectation that their children will take care of them when they become aged. This is a misunderstanding of inheritance or money.

The wealth of the sinner is meant to be inherited by the righteous. Proverbs 21:6 says,

> *"A fortune made by a lying tongue is a fleeting vapor and a deadly snare."*

Money made by falsehood, lying tongue, and wrong weights are purely a fleeting vapour and deadly snare.

According to Proverbs 10^2;

> *"Ill-gotten treasures are of no value, but righteousness delivers from death."*

This may sound unbelievable to you, but it is the truth. Any money or treasure acquired illegally does not last and has no value. Psalm 62^{10} says,

> *"Do not trust in extortion or take pride in stolen goods; though your riches increase, do not set your heart on them."*

This exhortation is a warning to all who trust in their own devices, fair or foul, to get what they want, rather than trusting God to sustain them. In the process of your acquiring wealth, you are advised not to set your heart on them when your riches increase, otherwise, if they dwindle or develop wings and fly off, you will break down and possibly die before your time. There are many who have died out of heartbreak because of business collapse or bank failure. Please remove your trust from money and put it in God.

Jeremiah 17^{11} says,

> *Like a partridge that hatches egg it did not lay is the man who gains riches by unjust means. When his life is half gone, they desert him, and in the end, he will prove to be a fool.*

The partridge did not lay the eggs, it did not work but wants to hatch the eggs. It wants to enjoy the benefits of hard labour, inherit good wealth and usurp what does not belong to him. This is akin to a man who gains riches by unjust means. At last, these unmerited gains will definitely disappear at the critical time when they are needed most. And that will prove him a spiritual and moral reprobate.

Three Major Mentalities Of Money

- The Poverty Mentality of Money
- The Prosperity Mentality of Money
- The Stewardship Mentality of Money

The Poverty Mentality of Money:

Persons with this mentality believe that possessions are a curse. They reject materialism in every form. Some people think that poverty is synonymous to humility, and accept that dressing shabbily and looking unkempt makes you humble. Some even believe that not brushing their mouth after meal and not keeping their hair tidy is a sign of righteousness. But such mentality is bankrupt and futile.

"For as he thinketh in his heart so is he" - Proverbs 23^{7a}.

The Prosperity Mentality of Money:

This group of people believes that it is a mandatory right to prosper. They have a lot of scriptures to back up their position and believe that God is obliged to prosper them. They claim promises, they believe and prosper in them, quite well. Many people I know that teach prosperity are actually prospering. We shall identify the secret for this later.

The Stewardship Mentality of Money:

This group believes that God owns the whole earth and everything therein and as such, spend their income within the framework of God's fear and influence. They see possessions as a privilege and not a right, and further believe that the rich are only God's channel to bless his people. They believe that all fingers are not equal. The longer fingers are there to help the shorter ones do what they can't do naturally. They display their wealth with constraint and manage their wealth under God's direction. These believe that the attitude of a steward should be that of a caretaker who only controls and distributes. They are more balanced than the other groups, and they enjoy God's abundant blessings. The stewardship mentality group believes in serving others with their wealth, and tend to obey the scriptural position on wealth than the other two groups.

Reflection On Chapter 6

Personal Notes:_____

___

=== Guided Action Plan ===

CHAPTER 7

Principles For Achieving Financial Freedom

In trying to achieve financial freedom, the believer is to adopt the following scripture-based principles to activate the obvious expected prosperity.

Obedience to God's Commandment

Essential to financial success is to have God's blessing on your side. The God factor cannot be overemphasized. Once this scriptural rule is not fully adhered to, God will cancel the other side of it. In Haggai 1^{5-9}, God warned them of the implication of disobeying him, which include the following; you plant, labour, invest and plan much, but it always turns out short of your expectations. You eat, but never get satisfied, never have enough. You drink to quench both your spiritual, material, financial, emotional and marital thirst but you remain unsatisfied, and without having you fill. You earn wages, salaries, and income that should enable you to meet your obligations and responsibilities, but you succeed in putting them in useless and unstable businesses that cannot return their investment principal, much more profit. You clothe yourself, cover your nakedness, put up a front for protection and still you are not covered or protected.

These are curses for the disobedience to God's commandment.

> *"You will sow much seed in the field, but you will harvest little because locusts will devour it. You will plant vineyards and cultivate them, but you will not drink the wine or gather the grapes because worms will eat them. You will have olive trees throughout your country, but you will not use the oil because the olives will drop off"* (Duet 28^{38-40}).

In Lev. 26^{18-20}, God described the unfruitfulness and barrenness of a land, nation, family, business and life judged by God,

> *"If after all this you will not listen to me, I will punish you for your sins seven times over. I will break down your stubborn pride and make the sky above you like iron and the ground beneath you like bronze. Your strength will be spent in vain, because your soil will not yield its crops, nor will the trees of the land yield their fruit."*

There was a sense of futility in every activity of the people whether it was legitimate or illegitimate business. This famine causes rise in the price of goods, because the law of demand and supply states, when there is increase in demand, more than supply, possibly as a result of poor yield, prices go up naturally.

According to Psalms 128$^{1-4}$, the man who fears God and careful walks in His ways shall be blessed, "Blessed are all who fear the Lord, who walk in his ways. You will eat the fruit of your labour, blessings, and prosperity will be yours. Your wife will be like a fruitful vine within your house; your sons will be like olive shoots around your table. This is the man blessed who fears the Lord." God promises good life, prosperity, long life and uncommon success for those who obey Him in regard to honouring their parents,

> *"Children obey your parents in the Lord, for this is right. Honour your father and mother – which is the first commandment with a promise that it may go well with you and that you may enjoy long life on the earth" (Ephesians 6 $^{1-3}$).*

Deuteronomy 28$^{1-12}$ provides a list of a litany of blessings of obedience while a list of woes to disobedience of God's instructions follows from verses $^{15-44}$, for the people of Israel.

This chapter in Deuteronomy is tagged choice chapter by some commentators: you choose what you really want. If it is blessings you desire, you have got to obey all simple instructions listed or catalogued from verses one to fourteen while if you choose otherwise; you suffer the consequences listed from verses $^{15-20}$. So, for a great financial success, God's factor is inevitable, that is obey God. In Joshua 1$^{7-8}$, God promises of prosperity and success required first and foremost obedience to God and his command. "Be strong and very courageous. Be careful to obey all the law my servant Moses gave you, do not turn from it to the right or to the left, that you may be successful wherever you go. Do not let this book of the law depart from your mouth, meditate on it day and night, so that you may be careful to do everything written in it. Then you be prosperous and successful". Success of any type was not guaranteed unconditionally, but it says, "be careful to obey."

Deut. 8^1 has a similar warning to Christians *"Be careful to follow every command I am giving you today so that you may live and increase and may enter and possess the land that the Lord promised on oath to your forefathers."* These scriptures are confirmed with God prospering Joseph in the land of Egypt, *"The Lord was with Joseph, and he prospered, and he lived in the house of the Egyptian master"* (Genesis 39^2). Similarly, Daniel was granted significant prosperity in Babylon, *"the king talked with them, and he found none equal to Daniel, Hananiah, Mishael, and Azariah, so they entered the king's service"* (Daniel 1^{19}).

Since sin is an obstruction to success and prosperity, those who want to grow in their finances should be able to confess their besetting sin; that is, those sins that easily beset them. Like Proverbs 28^{13} captures it, *"He who conceals his sins does not prosper, but whoever confesses and renounces them finds mercy."* Job while defending his righteousness, says, *"if I have concealed my sin as men do, by hiding my guilt in my heart because I so feared the crowd, and so dreaded the contempt of the clans that I kept silent and would not go outside...."* (Job 31$^{33\text{-}37}$). Confession of our sins, whether collective sins or individual sins, releases prosperity and financial blessings.

Again, right attitude towards work, promotion, financial gain and prosperity; and this will start when you first and foremost seek God's kingdom. Seek to please the "will" of God first, to be committed to the things of God first, to support his work on earth first. Allow God's concerns to become your major concerns, allow God's response to issues become your way of life response, allow God's attention to take the primary seat in your life. This will be accompanied with thankfulness and deliberate acknowledgment that God's hands are mightily involved in our prosperity which will enable us to delight ourselves in the Lord. The Bible made some promises of prosperity, Mathew 6 ^{33}, "But seek first his kingdom and his righteousness, and all these things will be given you as well." Great prosperity starts at the point of obedience and handing over our total being to him in reverence of His capacity and ability to return more than double that which is committed into his hands. This can only work when we first and foremost seek his kingdom principles and their righteousness workings and implementation.

The Solomon drama comes up here. After Solomon sought the Lord first through his offerings to God, God asked him to make a request of what he wanted in life. It was an open cheque for him to sign what he wanted. Solomon simply asked for a discerning heart to enable him govern God's people and to distinguish between right and wrong. God immediately mounted the platform and began to announce blessings upon blessings for him,

> *"So God said to him, since you have asked for this and not for long life or wealth for yourself, nor have asked for the death of your enemies but for discernment in administering justice, I will do what you have asked. I will give you a wise and discerning heart, so that there will never have been anyone like you, nor will there ever be. Moreover, I will give you what you have not asked for, both riches and honor so that in your lifetime you will have no equal among kings" (I Kings 3 11-13).*

Give God His Portion of Your Income:

This is what we usually refer to as tithe or paying God first. The most essential part of our stewardship is to give God the first part of our income. By so doing, you make Him (God), a partner and stakeholder in your finances. I really pity those of us who do not pay God first from their income. It is a command and an injunction, in both the new and old covenants. It has attachment of both blessings and curses for those who obey it and those who disobey it. The first of every part of your belonging, including our children, animals, crop, and wages, naturally belongs to the Lord. The struggle that is associated with this obvious mandate is a result of ignorance and greed. God permitted you to be in-charge of 90% of what he gave you and simply requested for just 10% of it, and we are reluctant to comply. He is not asking for your arrangement and consideration, neither is he hungry requiring you to feed him nor is he in difficulty expecting a bailout fund. Like apostle Paul will say to the Philippian church that their investment value of their gift to his ministry and the body of Christ is not primarily what Paul received, but the spiritual dividend they received, *"Not that I am looking for a gift, but I am looking for what may be credited to your accounts" (Philippians 4 ^{17}).* Like Paul, God is not looking for a gift or tithe from us for keeps; rather our tithing is primarily for our spiritual dividend. So, the first use of our finance is to pay God by giving him his own portion. Every income that comes our way, the Lord has the first part as the original owner, and that also expresses our readiness to take our positions as managers.

God expects us to obey scriptural injunctions by honouring him with the first fruits and then we will bask in prosperity, "Honour the Lord with your wealth, with first fruits of all your crops, then your barns will be filled to overflowing and your vats will brim over with new wine" (Proverbs 3 $^{9-10}$). The people of God were expected to give to the priests of God the first part of the olive oil, wine, and grain produced each year (Lev. 23^{10}; Num. 18$^{12-13}$), then the promise for those who obeyed this command, that is those who bring to the Lord their tithes and offerings as required, was God pouring out more blessing than they had room for, while in Malachi, God says he is going to open the floodgate of heaven to pour unlimited and unhindered blessings upon them. God expects us to give his portion of our income to him, not for his good, instead for our comfort and prosperity.

The struggle has been the attitude we adopt towards giving to God, often than not, we give God leftovers and still expect Him to appreciate it. Many have made vows without redeeming those vows but still, expect blessings from God. Many give despised gifts to God and still want to command God's blessings upon themselves. This is what distinguished the offering of Abel from Cain, his brother that led to envy and the first recorded murder. Cain gave to God from some of the fruits, while Abel offered to God from the fat portions of the firstborn of his flock. God showed favour to the gift of Abel because his sacrifice met the standard recommended while in the case of Cain, his sacrifice was ignored of God because it violated the principles of first fruit;

> *"In the course of time, Cain brought some of the fruits of the soil as an offering to the Lord. But Abel brought fat portions from some of the firstborn of his flock. The Lord looked with favour on Abel and his offering but on Cain and his offering he did not look with favour, so Cain was very angry, and his face was downcast" (Genesis 7$^{3-5}$).*

The NIV Study Bible states that the contrast is not between an offering of plant life and an offering of animal life as many theologians have argued, rather between a careless and thoughtless offering and a well-articulated and generous offering of Abel. Motivation and attitude of the heart are all important, and God looked with favour on Abel and his offering because of Abel's faith, predicated on obedience to the scriptural instructions and injunctions,

> *"By faith Abel offered God a better sacrifice than Cain did. By faith he was commended as a righteous man, when God spoke well of his offerings. And by faith he still speaks, even though he is dead" (Hebrews 11:4).*

Furthermore, Abel offered from the stock of firstborns, which indicate the recognition that all the productivity and labour of the flock are from the Lord and all of it belongs to him.

The Eucharistic prayer confirms the ownership of all we have whether it is authority, power, finances or honour when it says, "yours, Lord is the greatness, the power, the glory, the splendour, and the majesty; for everything in heaven and on earth is yours. All things come from you, and of your own do we give you." This prayer affirms God's ownership of everything. He has given us every good gift, and it is not a bad omen to provide him with portion of this gift. We can offer God first by supporting the ministry of God and church, and also by helping poor saints who are among us and beyond, provided they are genuine saints in need indeed.

Paul encourages this when he admonished the brethren at the Corinthian Church,

> *"Now about the collection for God's people, do what I told the Galatians churches to do. On the first day of every week, each one of you should set aside a sum of money in keeping with his income, saving it up, so that when I come, no collections will have to be made" (I Corinthians 16:1-2).*

Paul asked the churches, both in the Galatian and Corinthian churches, to prepare for the poor brethren, not an emergency offering, rather a deliberate, planned church offering to be properly kept aside for its mission. He said so that "when I come, no collection will have to be made." This unique offering, like St. Mathias offering of Church of Nigeria, is collected to support needy churches in Jerusalem. Then, of course, you know that Jerusalem is the headquarters church, but still, offerings are raised from small churches to support those brethren.

Severally, those who are favoured with financially buoyant churches have seen themselves as working harder than those whose churches are struggling to survive financially, but for Paul, he sees the struggling churches as the sole responsibility of the whole body of Christ. The shame of one church is automatically the total failure of the entire church irrespective of denomination. When the rich, whether persons or churches understand that wealth and riches come from God, our attitude to most of these things will change for the better.

You are not rich because you worked hard. No, it is the Lord who made you rich and honoured you with His wealth, "but the king replied to Araunah, *"No, I insist on paying you for it. I will not sacrifice to the Lord my God burnt offerings that cost me nothing" (2 Samuel 24^{24}).* David in several places in the Bible proved that God was the source of all his wealth. Little wonder he enjoyed long life, honour, wealth and permanent place in the dynasty of Israel. God expects every living person to be faithful in giving, whether poor or rich but according to your ability.

Giving must be done inclusively, cheerfully, willingly and according to ability. God is not expecting you to overstretch yourself or labour to give beyond your capacity. No! If this happens, then it may be manipulation from preachers, which for me, in a way, is witchcraft. Paul while admonishing the churches at Corinth, warned them not to offer offerings against their will or above their ability.

> *"For if the willingness is there, the gift is acceptable according to what one has, not according to what he does not have" (2 Cor. 8^{12}).*

For Paul, what matters is the willingness and eagerness of the Corinthians to face their Christian duty, no matter how little or significant the amount one could afford. He continued this crusade in 2 Corinthians 9^7 that people should not be forced or persuaded to offer God offerings that are not from their heart.

Can people offer gifts to God out of compulsion? Yes! Few years ago, a woman went to the church for a programme. When the man of God finished preaching and made an altar call for those who wanted to support his ministry, some people came out, including this particular woman, who made a pledge of twenty thousand Naira and immediately came back home and collected the husband's twenty thousand Naira (N20,000) to pay. As the husband returned that night and discovered that the wife had taken his money to redeem the pledge she made in the church, he quickly dragged his wife back to the church to meet the man of God for refund of the said amount, which the minister returned to him. For some people the man was mean, but that is a typical sign of not offering from the heart. Another case happened during the last investiture of knights in our Diocese. After the man of God finished preaching powerfully, and made altar call for those who would support the Cathedral building with the sum of one million Naira (N 1,000,000), over twenty people came out but up till now, we have not recorded up to forty percent (40%) redemption of those pledges. Such people were persuaded through the oratorical power of the man of God, and they responded based on that persuasion. Paul says in verse seven (v.7),

> *"Each man should give what he has decided in his heart to give, not reluctantly or under compulsion, for God loves a cheerful giver."*

Paying God first includes the responsibility to meeting financial needs of the poor, widows, orphans, the downtrodden and fatherless. Proverbs 19:17 states that giving to the poor is lending to God and God will always and deliberately payback to such people, not only in cash but also in various areas of life.

> *"Blessed is he who has regard for the weak; the Lord delivers him in times of trouble. The Lord will protect him and preserve his life; he will bless him in the land and not surrender him to the desire of his foes. The Lord will sustain him on his sickbed and restore him from his bed of illness"* (Psalms 41:1-3).

From the scripture above, over seven deliverances and blessings were associated with just kindness to the poor and weak. Think of many blessings and deliverance that have eluded us due to little carelessness over the poor and the vulnerable. When you give to the poor, you make a provision for God to intervene in your affairs in extraordinary ways. The gift given to the poor is the common or small gift that attracts uncommon provision and abundance of favour. The early church was a supportive church. She was marked for her welfare gifts to the ordinary in the church. The poor in the early church enjoyed a non-discriminatory fellowship. They had a fellowship where everybody was important, and nobody was hungry.

> *"The believers were one in heart and mind. No one claimed that any of his possessions was his own, but they shared everything they had. There were no needy persons among them. For from time to time those who owned lands or houses sold them, brought the money from the sales and put it at the apostle's feet, and it was distributed to anyone as he had need" (Acts 4 ^{32}, $^{34-35}$).*

That is why the church's challenge was not numerical growth rather space to accommodate inflow of new members. The first ever successful crusade took place, and over three thousand souls were crying out for their sins, repenting of them and accepting Christ as their Lord and Saviour. When the church does the needful, the obvious will emerge naturally. The early church was a caring church from all indications. The unity of the early church cannot be far from their ability to carry along the poor in their midst. One of the major characteristics of a spirit-filled church or a denomination will be their caring attitude to the poor in their midst.

> *"All the believers were together and had everything in common. Selling their possessions and goods, they gave to anyone as he had need" (Acts 2$^{44\text{-}45}$).*

The early church was indeed a **TALKING** and **DOING** church. Christian actions are called social action of the church. It is essential in church growth and influence in ministry. It proves God's love within us. Without this demonstration of love, we cannot claim that we are believers. Our claim as both believers and as a church is centered on our capacity to provide God's first gift from our income before any other expenditure. Our inability to bring this God's gift first also reveals our ingratitude and selfishness which is a direct reaction of greed. You cannot love without giving, but you can give without loving. The Book of 1st John captures it in a stylish manner when it says,

> *"If anyone has natural possessions and sees his brother in need but has not pity on him, how can the Love of God be in him? Dear children, let us not love with words or tongue but with actions and in truth. This then is how we know that we belong to the truth, and how we set our hearts at rest in his presence" (I John 3$^{17\text{-}19}$).*

This kind of Christian love in supplying the need of fellow believers does not in any way encourage laziness. The love of brethren we refer to here is genuine. In 2Thessalonians 310, Paul, while admonishing the Thessalonian believers, stated that lazy Christians should be allowed to starve, *"for even when we were with you, we gave you this rule: 'If a man will not work he shall not eat'."* Laziness should not in any guise be encouraged among believers. Laziness is very dangerous and needs to be fought against in the church. There are lots of people in the church doing nothing but going from house to house of members begging for food with very sympathetic stories. There is a particular case of a woman who went to members' houses to tell her stories for help which she obtained. Again, after about two weeks or thereabout, she went to other members with the same story and then, of course, got more gifts. However, one of the members caught her in another member's house with the same story. Such people need to be discouraged from such attitude, for it does not help us at all. Giving money to people is the worst crime you can commit against them. You encourage and enthrone laziness in an unlimited manner. Brethren should be encouraged to come up with what they want to do after then money can be raised to support such project or business so that in turn such brethren can become contributors to the general pool of funds.

Laziness is a battle all of us need to collectively fight if we want the church to assume its rightful place. It is a cancerous plague and feeds the body with a spirit that does not encourage taking initiative. It creates weakness in creativity, efficiency, and capacity. The Bible condemns it in totality, and the following scriptures point to that. In Proverbs 12[24], **"Diligent hands will rule, but laziness ends in slave labour."** Lazy people are always labouring for the diligent and making money for them while they receive peanuts as wages or salaries. Every lazy man has no plan for his life and those around him, including his children and wife, because they live a life without a sustained future plan. Lazy people are not the same as poor people who need help. While the Bible encourages us to support the poor, I am yet to see one instance in the same bible where we are encouraged to support the lazy.

The poor man needs to be supported while the lazy man needs to be helped out of his laziness. A lot of people who have assumed the status of poverty did so as a direct effect of laziness. If the church can deal with laziness, the rate of poverty and poor people will reduce drastically. Every scripture pointing to laziness does so negatively. Proverbs 12[27], even says that the lazy man finds it extremely difficult to lift his food from the dish to his mouth. 19[24] corresponds with this, **"The sluggard buries his hand in the dish, he will not even bring it back to his mouth."** This agrees with 26[15], **"The sluggard buries his hand in the dish; he is too lazy to bring it back to his mouth."** Laziness is very dangerous. When you have a staff who is lazy, it will affect management's target, vision, mission and the total efficiency of the company or church. It draws the string from one extreme to another and affects everyone in the extreme. It does not matter how smart and pragmatic you are; once a lazy person is in your team, it will affect the output of the entire team. Laziness is different from somebody being slow or weak. We have people who are hesitant or weak but eggheads, powerful thinkers, and creators at the same time. Lazy people are not creators.

Some people are always tired because of a wrong sleeping pattern, sleep deprivation, bad eating habits, thyroid problems, lack of exercise, procrastination, etc. If anyone is having struggles with fighting laziness genuinely, such a person should look out for these things first and deal with them. Laziness is clearly seen in the Bible as sin, and results in self-motivated poverty. Some people would prefer staying in bed all day to making a living, and this preference will undoubtedly bring their downfall. Laziness is a curse, but work is a blessing. Being a sloth brings down your confidence and motivation. Slowly you will start developing burn mentality which may lead to disastrous lifestyle. Work hard in everything you do because it always brings profit and honour, but too much sleep and laziness bring disappointment, shame, unfulfilled dreams, and disgrace.

When you are lazy, not only will you suffer, but other people will suffer as a result of it. Work hard to help others. Ask the Lord to strengthen your hands and to remove any slothfulness in your life and body. In any family where everyone is working hard in their assignments, things tend to be a lot easier than families where only a fraction take up the family responsibility while others tend to be idle.

John Henry Newman warned of the consequences of laziness when he stated,

- "A man would do nothing if he waited until he could do it so well that no one could find fault."

This is usually the lazy man's excuse,

- "I want to be thorough, or I want to take my time to do it, or I know what I am doing, or I am meticulous person or you know I want to come out superb."

Winkie Pratney said, "many say they cannot get God's guidance when they really mean they wish He would show them an easier way." An author has highlighted three types of laziness as "physical" which involves neglecting work and duties, "mental" which involves taking the easy way out, trying to take shortcuts, get-rich-quick schemes and "spiritual" which involves neglecting to pray, read scriptures, use God-given talents, etc. In Ezekiel, the sins of Sodom include laziness, for which she could not meet the expected needs of the poor and needy who require help. Sodom's sins were pride, gluttony, and laziness, while the poor and needy suffered outside her door. Lazy people ordinarily irritate people around them and even their employers. The reason is not far-fetched, they delay their team workers and as such delay the expected profit from the business, thereby causing failure of the whole organization.

> *"Lazy people irritate their employers, like vinegar to the teeth or smoke in the eyes" (Proverbs 10^{26}).*

From the scriptures you have seen how God regards lazy people. They have been likened to destroyers. This is divine indictment.

> *"Whoever is lazy regarding his work is also a brother to the master of destruction" (Proverbs 18⁹).*

Their paths are not smooth at all, they are prone to experience hiccups and bumps on their pathway,

> *"The path of lazy people is like a thorny hedge, but the road of decent people is an open highway" (Proverbs 15¹⁹).*

Lazy people are compelled to learn lessons of life's pursuit from the lowest creatures 'ants'. What a derogatory comparison! In Proverbs 66-⁹, lazy people are summoned to accept ants as their lecturers since they refused to learn from the circumstances and situations around them. Ants have no ruler, no boss, no commander, no administrator and no leader. But in the summer, they gather all of their food and save it, so that when winter comes, there will be plenty to eat. How long are you going to lie there? When will you get up? The desires of the lazy are not always coming to fruition, they can desire good things, claim people's beautiful homes, cars, and marriages, but hardly will they get theirs,

> *"Despite their desires, the lazy will come to ruin, for their hands refuse to work" (Proverbs 21²⁵).*

Few years ago, I was in a church service, and the man of God who was preaching asked us to imagine what we desired in our hearts, and then we should begin to claim them by faith whatever we claim, we will receive. Many of us claimed people's property, beautiful buildings, cars, peoples' estates, profession, careers, etc.

The day I read this scripture that the desires of a lazy man will come to ruin because his hands refuse to work, I just realized that we heard an impaired message.

People everywhere claim other hard workers' prosperity without working hard. Little wonder, Solomon said,

> *"The slacker does not plow during planting season, at harvest time he looks, and there is nothing" (Prov. 20^4).*

> *Paul, while admonishing his beloved spiritual son, Timothy said, "if anyone does not take care of his own relatives, especially his immediate family, he has denied the faith and is worse than an unbeliever" (I Tim. 5^8).*

Here Paul pointed out that laziness can lead a man not to fulfill his family and marital obligation, and to Paul, then of course to any moral person, it is a worse sin than unbelievers could commit. When you are lazy, you desire more of sleep and rest, and hunger is inevitable,

> *"Laziness throws one into a deep sleep, and an idle person will go hungry" (Proverbs 19 ^{15}).*

Even the scripture in Ephesians 5$^{15-16}$ captures it quite clearly when it states,

> *"So be careful how you live. Don't live like fools, but like those who are wise, make the most of every opportunity in these evil days."*

This warning is very vital and apt now than when it was first issued. From the scripture, it is clear that those who do not take advantage of every opportunity to maximize the time we are in, are regarded as fools. If this assertion is anything to go by, then we have many big-time fools.

Again, in Colossians 3:23, we were reminded to set our hearts to work wholeheartedly, as if we are working for the Lord,

> *"Whatever you do, work at it wholeheartedly as though you were doing it for the Lord and not merely for people."*

The warning on laziness continued by Paul to the church at Ephesus when he stated in Chapter 4:28,

> *"The thief must no longer steal. Instead, he must do honest work with his own hands, so that he has something to share with anyone in need."*

Was Paul actually talking about thieves outside the church? No, I don't think so! He was referring to the thieves in the church or among the brethren. He was referring to brethren made thieves by laziness. This thief was encouraged to do honest work with his own hands so that he would share the profit, wages, salaries and the outcome with the brethren in need. Such thieves as referred to here, include those who exaggerate figures of amounts of money. An instance would consist of building committee members who inflate harvest committee budgets, who ask for over-invoicing after purchase, who ask for ten percent (10%) from printers who print church publications, who connive with marketers to defraud the church, who squander pledges redeemed through their offices, who betray the church's confidence, who always carry out assignments from the church with an eye for pay, etc. Paul counsels them to stop stealing but to engage in meaningful ventures with their own hands so that other poor brethren would be supported by them.

There is another kind of thief Paul highlighted; these are those who use their places of pride to defraud the church by making unnecessary demands from the church. They even put their own personal projects or responsibility on the church or Diocese. In a way, they are thieves and have been advised to desist from stealing. For instance, if my children need to go to school every morning, I should be the one to arrange for how they will go to school, by either fueling the vehicle or procuring a car and hiring a driver whose duty is to take them to school and bring them back. It is entirely out of place that I will use the church vehicle, church fuel, and church driver to do all of these at the expense of the church. You are paid salary as every member who works is paid salary. So if other workers are able to take care of their challenges, you ought to take care of your own. Even in the outside world, nobody uses official vehicles for private use and patronage, more so now that some of the salaries of clergy is far bigger than most of the minimum wages in this country. If the Council does not approve the use of the church property, including their employees by you, if you use them without their official approval, Paul says you are a thief, and you are advised to stop stealing.

Slothfulness Leads To Procrastination And Excuses

Both Proverbs 22^{13} and 26^{13} form the background to the next dangerous challenge of laziness. The Slacker says,

> *"There is a lion outside. I will be killed in the public square and the next, "the lazy person claims, "There is a lion in the road. There is a lion in the streets."*

For the lazy man or sloth, this is enough and sufficient excuse not to go out that day, and as such, every assignment and assigned duties should wait for a future date. The Ecclesiastic stated in chapter 11:4, **"Whoever watches the wind will not plant, whoever looks at the clouds will not reap."** Commentary on this verse admonishes us not to toy with 'maybes' and 'might-have-beens.' That we start from where we can and put to recognition our limited paths in all of this. The lazy has always used weather interpretation to perpetuate their laziness dotted with lots of excuses. In discussing procrastination and excuses, the preacher states in Proverbs 24^{30-34},

> *"I passed by the field of a sluggard, by the vineyard of a man lacking sense, and behold, it was all overgrown with thorns, the ground was covered with nettles, and its stonewall was broken down. Then I saw and considered it, I looked and received instruction. A little sleep, a little slumber, a little folding of the hands to rest, and poverty will come upon you like a robber, and want like an armed man."*

Personal Savings:

Income without savings is futile and baseless. Various nations have portions of their earning as savings to sustain them during economic recession or at least, during adverse economic conditions. For instance, the Americans save up to 4% of total earning for raining days; Germany about 14% for the same purpose and of course Japan is the highest saver with as much as 20%. Our country's lack of savings was the direct cause of what we suffered during the economic recession that hit our nation in 2016, though it started gradually from 2010 and went full blown in 2016 because of poor managers of our economic policies. Any organization, whether secular or sacred, that does not maintain savings as a fundamental policy may not survive the next generation.

A one-time finance minister of Nigeria had talked about a sovereign fund which was to be grown from earnings from our external foreign reserves, but Nigerians, through some of her political leaders, sabotaged the move, and the consequence of that action is what we all suffered in the recession.

Saving is of vital importance in any organization that wants to survive the pressure of future demand. Families that never planned to save regret at later times in their life. Individuals who never put it into practice, die fast, as soon as they retire. The importance of savings cannot be over-emphasized as it is a "SEED" to each organization, family or church. Without savings, there will be no investment, and if there is no investment, there will be no harvest, and if there is no harvest, it means there will be no continuity. Savings is intended for continuity. When your savings grow, you invest it, and when your investment matures, it yields proceeds. Savings is like a seed which when planted starts small but with time, grows into a plant of wealth that builds branches for other people to build upon.

Savings is not a recommendation or a choice; instead, it is a commandment of Almighty God to the family. It serves the purpose of inheritance as recorded in Proverbs 13[22], ***"A good man leaves an inheritance for his children's children, but a sinner's wealth is stored up for the righteous."*** How would a good righteous and kind-hearted man leave an inheritance for his children, if not through saving? The same happens even at church level. It is expected that churches or organizations and even nations should make adequate plans to provide for the future, for reasons of continuity. A good country, organization and indeed a good church, should as a matter of mandate, keep an inheritance for its successor.

Savings is also for the purposes of emergencies. There are emergencies all over the world and in various households and churches. The monies set aside as savings are usually used to cushion the effects of emergencies during crisis. To handle emergencies, Apostle Paul admonished the Corinthians church to learn the habit of saving in order to avoid embarrassment.

> ***"On the first day of every week, each one of you should set aside a sum of money in keeping with his income,***

> *saving it up, so that when I come no collections will have to be made" (I Corinthians 16[2]).*

Paul had a very wonderful and overwhelming insight into the workings of finances. So, he had to set out plans how to have ready funds for the work of God without being disappointed.

Again, savings will be of tremendous importance when it comes to supporting poor churches, rural churches, and poor saints. The Apostles in the Acts of the Apostles demonstrated that savings can be of great help in time of need,

> *"There were no needy persons among them. For from time to time those who owned lands or houses sold them, brought the money from the sales and put it at the Apostles' feet, and it was distributed to anyone as he had need" (Acts 4:34-35).*

I am very sure you would not dispute that these lands and houses sold by the disciples or brethren to solve the financial needs of other brethren were direct proceeds from savings invested over time. Proverbs 21[20], slighted those who are not given to saving, **"in the house of the wise are stores of choice of food and oil, but a foolish man devours all he has."** The strategy that provides the choice of food and oil in the stores of the wise is that he knows how not to consume all income at once, while the foolish, those who don't have long-term perspectives or vision, consume all they get at once, and automatically become slaves to the wise.

The difference between the rich and the poor or wise and foolish is the ability and capacity to set aside something in every season, no matter the circumstances and economic condition of the moment. Even King Solomon, the wisest, the wealthiest, and possibly the most "successful" king on earth, both among the dead and living, asked all of us to learn saving principles from the "ants", *"Ants are creatures of little strength, yet they store up their food in the summer" (Proverbs 3025).* The ants are aware there will be moments they will be helpless, and a season they cannot work even if they may want to but the circumstance will not allow them, so they prepare to cushion the effect of that future time using the present availability to prepare.

Saving will help you preserve the future, because not saving or setting aside during the time of abundant provision by God is a grave sin because when you need it, it may not be available, so Solomon warns us again in Proverbs 2724, *"For riches do not endure forever, and a crown is not secured for all generations."* Even, in the church calendar, there are seasons or months of slim income to the church while there are moments of abundance. It is expected that a good church manager should study the cycle and save during the abundance as much as he can, to be used during the time of scarcity.

Saving must be a planned and prioritized agenda in anyone's life, not an option or legislation to be considered after other expenses would have taken place. In short, saving is "number one" expense before any other one. That is why immediately after giving God his due from your income, the next is saving, that is, paying yourself from your income. If you don't decide to save before you begin to spend from your income, the chances that you will not be able to save is 99%. I advise that a proper commitment to savings be made before spending is allowed. Some persons I know issued a standing order with their financial institutions to debit to an amount of money at a particular day in the month, and I want to recommend that to you so that savings can become a lot easier.

There are some persons who would not be able to set anything aside immediately the cash enters into their hands. We advise such people to seek the help of their employer to deduct a certain percentage of their income at source and transfer same to their account in the bank. There is another one called Esusu - a small co-operative group of people who decide to be pooling an amount of money together every month. Each month's total pool or collection is given to a particular member to solve his or her financial problem. This is also good if members are all honest people and have respect for integrity. Every intelligent man or woman must be able to ask himself or herself this sincere question, "how much of my income do I have at my less active involvement from my sweat, toiling, deprivation, sacrifice, and frustration?" Let your savings grow from daily Kobos to daily Nairas. To achieve this, you must decide to live on half of your income monthly or as the case may be, do not use your savings except in extreme emergencies. This allows you to have employees to work for you while you rest, it gives you an edge over your peers, but it requires time, consistency, discipline and sacrifice and above all, it gives you the advantage to maximize opportunities that will come up unexpectedly.

How do we define SAVING and SAVINGS?

Savings has been defined variously, and we will be humble enough to state that we cannot offer an all-encompassing definition of savings here. Savings is income not spent, deferred consumption or procrastinated expenditure. Mostly, it is put in a deposit account form, pension account, investment fund, collectibles, drafts, equities, money markets, bonds or as cash. It is deliberate reduction of expenditures.

However, there has been misunderstanding of saving and savings. Saving refers to increase in one's assets, while savings is increase in one's one part of assets, typically, deposits in savings account. Saving refers to an activity occurring over time, a flow variable, whereas savings refers to something that exists at any one time, for instance, stock variable or buying. Saving could be said to be physical investment because it provides funds for savings. By not spending some part of one's income to buy consumer goods and services, it is possible for such resources to be instead invested by being used to procure fixed capital, such as factories and machinery. Saving can be vital to increase the amount of fixed capital available, which in turn contributes immensely to economic growth.

Point of note: increased saving does not automatically translate to increased investment. For instance, if savings are slashed or kept under a mattress or otherwise, not deposited into a financial institution or intermediary such as a bank, there is no chance for those savings to be recycled as investment by business, and as such, it is useless to both the economy and individual savers. This proves that saving may actually increase without necessarily increasing investment, causing a shortfall of demand rather than to economic growth. In the short term, if saving falls below investment, it can lead to an increase of aggregate demand and possibly economic boom, but not so in the long-term. In the long-term, if saving falls short of investment, it eventually leads to reduction in investment and drastically affects future growth. Future growth is made possible by foregoing present consumption to increase investment but if the foregone alternative (consumption) and the financial value is not invested, it amounts to interest-free non-recycled loan to the Central Bank, and as such, turns useless to economic growth.

Classical economies posit that interest rates would adjust to equate saving and investment, but a rise in saving would automatically cause a fall in interest rates and stimulate investment, hence investment would equal saving. But Keynes has a different opinion. They argue that neither saving nor investment has any influence on interest rate, that is, both were interest inelastic so that significant interest rate charges were needed to re-equate them after one changed. Again, in the short run, it was the demand for and supply of stocks of money that determined interest rates. Peradventure saving exceeds investment for significant amounts of time, then it will lead to a general glut and a recession. In personal finance, the act of saving relates to nominal preservation of money for future use. A deposit account paying interest is typically used to hold money for future needs, like an emergency fund, to make a capital purchase (car, building, etc.), or to give someone, for instance, children's school fees or to pay utility bills, etc.

Generally speaking, in economics, savings are defined as income minus consumption. The rate at which people can be expected to do this is called the marginal propensity to save or average propensity to save. The rate of savings is directly related to both the interest rate and investment, mainly by way of the capital markets. If investment merely replaces depreciated capital stock, rather than increasing the capital stock and workforce, it is still considered part of savings.

We have read from different papers and articles reasons why many people cannot save money, but the point is that most of these excuses are honestly not valid. I have met different people with different levels of salary structure, some with very high salary earnings while some, a little above average income, who have informed me of their handicap in saving, and actually, have discovered that they lack willingness to get started with the business of saving. One thing that is obvious and we must accept is that our needs and wants are unlimited and there will always be a reason why we should spend instead of saving part of your income today. The temptation has always been, we will start next month, next year, next week and on and on. The absolute and uncompromisable truth is that the only possible way to save some part of your income is to decide and determine to start now and today. Come to think of it, who actually benefits from the saving? Hope you know that the answer is simply "you!"

Warren Buffet maintains that we should not save from the leftover, when he stated,

- *"Do not save what is left after spending but spend what is left after saving."*

The popular Chinese proverbs says,

- *"Do not wait until you are thirsty to dig a well."*

From this proverb, it is evident that saving has significant benefits to the saver. Let us mention few of such benefits.

It Creates Some Financial Independence: Saving impacts a level of happiness according to some researchers. With some savings to cover our future expenditures, you do not have to bother or worry much about relying on someone else. One honour I wouldn't want anybody to deny me is the pride of settling my bills. There is a lot of joy that radiates within each time you pay your bills without much stress or dependence on anybody. With savings that leads you to financial independence, you may have solved one of the most critical causes of stress in life and thereby reduce family pressure. Probably you might have heard that severe stress can cause ulcers, high blood pressure and generally impact negatively on both productivity and efficiency. To avoid this experience, start now to save money, and you will be sure of financial security in the future. Economic independence brings reassurance of a future and creates a level of confidence and self-worth.

Expect The Unexpected Emergency: Life is full of ups and downs, mountains and smooth levels, emergencies from families, relations, unplanned disasters, etc. This may include early retirement, termination of employment, downsizing, reshuffling, and incapacitation, which may render one inefficient and redundant such that he becomes economically useless, out of business of the organization's goods and services, etc. So, you should naturally expect or plan for the unexpected at any time. This is why you have the concern to save substantial parts of your income for unforeseen coincidences. Further, your emergency fund can be used to cover unexpected car repairs, raise children's school fees, sudden increase in exchange rates, medical bills, procurement of landed property, handle successful transactions, house renovation, etc. Experts have recommended that at least between three to six months of your living cost should be saved into an accessible account as an emergency fund.

Starting Your Own Business: Accessing capital outside to commence a personal business is not always easy, but personal savings can kickstart the business. People naturally don't commit their money to any business they are not sure of, especially when the person involved is not an established or successful entrepreneur. So many successful entrepreneurs started their businesses with their personal savings, before engaging others.

Planning for Education Fund: This is one area many people do not consider in their income. Some begin planning immediately they get admission into the university. You need to seriously commence saving for the children's higher education and possibly the kind of university and course you think they should study. It is mere shortsightedness to begin savings after the children have been admitted before you think about the acceptance and tuition fees. You should start immediately. It does not matter how much you earn; you can start from that amount to save money towards fulfilling the dreams and aspirations of the children and possibly you or your wife. You can still save money to support your uncles, brother's children, or even widows, orphans or the village development project. There are lots of needs waiting for us to cushion, and the only way to handle them is to start saving on time.

Beyond Active Service: Many of us forget that we commence our retirement from the first day we start. Hence we refuse to plan for it. The sooner you start thinking about retirement, the better for your future, that is, if you are not late already. Retirement is something that happens daily, and it is going to be disastrous if you retire without enough savings to take care of your needs. One thing about retirement and why we need to treat it as priority is this: at retirement; you are directly or indirectly weak, unproductive with very insignificant attraction to be hired. You are encouraged to begin to put some money aside now for your retirement. Again, at retirement, most of the extra benefits or official allowances or stipends disappear. So, it is better than those allowances or stipends are saved now in order to sustain you in future. God has given us the capacity to plan and stated that there is time for everything under the earth. Make use of your time now to save for your tomorrow.

It Makes You To Be Contented: When you save, it brightens on your level of dedication and delight; hence your exit from anxiety and displeasure. You come to a state of contentment and have the comfort of knowing that you have your financial needs under control. You won't have to worry about unexpected expenses. Paul while addressing his spiritual son, Timothy, exhorted him by saying, "but godliness with contentment is great gain" (I Timothy 6^6). In essence, Paul is saying that contentment in the sense we are advocating has nothing to do with desired satisfaction that comes as a result of acquisition of more wealth or property. He corroborated this in Philippians 4^{11},

> *"I am not saying this because I am in need, for I have learnt to be content whatever the circumstances."*

Hence, Paul said to the church at Philippians, I appreciate the gift from you, but I am not ultimately dependent on them. Saving makes you to rely more on the grace of God, you know why? He sustains the economy of every nation, so depending on Him to sustain or make your savings relevant is an emphasis not taken too far. The following may somewhat help us to adjust to fit into the purpose of God for you through your saving:

Contentment Brings Gratitude: I stand to be proved wrong that it is almost impossible to develop contentment without gratitude. They are inseparable. Grateful persons are ones who have learnt to focus on the good things in their lives, and not the things they lack. When you begin to question what you have instead of being grateful to God, just start making a list of all the goodness of God's in your life. Always be grateful to God, the giver, and reduce your items of demand to satisfy self; you will undoubtedly shift your focus back to the many good things you already have. The simple capacity to commence is indeed the supernatural grace of God. Contentment drives you to begin to save and teaches you to be satisfied with what you have. Competition has been proven as one of the primary reasons why it seems difficult to start saving.

Engage Your Lifestyle: Take control of your attitude. People who lack contentment are not always organized. They have an ad hoc approach to life. They always get involved in "when-and-then planning" "when-I-get, then-I-will-be-happy." Their happiness is determined by what they have. They see happiness as a subject of what they acquire. Remember, your happiness is not reliant on the acquisition of possession, rather your happiness is based purely on your decision to be happy. Happiness is a temporary attitudinal pleasure decided by its host. There is nothing extraordinary that produces happiness rather a deliberate decision to be happy. Those who have decided to buy happiness by going for everything they feel will introduce happiness, have long been disappointed by its permanent exit. Nothing on earth helps happiness. A typical example is Esther 5^9,

> *"Haman went out that day happy and in high spirits. But when he saw Mordecai at the king's gate and observed that he neither rose nor showed fear in his presence, he was filled with rage against Mordecai."*

A derived happiness does not last. Such happiness is influenced by circumstances. When they are favourable you are happy, otherwise you are not. There are many of us, whose happiness mounts its wings when we are flattered and praise-tongued. Unfortunately, the church is not spared in this perils superstition of achievers. Take control of your attitude and decide to be joyful irrespective of the circumstance and situation. Situations and circumstances come and go, but joy remains a constant factor. So, control your life by choosing to be joyful always, regardless of the circumstances.

Diffusing Discontentment Is Useless: Break the habit of trying to satisfy your discontentment by acquiring more acquisitions. For many of us, it has been ingrained into our lives that the proper way to diffuse discontentment is to procure the outward items that are perceived to be responsible for the discontentment. The root of discontentment is not farfetched. In most cases, when we are dissatisfied with our wardrobe, or the performance of our car, we quickly go for replacements. We need to break this habit before it wrestles us down permanently. Break the pattern of using acquisition to solve the challenge of discontentment; it does not work. In short, it is outdated, obsolete and moribund. Know this that no amount of material possessions will fully satisfy the desires of your heart. You are counseled that next time discontentment rears its ugly head, smash it and commit to better understanding of yourself and why the lack of that item is causing discontentment. Only after you deliberately break this yoke of discontentment that true and acceptable contentment will begin to surface. Nobody achieves contentment through acquisition; rather you will compound the problem and increase the appetite of discontentment.

Reject Rat-Race: Remember that you are not living your life on another person's wristwatch. No one should live your life for you or determine the pace of your life. Comparing your life with someone else's will always lead to dissatisfaction and discontentment. There will always be people who would "appear" to be better off than you and seemingly living the perfect life. At least the environment presents as such. Though you may be disappointed, by the time you get closer to them, you will discover that you are far better than they are. The challenge is that you have allowed your mind to decide the narrow road of inferiority or superiority complex. Your thinking may misdirect you to take a debased, inferior and non-consequential path. Remember, you are unique and special. The mould used for you was broken after you were carved. In the whole of this world, you are the only person God created to be you. There is no duplicate of you anywhere in the whole world. Some people may 'look' like you but cannot be you.

Increase Your Net Worth: Your net worth is the difference between what you owe and what you own. A conservative approach to net worth does not include the value of any real estate, your home, and cars. Personal assets don't have an effect on your credit balance. However, those assets are considered when you are applying for a personal loan. Using some of our personal savings to pay down debt does somehow improve your credit balance or value. Personal savings give you a head start on retirement as well.

Maximizing Savings: You earn more money via savings. Savings don't earn much, but they do earn some interest. A bank savings account may earn only a percentage point depending on the rate of interest at the time, but a money market fund earns a bit more and a certificate of deposit slightly more much more. The interest rates fluctuate over time. Some banks have a non-fee policy if you keep a minimum balance in your checking account. Increasing the balance in your checking account may exempt you from paying service fees. That amount is an income to your savings.

Reduce Expenses: The first and foremost discipline of anyone who wants to achieve financial success is to know how to reduce expenses drastically. Most things we crowd ourselves with are not actually what we need at the time. Your financial success starts with the ability to tell yourself 'No' to imposing needs that do not contribute to your finances wellbeing. Avoiding unnecessary expenses is an income for saving, and a potential proceed for investment. Learn to use income as wisely as possible for other goals. Proverbs 21[20] highlights the challenge of the foolish man as his spending habit. ***"In the house of the wise are stores of choice food and oil, but a foolish man devours all he has."*** The foolish man is a symbol of a squanderer who does not spare for tomorrow. This foolish man is not a designated fool, but his attitude and character portray him a fool. A foolish man does not plan for tomorrow. In the house of a man who remembers, there will be tomorrow; he spends, with caution as a watchword but a foolish man devours all he has.

We should watch our spending habits. They will either lead us to be financially successful or make us failures in financial matters. Unfortunately, many are already downward, financially. Habits, they say die hard, but I believe that habits that ridicule us should be terminated from the root. Decisions are choices we make each day, including our spending habits. There is no wonder or gimmick, instead a deliberate decision to say "No" to poor financial habits. Indiscipline spending habit is the most common factor today, both at individual and corporate levels. Arbitrary spending is a bad habit that should be deliberately avoided by anyone who wants to live a successful financial life. People are not ruined by high cost of living. They are destroyed by the cost of high living. So, to achieve the expectation of financial success, we should learn how to live sacrificially and be disciplined enough to give up desires that does not contribute to our survival. There are materials or properties that add no value to your existence. Do away with them because you don't need them. Give up those desires that are spurred by competition, imitation and copycat lifestyle. Indiscipline spending habit leads to waywardness and class stratification.

Proverbs 189 states that impulsive, foolish, unplanned, eye-catching and wasteful spending makes you a brother to the slothful, "one who is slack in his work is brother to one who destroys." Solomon continues in Proverbs 2117 to exhort against spending without limit, "He who loves pleasure will become poor, whoever loves wine and oil will never be rich." When a man loves pleasure, he tends to commit his finances without considering its effect at long run. Pleasure is one thing we should watch; it goes with the love for wine and oil, the characteristics of feasting lavishly. Most times those who love pleasure are indebted to the suppliers of pleasure; they are driven to indebtedness by their desires for pleasure. They often spend their money before they receive it. They live a life of pretense and live to please their admirers. They are impulsive purchasers, known as buyers of today and payers of tomorrow.

The following steps will help you reduce expenses if you strictly adhered to them;

- Limit the opportunities advertisers have to seduce you for their goods and services,

- Question the "season sales" and avoid buying things not needed in order to save the money. You know during sales, people flood the market to buy things at cheap prices but often times those things are not actually needed at home,

- Target unnecessary expenses and neglect them from the outset as never required in the house,

- Learn to prepare local dishes and snacks. Moi-moi (beans

cake) should not be bought from the market. Every household should be able to prepare it,

- Shop less and buy bulk if you have a disciplined family, otherwise buy daily. There are some families who cannot keep bulk purchase. They may likely finish a bulk purchase meant for one month in less than a week. Only purchase what is needed for such families,

- Plant vegetables, pepper, plantain, etc., at your backyard,

- Learn to do some basic household repairs,

- Avoid unbudgeted and impulsive purchases or what is called superfluous buying,

- Compare prices from different dealers; you can save as much money as possible. For instance, few years ago, we wanted to procure some doors to fix in the house. When we priced at our base, the total sum came to three million, two hundred and eighty-five Naira (N3,285,000), but when we compared prices from Lagos, we were getting almost one million, one hundred thousand Naira only (N1,100,000) as difference so buying from Lagos helped us to save nearly N1.2million. So, comparing prices will enable you most of the time to save money.

- Put up with a little pain before rushing to a clinic. Medicine does not prolong life.

- Getting out of debt, when you are unable to pay an entire bill in an account or if the amount you owe on an item exceeds its asset value, you have joined the list of debtors.

In his book, *Your money; frustration or freedom?* Howard L. Dayton, Jr. suggested eight steps for getting out of the entrapment of debt hence reducing your expenses:

Establish A Written Budget: A budget allows you to analyse where you are to plan where you want to go and to control impulse spending. Rarely, people who follow a written budget get into financial trouble.

Make A List Of All Your Assets: Include cash and assets readily convertible to cash, real estate, automobiles and other personal property, investments, and receivables. Evaluate each of these to see if there are any you can sell to cut your indebtedness.

Make A List Of All Your Debts: Most people do not know what they owe. Write down the monthly payment, the interest rate, and the balance due. The goal is to pay off the items that have the highest interest rates first.

Establish A Repayment Plan: Schedule for each debt you have, include the creditor, monthly payment, months remaining and balance due. This requires discipline and effort, but it's worth it. It is encouraging when you can tear one of these schedules up.

Consider Possible Sources Of Additional Income: This will help you to get out of debt more quickly. The only way to get out of debt is to reduce spending and increase revenue. If you find a way to supplement your income, be sure to use it to retire debt and not to spend more.

Be Content With What You Have: Since advertising is designed to create a lack of contentment, try to expose yourself less to the temptations caused by television commercials, newspapers and magazine advertisements, catalogues and window shopping.

Ignore And Avoid Competitive Lifestyle: You are not living your life for somebody else, hence do not allow another person's wristwatch to determine and decide how you live your life.

Hard Work Rules The World

Severally, there are places in the Bible we are admonished to work hard. Beyond the Bible, hard work has always been a yardstick for promotion and assignment of duty. Those who work hard have consistently climbed the ladder of promotion with ease. So, hard work is sine qua non for leadership position. Hard work is not only activities, it also engages mental capacity, the ability to become creative, to manage other levels of leadership and managerial capacity to coordinate other factors of production, the ability to forecast the policy advancement, to position the organization in a more competitive manner and provide corporate advantage over competitive rivalry.

Hard work requires patience and diligence and over time, by God's rule, brings gain. God did not only suggest hard work, but he commended hard work,

> *"Whatever your hands finds to do, do it with all your might, for in the grave, where you are going, there is neither working nor planning nor knowledge nor wisdom"* *(Ecclesiastes 9:10).*

In heaven, we don't need all these virtues because they are needless and have no value. So, we are admonished by King Solomon, that this is where we need to work hard in every area or aspect of our calling because where we are going, they do not exist. Paul, while addressing the church at Rome, asked them never to be lacking in zeal, but to *"keep your spiritual fervor, serving the Lord"* (Romans 1211). Again, while talking to the Corinthian congregation, he did remind them that he worked hard with his own hands, *"we work hard with our own hands, when we are cursed, we bless; when we are persecuted, we endure it"* (I Cor. 412). Paul never imposed himself and his financial demand on the church; rather he set an example. He was a tent maker, a trade he learnt to support himself in the ministry thereby reducing dependency upon the church at Corinthians. Then, of course, that earned him some respect. He could boldly ask them (his disciples and followers) to accuse him of any fraudulent practice while he ministered among them, and even ask them to follow him as he followed Christ. This is the courage of a person whose credibility is impeccable and blameless. He counseled the church at Colossians, *"whatever you do, work at it with all your heart, as working for the Lord, not for men"* (Colossians 323). 1Thessalonians 411-12, says,

"Make it your ambition to lead a quiet life, to mind your own business and to work with your hands, just as we told you, so that your daily life may win the respect of outsiders and so that you will not be despondent on anybody."

When we work hard, we do an indirect evangelism. From the scripture, Paul informed the brethren on the importance of and vitality of hard work. He mentioned minding your own business. Those who work hard don't have time for gossip or blackmail. They are focused and dutiful to their own business. Busybodies are lazy workers, tale bearers, and gluttons. He said; work with your own hands, meaning be engaged in whatever you have accepted to do. The third thing he said, so that your daily life may win the respect of outsiders. When you show a level of seriousness with your duty, unbelievers tend to respect you and your God. Finally, he said, so that you will not be dependent on anybody. This is a boast Paul never wanted anybody to rob him of. There is a great honour in dignity in solving your financial needs from your personal sweat and struggle. It gives one a sense of fulfillment and boldness. Paul warns all his followers of the dangers of depending on someone else for the propagation of the gospel. He advocated for self-propagation, self-sponsorship and self-finance. In the final instruction to the church in Thessalonians, the author admonished the church to respect those who work hard among them, *"now we ask you, brothers, to respect those who work hard among you, who are over you in the Lord and who admonish you"* 1 Thessalonians 512.

Paul continued his protest against lazy workers when he counselled in 2 Thessalonians 310, *"For even when we were with you, we gave you this rule, "if a man will not work, he shall not eat."* Paul had to remind the Thessalonians brethren of a principle he taught them while he was with them in Thessalonians that working for your meals, upkeep, and wellbeing is a biblical principle. This warning and admonition had to come because the Thessalonians' attitude to work was irrational and the excuses some of them gave for not working was that Paul taught the imminent return of Christ and that He (Christ) might come back momentarily. When they waited for the imminent return, which of course did not happen, they ran out of financial resources and started sponging off their fellow Christians, causing relational problems in the church. The major issue is not their expectation of the return of the Lord Jesus Christ. It was their obstinate attitude towards the subject of working for their food. Laziness goes against many biblical principles. The question here is not refusing to give aid to those who cannot help themselves or support to those who truly need the support but those who, under the guise of church's welfare package, defraud the church of her resources as helpless brethren.

Paul was not referring to people who cannot find a job or people who do not have the physical ability to work. The charge is against people with capacity and opportunity to work but who live exclusively off the graciousness of other people's wealth and gesture. To be tough on those who do not want to work or who choose to disregard the principle of work is to be kind to other individuals and to the church. God provides resources through our work. A principle of God's creation is to work for our welfare, except people who cannot work for themselves.

Diligent labour has the promise of many blessings and reward, both in the Bible and workplace. Promotions do not come to the slothful but to the diligent worker. No organization puts a mentally weak person in their driver's seat. Proverbs 12^{24}, **"The diligent shall gain in authority, but the slothful to greater servitude."** Further to that, Solomon said, *"A man diligent in business shall stand before kings instead of mean men,"* (Proverbs 22^{29}).

In support of this verse, another author posits, "I believe success in life is within the reach of all who set before them an aim and an ambition that is not beyond the talents and ability which God has bestowed upon them. We should all begin life with a determination to do well whatever we take in hand, and if that determination is adhered to with the pluck for which Englishmen are renowned, success, according to the nature and quality of our brain power, is, I think, a certainty. Had I began life as a tinker, my earnest endeavour would have been to have made better pots and pans than my neighbours, and I think I may venture to say without any vanity that, with God's blessing, I should have been relatively successful.

The first step on the ladder that leads to success is the firm determination to succeed; the next is the possession of that moral and physical courage which will enable one to mount up, rung after rung, until the top is reached. The best men make a false step now and then, and some even have very bad falls. The weak cry over their misfortunes, and seek for the sympathy of others, and do nothing further after their first and second failure, but the plucky and the courageous pick themselves up without a groan over their broken bones or their first failures, and set to work to mount the ladder again, full of confidence in themselves and with faith in the results that always attend upon cheerful perseverance."

Gill (www.bible.com) in his commentary of the verse, stated "such a man be it in the business of his calling, be it what it will, whether for himself or his master, constant in it, swift ready, and expeditious at it, who industriously pursues it, cheerfully attends it, makes quick dispatch of it, does it off hand, at once, and is not slothful in it, nor weary of it, when you have observed and taken notice of such man, which is not very common, you may without a spirit of prophecy, foresee that such a man will rise in the world. Such a person who is diligent will cease to work for ignoble persons or work with them, instead he shall be taken into the services of princes and noblemen, men of substance, and be admitted into their presence and receive favours from them, as Joseph who was industrious and diligent in his business in Potiphar's house, was in process of time advanced, and stood before Pharaoh king of Egypt (Gen.39[4]).

Likewise, men of God who are diligent in teaching, steadfast and immovable always abounding in the work of the Lord, are ready to every good work, heartily engaged in it, and continuously at it, shall not be company for the sons of darkness, unregenerate men, who are in the dark, and darkness itself. What communion has light with darkness, with works of darkness, Or have any fellowship with the prince of darkness, from whose power they are delivered, but shall have society with the saints, who are made kings and priests unto God; shall be admitted into the presence of the king of kings now, and have communion with him, and shall stand before him at the great day with confidence and not be ashamed, shall stand at his right hand, and shall be forever with him. Proverbs 19^{15}, states that slothfulness always and all the time, leads to more laziness. So, for you to stand before Kings and authorities, you must deliberately break the cycle of this sin called slothfulness, **"Laziness brings on deep sleep, and the shiftless man goes hungry."** So, you are implored to deal with the sinful cycle of laziness, though the body needs sleep but not as much as we offer to it, energy comes from activity not sleep. God, through the Bible, makes a mockery of laziness and lazy people. The pictures painted of laziness and lazy people tell me that God will surely judge all sloths and laziness. In several scriptures, God mocks lazy men with sarcasm and hyperbole for their sloth. You do not abscond from a job because you think it is difficult. If you do, it shows you have little strength, but if the righteous is as bold as a lion as enshrined in the scripture, you ought to guard against fear of obstacles (Prov. 28^1) and rule out of your life all routine procrastination (Prov. 20^4).

Drastic Reduction Of Debt

People of wisdom try to minimize the amount of financial debt they incur. The bible has a lot of pictures of debtors and the effect of their indebtedness. Look at the picture of a borrower painted in Proverbs 22^7, *"The rich rule over the poor, and the borrower is a servant to the lender."* From this scriptural position, it seems that 'ALL' borrowers are slaves to the lender. Then, of course, you know that in the modern world, you cannot borrow without collateral, which is one of the reasons putting up security for someone else is frowned upon in the bible. Whoever you borrows from controls your life and how you live your life until you pay off. God considers indebtedness a great curse,

> *"If only you fully obey the Lord your God and are careful to follow all these commands I am giving you today. For the Lord, your God will bless you as He has promised, and you will lend to many nations but will borrow from none. You will rule over many nations, but none will rule over you"* (Deut. 15 $^{5-6}$).

This same posture against the spirit of indebtedness is emphasized in verses 11-^{13} of Deuteronomy 28, especially verse. ^{12},

> *"The Lord will open the heavens, the storehouse of his bounty, to send rain on your land in season and to bless all the work of your hands. You will lend to many nations but will borrow from none."*

God continued His detest for indebtedness in verses 37-46.

In reducing your debt, you must begin by discarding irrelevant wasteful needs and concentrate on needful needs. There are things you can do for yourself as part of the strategies to reduce debt. Many people, not just the less privileged, but also the very much privileged people were engaged in local, domestic and hobby-farming behind their homes. Many of them, you will not believe it, are highly placed people in the society who do not buy vegetables, tomatoes, pepper, plantain, yam, and garri from the market over years.

The state of debt clearly is seen whenever you spend more than your normal stream of income. Whenever you buy to pay later, you are in debt. Whenever you are unable to pay your bills, you are in debt. Whenever you cannot pay the children's school fees naturally, you are in debt. Whenever you complain that your expenses are draining your income to the less break-even point, you are in debt. Whenever you cannot comfortably cushion your needful demand, either for the family front, extended family, neighbouring support, and environmental evangelism, you are in debt.

Debt does not only mean all the above, debt is also incurred when you borrow to spend on consumption, eatable and cloths; when you load your credit card with borrowed fund from bank or financial houses and after your vacation, it takes over twelve (12) months to pay back, you are dangerously in debt. It is also noteworthy that you are in debt when you borrow funds to execute a wedding, celebrate your birthday or child dedication, or burial ceremony or when you sell your property or liquidate your investment for celebration. All of these have no pay-back period and are called needful waste. A greater percentage of our limited income is spent this way.

Few years ago, a young man in a bid to please his wife-to-be and parents-in-laws, borrowed from different individuals to execute a supposed society wedding with all kinds of irrelevancies only to continue to pay debt five years after wedding. To my mind, that is a needful waste. There are many families who are dragged into needful waste during the burial of their loved ones. They borrow money to bankroll a burial that does not contribute anything to the economy of the family except flattery praises. Some sew different kinds of uniforms for the dead who was never loved and catered for while alive. The recent trend is the printing of different types of burial programmes such as burial service programme, burial photos-peak, burial condolences, burial choice hymns, etc. Do you know what? Some of these programmes do not go with the people. Immediately after the burial service, the people drop the programmes behind in pursuit of food and drinks. A family in trying to set a record for organizing the most expensive burial in their community ran into debt worth several millions of Naira. After seven months of the funeral, they were dragged to my office for settlement of the debts incurred during the burial. What a waste!

Though negative, but I think the economic recession is frankly putting people back to shape and appropriate status. Needful waste is a disgrace and a corrupt spirit. It thrives most on competition and demonstration. It has no mind of its own; somewhat depends on the outside influence to grow its tenacity. Chase it away from your home and business and lifestyle through drastic reduction of needful waste by practicing debt minimization. Most of this borrowing is done with high-level interest rates, which will not stop running until the borrowed principal amount is paid fully. Borrowing at interest will always cost you more than saving with interest to buy or execute your projects. In borrowing, you spend to maintain the money borrowed, while in savings you gain income as interest is paid to you.

To achieve the drastic reduction of debt, which is an attainable goal in staying financially afloat, you need to redefine what is truly important that will lead to wealth, rewarding, fulfilling, Christ-centered and balanced life. Covey (1999) in his book, First Things First states how to set and achieve principle-based goals. Without principles, goals will never have the power to produce quality life results. You can want to do the right thing, and you can even want to do it for the right reason. But if you don't apply the proper principles, you can still hit a wall. A principle-based goal has three dimensions: the right thing for the right reason, in the right way. The person who wants to reduce debt drastically must develop the right things, for those right reasons and do it the right way. Efficiency is the manager of all life endeavour and flavour of mystery is the ability to know when to stop and when to say no.

There are four significant human endowments, and all of them are required to achieving a principle-based, goal-setting for drastic reduction of debt.

Conscience: With the conscience, we connect with the passion of the vision and mission of expected goal and the power of principle. This is so when you have the passion of vision and mission to live a life free of debt, then the power of principles will level you to contentment, deliver you from competition and save you from acquiring materials you do not need.

Creative Imagination: This helps us to envision and design possible ways that can be supervised and more profound, ways for creatively achieving deserved results.

Self-Awareness: This helps us to understand who we are and what we are capable of doing. When one does not know his ability and capability, it is dangerous. When you hear people say, "he has bitten more than he can chew," they are simply saying that you are not aware of who they are; they don't understand their limits, and don't have a value system. Likewise, when one lives above his income, he is as good as someone who does not understand the psychology of his composition and as such could be referred to as a fool. Self-awareness helps us to set goals and targets with realistic stretch and stay upon conscience-driven change or alternative.

Independent Will: Nothing on earth should be our master apart from our Master and Lord Jesus Christ. Independent will, tells you that you are master of your environment and a creator," by making purposeful choices and decisions and carrying them out for the ultimate achievement of the expectation and by so doing, have the integrity to walk and talk. Independent-will is the divine capacity of God imputed in every creature to make choices and take responsibility for such choices. God created man in His image and after His likeness. From the nature of creation and the mandate to man to coordinate the universe for the ultimate owner, man has been called to be independent, but this is not without associated consequences if he makes wrong decisions and choices. Whatever happens, man should not be entirely independent from his creator.

So, try to be out of debt by avoiding debt traps. Borrowing to solve a challenge is one side of the coin but taking on financial obligations one can't but keep - buying beyond your ability to pay, is another side of the coin. Psalm 3721, says **"the wicked borroweth, and payeth not again."** The minute a person goes into debt, he loses a part of his freedom, boldness and courage. Proverbs 227 captures it practically when it states, **"The rich ruled over the poor, and the borrower is servant to the lender."**

Too many people think you can buy now and pay later, which is very common among our civil servants, but that has not really worked out. I have also discovered that easy money or credit now makes people uneasy later. You pay more for the use of borrowed money than you get in interest for saving. There is a product plan launched by MTN called beta talk. At face value, you will think you are saving money, but soon after you finish the two hundred (200) percent bonus, the way your main credit will be exhausted is at the speed of light. To make sure you pay back double of the 200% bonus, you are not allowed to transfer the bonus to anybody, and you are to finish it within a few days from the day you top up.

Self-Awareness

Self-awareness is really just about being aware of who we are, which may relate to knowing our values, beliefs, personal preferences, and tendencies. You know how famous people always say, "stay true to yourself." This is indeed an essential advice, but it is not easy to tell yourself the truth if you don't know who you are. By becoming self-aware and understanding your strength and limitations, you open up opportunities that are ordinarily not available if you don't know yourself. You are also able to have more honest and genuine relationships because the people you are attracted to will be drawn to you for who you indeed are.

Covey (1999) defines self-awareness as *our capacity to stand apart from ourselves and examine thinking about our motives, our history, our life scripts, our actions, habits, and tendencies. It enables us to take off our glasses and look at them as well as through them. It makes it possible for us to become aware of the social and physical history of the programmes that are in us and to enlarge the separation between stimulus and response.*

Self-Awareness Empowers Us To Build Integrity

Our trustworthiness is only as high as the balance in our personal integrity account. Sequel to our integrity being the basis of our confidence in ourselves and the confidence we inspire in others, one of the most significant manifestations of effective personal leadership is the exercise of care and wisdom in building a high positive balance in that account. Hence, self-awareness establishes the link of confidence to achieve self-confidence, both in ourselves as leaders and those we inspire to follow us. Without self-awareness, we will hardly develop followers.

Primarily, we build this integrity through the exercise of independent will in making and keeping commitments. But without self- awareness, we don't have the wisdom necessary to manage such an account. We may set our goals too high, turning potential deposits into huge withdrawals when we fail to achieve them. Again, we may set them too low, depositing Kobos when we could be depositing Nairas. We may miss daily, weekly, quarterly, and moment by moment opportunities to make deposits because we are too busy blaming circumstances or other people for our failure to achieve our goals. Self-awareness prompts us to start where we are; no illusions, no excuses and helps us to set realistic goals. On the other hand, it also doesn't allow us to cope with mediocrity. It helps us recognize and respect our need to stretch, to grow and push beyond limits. Since much of our frustration in life comes as a result of failed expectations, the ability to set goals that are both realistic and challenging goes a long way towards empowering us to create peace and positive growth in our lives.

Self-awareness is an ear to the voice of conscience. It helps us to recognize that there are principles independent of us, to understand the futility of trying to become a law unto ourselves.

It helps us to be humble and open for growth and change, to realize that we are neither omniscient nor omnipotent when we set a goal. To the best of our awareness at the time, out of all the good things we could do, we choose the best thing, for the best reason, and we plan to do it in the best way. Self-awareness empowers us to ask questions that affect our personality: am I allowing the good to take the place of the best? The best may be the goal we set. The best may be in the unexpected opportunity, the new knowledge, and understanding. If change is driven primarily by urgency, mood or opposition, it takes us away from the best, but if it is moved by mission, conscience, and principles, it moves us towards the best.

To have self-awareness is to know the difference between the good and the best and to act based on mission, conscience, and principles. It is to make the most significant deposits in our personal integrity account. Integrity means more than sticking to a goal, no matter what. It is integrity of system, an integrity process that creates an open connection between the mission and the moment. Self-awareness is understanding your own needs, desires, failures, habits, and everything else that makes you tick both now and after, long term and short term. The more you know about yourself, the better you are adopting life changes that suit your needs. It is a huge part of both therapy and philosophy. It is also the basis of the quantified self-movement, which assumes that if you collect data about yourself, you can make improvements based on that data.

The New York Times breaks down the roots like Socrates Ukase was "know thyself." Though it may come as a surprise to some philosophers, self-knowledge requires more than intellectual self–examination. It demands knowing something about your feelings. In my experience, philosophers are, in general, not the most emotionally attuned individuals. Many are prone to treat the ebb and flow of feelings as though our passions were nothing but impediments to reason. Fraud, more than the sage of Athens, grasped the moral importance of emotional self-transparency. Like the Greek tragedians, but in language, that did not require an ear for poetry, he reminded us of how difficult it is to own kinship with a whole range of emotions. Mostly, the more you pay attention to your feelings and how you work, the better you will understand why you do the things you do. The more you know about your own habits, the easier it is to improve on them. In most cases, this takes a little experimentation.

To explain self-awareness, the New York Times adopted a method called double-loop learning. Less common but vastly more effective is the cognitive approach. However, Professor Argyris questions every aspect of our approach, including our methodology, bases, and deeply held assumptions. This more psychologically nuanced self-examination requires that we honestly challenge our beliefs and summon the courage to act on that information, which may lead to fresh ways of thinking about our lives and our goals. When you develop your self-awareness, you have a wonderful opportunity to move beyond petty jealousies and all the garbage that creates conflict, chaos, confusion, and misery in your life and focus instead of a loving, kind, joyful, profoundly, introspective and fulfilling existence.

You heal the hurts from your past; you are in touch with your emotions and are able to feel them and use them to move in a positive direction.

You are also comfortable with other people's emotions, you understand your strengths and areas for improvement; you treat yourself and others with kindness, empathy, and compassion; you do things to make the world a better place; you focus on the more profound things in life rather than living superficially; you get to know the real you and live your life accordingly; you let go of the need for power and control and focus instead on being the best person you can be without dominating others or having to win. With this attitude, people will like you both at home and at work. You won't have the constant internal conflict, saying one thing and doing a different thing entirely. Again, you are generally happy and balanced even in difficult situations. You understand why you feel, think and do things; you learn and grow each day; you become a better person, and enjoy your life and that of those around you, family and friends.

Daniel Goleman (1995) says, "if your emotional abilities are not in hand; if you don't have self-awareness; if you are not able to manage your distressing emotions; if you can't have empathy and have effective relationships, then no matter how smart you are, you are not going to get very far. Self-awareness is the beginning of emotional intelligence. It is the first priority upon which all the other parts are developed.

According to Robert Jerus (2014), in his book, Mind matters and the EIQ-2 learning systems, there are five (5) contexts of self:

Deep self (core): This is the core of human attitude that remote controls all other parts. The deep self is where definition and identity are created. This is the stable, immutable core. It is the personal characteristic that remains stable throughout life. This includes primary personality traits, integrity coefficient, potential and what defines who you are and who you are not. This deep-self differentiates the 'you' from the real 'you'. The 'you' people see is not really the 'you' that controls you. This sets the foundation for performance, communication, relationships and life's adventure.

Self in Time (Story): This is your personal story or testimony which forms the background of your actions and inactions. These personal testimonies go a long way to pattern how we behave towards things around us. It starts with individual history and experience. This includes the following: **education, civilization, training and nurturing.** It references feelings, thoughts, performance and associated cause and effect. History is the set of events that has moulded the present. The present is today's mindset, thinking, behaviour, attitudes and lifestyle that shape how life plays out later on. While the past provided the "why" the present directs the "how." It is the active framework that has been formed by the consequences of yesterday.

So, when we refuse to form our present, we are denied of tomorrow, and we will not experience the past and hopelessness associated with the yesterday. So today or the present, is the mother of the past and gives birth to yesterday. Thus when one refuses to make use of his experience, strength, resources, and ability to create his past and yesterday, he labours in sorrow and suffering in the future and tomorrow. No tomorrow without adequate plan for today. You want to enjoy the goodies of the past in the tomorrow; you must sacrifice for it today.

Today is significant in the type of life you would want to enjoy tomorrow. The future is formed by dreams, aspirations and coordinated for tomorrow. It is based on expectations and anticipation. It is moulded by preparation and plans.

Self-Construct (Developed): The self-construct is developed and decided by the individual. It is not imposed on you instead you make the choice, and of course, you reap the consequences. It includes the self-concept and image, that is, who you see yourself as; predispositions that pattern thinking, emotion and action that enhance self-construct, preferences which include your likes and dislikes contribute to your self-construct, secondary personality characteristics, which are the changeable traits subject to shift, transition, and transformation, values and principles, that is, chosen courses to implement integrity, motivation, focus; and an array of self-selected factors.

Processing-Self (Behaviour): The processing-self manages operations of the whole self. It governs sensory perception: how information is taken in, decoded and understood; thinking: assumptions, beliefs, cognitive frameworks, paradigms, interpretations and evaluations; feelings: negative, positive, primary and secondary, moods; attitude: relatively permanent patterns of dealing with the world; performance: cause of action designed for targeted results; motivation: engaged drives to particular ends.

Dynamic-Self (visible): The dynamic-self that is most readily viewed and understood by the self and others. This is presented externally. It is based on tangible qualities like relationships, ownership, position, authority, and their value and implication. It is also predicated on interests and opinions, with their subsequent implications; individual strengths, weaknesses, opportunities and threats and their subsequent effects on action; synthesis and application of the total self. Finally, it creates a personal definition of reality, cause and effect, and pattern to cope with life.

The benefits of self-awareness according to Robert Jerus:

Deliberately become the person you want to be: Make choices, exercise self- selection. Do not drop your life to the world to decide what you want to become. No, you must be deliberate about it.

Act Consciously instead of reacting to people and event: While the subconscious is creative, conscious action is far more effective at directing performance to targeted goals. It is also better at coping with daily life.

Create self-esteem, confidence, and self-worth: Self-assurance and efficacy, learning and improvement focus on desired results. Patterns of achievement are recognized and celebrated.

Be authentic and make active choices: Self-knowledge enables being genuine. It allows for the choices of thoughts, feelings, and performance that are consistent and designed with who you truly are. Active choice is enabled by exact knowledge of your person and capacity.

Having greater depth of experience and enjoyment of life: Self-awareness allows wisdom to choose positive emotions and constructive paths. It sets the tone to create a personal agenda and pathway.

Manage the ability to redirect your negative thoughts and emphasize positive ones: If it cannot be recognized, defined and labeled, it fosters confusion and disengagement. Awareness empowers active, selected achievement. It allows realistic optimism.

Relate effectively to others with empathy and understanding: Connecting with the self-facilitates resonance and rapport with others. This permits the development of quality interaction and enhances relationship skills.

Understand yourself and exercise self-care and compassion: Intrapersonal kindness and tenderness allows for personal forgiveness. It releases regrets, worry, anxiety, and negative feelings, allowing self-nurturing and a more fulfilling life journey.

Reduce internal conflict and perform assertively: Internal ambiguity results in a lack of direction, ineffective action, misguided efforts and results that are less than satisfying. Focused performance gains high-quality objectives in both the short and long term.

Identify and come to peace with who you are and who you are not: Consequence of thought, communication, emotion, and performance generate harmony, balance and tranquility.

The Doctrine of Prosperity

Reflection On Chapter 7

Personal Notes:

===== Guided Action Plan =====

CHAPTER 8
The Budget As A Regulator

"Control is the name of the game. It is one thing we must learn to do, the ship no matter how large and driven by strong winds, is steered by a very small rudder wherever the pilot wants it to go."

There are lots of people who do not believe in budgeting. However, their unbelief does not change anything. So many businessmen and women do not consider budgeting as a critical factor in sustainable financial success. Some see it as a sign of stinginess. But it is not. It is supposed to be a way of life. A life without a budget is a disorganized and chaotic life. A business without a budget will end up in bankruptcy. A marriage without a budget will end in catastrophe. A career without a budget will end in a frustrated future. A profession without a budget will end up producing quack. A contractor without a budget will end up spending both his capital and profit and will make more money for banks in regard to interest rate.

Budget is an essential aspect of our lives that needs a closer attention. Everything we do requires a budget if we desire continuity. Budget is not only for professionals but also for individuals, churches, fellowships, institutions, families, and communities, to enhance their development. It is so essential in the life of anything that expects success. Without budget, there will be no posterity, no tomorrow, no continuity. Budget harmonizes our inflows and outflows.

What is a Budget?

There are different definitions of budget, but they all seem to mean the same thing. A budget is defined as; "An estimate of individual, government, family, company or institutions, expenditure, and revenue for the financial year."

- From the definition above, we draw the following conclusions;
- Budgeting is an interaction between the inflow and outflow.
- Budgeting is nothing more than planned spending.
- Budget is taking control of your money.
- Budget is managing and controlling your cash flow.

A close observation of all the points above reveals the four major concepts of budget.

- Income
- Expenses
- Control
- Choice

The Budget As A Regulator

Budget is not zeroed down to money only. Your time, your talent and, even your skills can be budgeted. You can decide on the month or year to begin to employ your skills. Your time, for instance, can be segmented into modules of five years or ten years. For example, you may plan to get married or build a house, between the ages of 20-25 or 25-30. You may plan to buy a car between 35 - 40 years. You may want to start an investment between your 50-60 years. You may plan for your retirement. These are instances to prove that we don't only have to budget money, we can also budget our talents, time and skills. And if they are appropriately budgeted for, they will yield revenue.

> **Budgeting was first practiced in the Bible by Joseph in** Genesis 41[11], **"when King Pharaoh had his dream of seven cows, fat and sleek; and another seven cows, scrawny and very ugly and lean, and fat cows. The king shared another dream where he saw seven heads of grain, full and good, growing on a single stack. And the king continued that the lean, ugly cows ate up the seven. Later another seven heads sprouted, withered and thin and scorched by the east wind. The thin heads of grain swallowed up the seven good heads."**

In the interpretation, Joseph said the following: That the dream of King Pharaoh are one and the same and that the seven good cows and the seven good heads of grains represented seven years of abundance, while the seven lean, ugly cows that came up and the seven worthless heads of grain scorches by the east wind represented seven years of great famine. He went further to say that God had to bring this message in two forms just to prove to the king that the matter had been firmly decided by God and that God would do it soon.

The Budgeting Time and Resource

When Pharaoh employed Joseph to manage the seven years of great abundance and the seven years of great famine, he said,

> *"Since God has made all these known to you, there is no one so discerning and wise as you. You shall oversee my palace, and all my people are to submit to your orders. Only with respect to the throne will I be greater than you."*

Joseph practiced the principles of budgeting when he was discharging this onerous task from the king. Since it is the interaction of inflows and outflows, he practiced planned and well-calculated expenditure. He saw the seven years of great abundance as the years of inflow, and made use of them accordingly, and saw the years of severe famine as the years of outflow. The seven years of great abundance could as well be the years of enormous inflow of cash or revenue, while the seven years of severe famine were seven years of economic austerity. Whatever you do with your years of great abundance will unavoidably affect your years of famine. We have seen people, who unduly increase their wardrobe and feeding expenditure just because their income was slightly increased. Joseph did not allow the seven years of great abundance to blindfold him. He did not spend outside the budget for each day because he had plenty of revenue. Additional revenue does not mean extra expenditure but proper planning and budgeting.

What Joseph Did

During the seven years of great abundance, Joseph collected all the surplus and plentiful of the land and stored them in cities. Not only in one city, but in many cities. Suggesting that we should not put our eggs in one basket, we should as a matter of urgency spread our investment across board. Some people have all their eggs in one basket. Some have set up their business empire in one city or state. Some in one line of business and cannot diversify, while some others consider diversification as a weakness of the mind and brain.

For Joseph, he did not store the harvest of the seven years of massive financial prosperity in one city, instead, in many cities. The Bible said,

> **In each city, he put the food grown in the fields surrounding it (V. 4^{5b}).**

He stored up so much goods and vast quantities of grains that he could not keep records again. Suddenly, the years of abundance came to an end and the years of famine took over as predicated by Joseph. People who did not develop long time perspective mentality enjoyed the few quantities of grains they stored thinking that the famine would last but a few months. The famine continued till one year, and their hopes began to fail them. The Egyptians who had the opportunity of hearing the interpretation of the dreams enjoyed their provisions for a while.

> "There was famine in all the other lands, but in the whole land of Egypt, there was food" (v.⁵⁴ᵇ).

But for how long would what they stored serve them? There are many people who only think of today, and if anything, negative happens to them, you will see them begging for food from the first day of the problem. Budgeting forces you to think in the long-distance perspective. The Bible did record that the whole of Egypt enjoyed food **for a short time**, because they did not store enough even when they heard the interpretation of the dream.

> "When all Egypt began to feel the famine, the people cried to Pharaoh for food. Then Pharaoh told all the Egyptians, go to Joseph and do want he tells you" (v.⁵⁵).

Between the time the famine started and the time the Egyptians ran out of food was quite a short time. During this period, Joseph did not open the storehouse preserved for the period of famine until they ran out of stock. Then the people cried to the king for food. What you are storing in your time of abundance should be big enough to sustain you in the times of adversity. They ran out of stock and death took over but for the storage of Joseph in a wise budget. The people went to Joseph and bought food until their money was exhausted.

> *Genesis 47:13-14.* "There was no food, however in the whole region because the famine was severe, both Egypt and Canaan wasted away because of the famine. Joseph collected all the money that was to be found in Egypt

> *and Canaan in payment for the grains they were buying, and he brought it to Pharaoh's palace."*

The people used up their money and began to buy with their livestock and their landed properties, and finally started selling themselves to Joseph who in turn made them become Pharaoh's slaves. Reading this in Genesis 47$^{23-24}$ will interest you;

> *"Joseph said to the people; Now that I have bought you and your land today for Pharaoh, here is seed for you so you can plant the ground. But when the crops come in, give a fifth of it to Pharaoh. The other four-fifths you may keep as seeds for the field and food for yourselves and your house and your children."*

Hear their reply; poverty is dangerous: *"You have saved our lives; they said, may we find favour in bondage" (v.^{25})*. Please do not settle for poverty. It is entirely different from suffering for Christ. Its influence is overwhelming and cruel.

Lack of budget produces servant-hood mentality. Without budgeting and targeted expenditure, you are bound to be somebody's slave throughout your life. The Egyptians were looking for favour in bondage. There are people whose hope is only in servant-hood, they hardly aspire a better future other than servanthood.

Joseph gave seed to each of them to plant the ground. The seed was saved in the budget planning. Each budget plan has two major sides to it. The income and expenditure sides; the asset and liability side; the injection and leakage. The interplay between the two sides is what we call budget planning. The concept is not new, but few individuals accept it because some believe you don't need to budget with small money unless when the money is large enough.

An average man once asked me this question: "is it not when you have enough money in your pocket that you will budget? How does one budget when what he has is not enough to cushion his daily expenditure"? This is precisely the mentality and mindset of many people. Listen, budget starts with nothing and grows to something. If you cannot budget with N10.00, you may not be able to budget with N100.00. Consequently, you may not be able to budget with N100,000 or N1,000,000, because there are overwhelming needs and problems waiting to swallow up all the money. Poverty starts from mentality, for wrong mentality towards budgeting leads to financial crisis. Between the rich man and the poor man is a tiny line, the rich man spends according to budget while the poor man believes there is no need for budget since the money is small. Most affluent men and women hardly have time to eat, but poor men and women eat to stupidity. If you know any man or woman who is rich, watch his eating habit and compare it to the appetite of the poor man, you will undoubtedly observe the cause of poverty.

Let us look at the different types of poverty:

- Appetite induced poverty
- Government enforced poverty

- Lack of planning enforced poverty
- Inadequacy compelled poverty
- Budget-less enforced poverty

Appetite Induced Poverty: Appetite is defined as an inherent craving, an insatiable desire for food or material possession. Anything you have uncontrollable appetite for will undoubtedly lead to poverty. Few months ago, I travelled with a group of people, and during the trip, I observed that one of us was busy satisfying his appetite by eating over ten pounds (£10) per meal. I had to call him to order. There are some people who cannot cope without buying everything they set their eyes on. Some go to the market, and before they attend to their shopping list, the money budgeted for purchases is exhausted in buying things that were not in the original list. Uncontrolled appetite leads to poverty.

Government Enforced Poverty: When a government cannot provide the necessary social amenities, infrastructures, and energy to enable the private sector create employment for the masses, automatically the resultant effect is primary poverty. There will be hunger and suffering. When a people cannot feed in their country or at least enjoy basic infrastructure like good roads, healthcare scheme, pipe borne water, shelter, and at least three-square meals a day, such a people are said to be suffering from primary poverty enforced on them by their government.

Inadequacy Enforced Poverty: Inadequacy is defined as insufficiency or deficiency. When people who are entrusted to run the government, company, organization, community or parastatal, are not sufficiently trained or lack the required capacity, they deliver inadequate services to the people, hence will create its own poverty-environment which will lead to the citizens, suffering. This is called inadequacy enforced poverty.

Budget-less Enforced Poverty: As the name sounds, its meaning becomes obvious. When you refuse to budget, it is assumed you have accepted to fail. When you buy anything outside your perceived list, you are budgetless. When you buy out of impulse, it means you are budgetless, and when you spend outside of planned expenditure, it shows you are budgetless because you don't have respect for your budget. By this lifestyle, you can enforce poverty without knowing it.

Budget Management

In the process of planning a budget, the implementation of the budget should be topmost in the list of priorities. You can have an excellent budget, but if you have not resolved how to manage it properly, your budget will crash, and your goals, dreams, and aspirations will be destroyed without hope of restoration.

As a Pastor, I have seen people who started the year with a clear-cut budget vision of everything they wanted done for that year, only to abandon it in the first quarter of the year. Foundation speaks volumes, not just in our lives as many speakers have made us to understand, but also Jesus spoke about the foundation of houses which represent businesses, future, marriages, budgets, and investments.

The Budget As A Regulator

Several times people have made budgets but lack adequate aptitude to implement them. If you have not planned to restrict your spending to your budget, don't bother budgeting. It is mere mockery of budget and planning. The implementation of budget is the realization of the four major concepts of budget. Namely:

- Income
- Expenses
- Control
- Choice

By this, budget implementation and management must involve the following steps:

To ascertain your daily income stream: That is, all the sources you expect income from whether daily, weekly, monthly or yearly. Your income includes:

- Your salary, if you are a worker of any sort.
- The cash that comes to you through transport if you are a taxi or bus owner.
- The cash that comes to you through your investments, i.e. dividends, bonus shares, interests, and debentures.
- The cash that comes to you through real estate, if you are an estate owner.
- The cash that comes to you through your publications, royal-

ties, and copyrights, if you are a writer.
- The cash that comes to you through retirement benefits and gratuity.
- The cash that comes to you by easily converted money like credit account balance, traveler's cheques, treasury bills.
- There are many more sources of income peculiar to different individuals, but let us make do with these for now.

To establish your expenses' limits for each expenditure pattern: In budget management, the manager is expected to come to terms with his major expenses, minor expenses and can-do-without expenses and stick with the budget, it does not matter what people around say. Often, we have been influenced by the opinion of people around us. Some have been called funny names like: superglue hand, stingy man, economizer and when it is time for borrowing, the same people come to the stingy man and super glue hand man to ask for financial help. If he was not super glue handed, he may not have kept money enough to lend in time of need. Everyman should develop one way or the other of becoming super glue hand for the rainy day.

Many people find it difficult to state categorically the type of expenses they want to get involved in for a time. For instance, if you are about to shop, state from the house, what and what you need and what to buy. You cannot satisfy all your needs throughout your lifetime, so why do you want to buy up the whole supermarket in a moment of purchase. Stating the limit of your expenses will help you to be focused and reasonable in your demands and purchases. I have observed cases where after people have written what they wanted to buy from the market and collected the expected amount of money they think will sponsor that list, when they get to the market, they will start buying things that were not in her original list and by the time they open their list, the money is three-quarters spent. Often, they are gone back home with their list unattended to.

To deliberately stick to your budget by controlling your daily expenses: This is almost impossible with some persons. My wife will ask me: 'why keep money when there are needs in the house to be solved with money'? And I will reply; *when are you going to finish these needs so that we can keep some savings behind for the future'?* "It is totally against the spirit of financial favour to spend according to needs, rather according to budget". There are many people who are in severe financial burdens because they prefer spending according to needs rather than according to budget. *You cannot satisfy your needs, but you can satisfy your budget and feel fulfilled.* You must check and balance your attitude towards your expenditure by asking yourself relevant questions like:

- Do my expenses really reflect my exact priority?
- Do my expenses give me opportunity to pay myself salary?
- Are my expenses more than my monthly income?
- Are my expenses allowing me the opportunity of satisfying my choice?

You can deliberately stick to your budget by controlling your expenses by doing the following:

- Write down your needs.
- Write down the sum amount you need to satisfy them.
- Ask yourself, will all of them be bought the same day?
- Ask yourself, what are my preferences?
- Ask yourself, can I make do without any of these?
- Take a monthly, quarterly, yearly review of your expenses and match them with the current prices in the market as induced by market forces of demand and supply.

To compose your choice: This is an area of concern, because the power of choice is independent of the amount of money you have. There are poorly paid people, but their menu list will shock you. If they tell you their choices value, you will be dumbfounded. Somebody whose salary, that is, his take-home-pay is about N30,000 (Thirty thousand Naira), is desiring to buy a jeep in the next few years of work. Of course, you know as much as I do that choices have led people into all kinds of things. Choice has been associated with lack of contentment and other vices connected with it. Choice is an important area that can affect our budgets negatively. The power of choice is a major problem that can promote poverty. There are people who have been struggling to have a meal a day, but soon after their salary is increased, their total expenses will increase and everybody around them will notice that something has happened. This evil of demonstration effect is deeply-rooted in our members, in every one of us. It manifests when there is a little positive change in the amount of money in our coffers.

There are people who buy more than they budgeted for merely because the other person has it. On my way to Aba one day, in a public vehicle, I observed one lady who bought something in every traffic jam (hold-up), and I was wondering if she had planned to spend such an amount of money on her way to buy fabrics for sale. The issue that was bogging my mind was whether she would be able to make any profit after all the expenses of purchasing cost, transport cost, time cost, health cost and extra buying cost.

The power of choice must be conquered if you must maintain and manage your budget. Some people buy anything the ware dealers present to them through the window of the vehicle; whatever that flashes their way is for consumption. In Cameroon few years ago, I was traveling from Douala to Bamenda in a luxury bus, and I had on board this lady that bought almost everything that the traders presented to us, to the extent that people who were traveling with me nicknamed her 'minister for buying.' The eye concept of choice that enslaved Adam and Eve is still enslaving men and women today.

How Do I Reduce My Expenses?

There are lots of ways to reduce your expenses because not all expenses are necessary. You must:

Target unnecessary expenses and neglect them from the onset.

Learn how to prepare local snacks e.g. moi-moi, akara, meat pie, chin-chin, fish roll, and the like. If you get into any eating home, you buy a plate of moi-moi at N100.00, and if you are about four in a family, you will need at least N400.00 for everybody to have a bite of it. But if the same family would prepare moi-moi by themselves which can easily be done with N100.00, everybody in that family will eat at least more than one plate of moi-moi. The same thing applies to akara. Learn how to prepare something local. You must not buy all you need from the market.

You can plant vegetables, pepper, and okro. You can manage yourself. You don't need to buy vegetables; you can grow them; you can cultivate maize, egusi, and okro. Each family should have a garden where these things can be produced.

Learn to do some basic household repairs. e.g. mending your children's loosed dresses, using needle to adjust oversized dresses and doing minor domestic maintenance by yourself. For example, repairing your electric iron, touch lights, umbrellas, etc.

Avoid unbudgeted, impulsive or what is called superfluous buying. Most women have this problem. Once they see another woman buying something, they will draw nearer and say, 'this thing is fine,' and from that to 'how much' and then to ' I don't have money now, can I pay at the end of the month? Some women finish spending their salary on credit before the end of the month and often times, they don't need those things.

Locate shops that sell goods at cheaper prices and buy from there.

Avoid buying inferior materials because they are cheap. The reason behind this point is that one quality material will outstay three to four inferior ones. There was a time a friend of mine bought one original shoe at N6,000, and I bought the same type of shoe at N1,500. I was wondering why he spent such amount of money when he could buy the same shoe at N1,500. It was after about two months that the difference became obvious. His shoe lasted for about five years while my own did not survive the same year it was bought.

Pay off your debts fast and don't save when you are still in debt because you will only be deceiving yourself and your finances because what you claim you have is not really yours, but another's.

Don't embark on trips just because you want to have some good time. Let every of your trips be targeted at something.

Learn to take your lunch to your office. It is cheaper and healthier to eat your meal from the source you are sure of instead of eating from public places where you are not sure of their hygiene standard.

Avoid buying seasonal fashions that last only few months and lose value. There are some wrappers women buy that do not last up to a year. It will come out that year and phase out that year. Tell me, how many years did your 'Washable', 'Madam pass Madam', 'One Million George', etc., last before they became obsolete?

Sew your dresses with allowance to your body fitting so that peradventure you add weight, it will still be relevant at least for upward of two years. There are people who make one blouse or skirt today only to drop it next week because they just added weight and cannot wear it again. Avoid waste, for you shall give account to God Almighty.

Avoid middle persons in your buying, try to go to the source and buy directly from them and again, if it is possible, use direct labour to do your work. The western world uses direct labour; even the government uses direct labour.

Study your family make up and if your family is the type that cannot control their desire to eat if the food is at home, then don't buy things in bulk at all or you will end up quarreling with your wife always. There are people who cannot be restricted from eating what they have around even if they are full. Until that available food is finished, they will not rest. Such families should not try to do bulk purchase at all, else they will spend double on feeding.

The women should be in control of their store and the kitchen because some brothers-in-law, sisters-in-law, brothers, and sisters see it as a right to enter a woman's kitchen and eat whatever they want to eat. It should not be so, and if a husband refuses to handle the matter, he is only putting himself and his wife into trouble.

Don't allow advertisements and marketers to detect your choice or control your desires.

Finally, become contented, it is the only virtue that can enable you to cut down your expenses.

Cash Flow Chart

This is another tool to control both your expenses and income. It is when you know your income stream and your expenditure pattern that you can talk of budget. We are going to look at three major cash flow charts of different classes of persons. The rich class, the middle class, and the subsistence cash flow chart.

Chidi's Family (Rich Class)

Cash Flow Statement for the Year Ended 31st December 2005		
INFLOWS	$	%
Salaries	8,400,000	84.6
Interest on savings and deposits	662,000	6.7
Return on investment	860,000	8.7
TOTAL INFLOW	9,922,000	100.0
OUTFLOWS		
Savings and investments	1,000,000	10.1
Loan Payments/Insurance Premium	1,399,800	14.1
Food	1,080,000	10.9
Taxation	924,000	9.3
Education	1006,800	9.3
Medical	340,000	3.4
Transportation	624,000	6.3
NITEL/Electricity	884,000	8.9
Personal Effects	950,000	9.6
Entertainment	1,049,000	10.6
Beneficiaries	376,400	3.7
Miscellaneous	297,000	3.0
TOTAL OUTFLOW	9,922,000	100.0

The Budget As A Regulator

Clement's Family (Middle Class)

Cash Flow Statement For The Year Ended 31st December 2005		
INFLOWS	**$**	**%**
Salaries	2,100,000	84.6
Interest On Savings And Deposits	165,500	6.7
Return On Investment	215,000	8.7
TOTAL INFLOW	**2,480,500**	**100.0**
OUTFLOWS		
Savings And Investments	1250,000	10.1
Loan Payments/Insurance Premium	349,950	14.1
Food	270,000	10.9
Taxation	231,000	9.3
Education	251,700	9.3
Medical	85,000	3.4
Transportation	156,000	6.3
NITEL/Electricity	221,000	8.9
Personal Effects	237,500	9.6
Entertainment	262,250	10.6
Beneficiaries	91,850	3.7
Miscellaneous	74,250	3.0
TOTAL OUTFLOW	**2,480,500**	**100.0**

Igoni's Family (Subsistence Class)

Cash Flow Statement for the Year Ended 31st December 2005		
INFLOWS	**$**	**%**
Salaries	525,000	84.6
Interest on savings and deposits	41,375	6.7
Return on investment	53,750	8.7
TOTAL INFLOW	**620,125**	**100.0**
OUTFLOWS		
Savings and investments	62,500	10.1
Loan Payments/Insurance Premium	87,487.50	14.1
Food	67,500	10.9
Taxation	57,750	9.3
Education	62,925	9.3
Medical	21,250	3.4
Transportation	39,000	6.3
NITEL/Electricity	55,250	8.9
Personal Effects	59,375	9.6
Entertainment	65,265.50	10.6
Beneficiaries	22,962.50	3.7
Miscellaneous	18,562.50	3.0
TOTAL OUTFLOW	**620,125.00**	**100.0**

The Budget As A Regulator

Each time I tell people or congregations wherever I teach on Financial Management that I know the total amount of money I spent in school during my university education from: transport, snacks, clothing, inner wears, school fees, offerings, tithes, vows, handouts, term papers written, project, feeding, toothpastes, soaps, creams, etc., they seem to be surprised but for me, it is an embarrassment to spend without writing it down.

I advise you, learn how to write down each money you spend, no matter how small the amount is. *The smallest fraction of your money spent is a whole part of the entire income. Little by little, you are spending your money without knowing it.* Learn to take control of your finances and your finances will learn to respect you and double in value. Highlight areas of excesses and cut down on them. Make assurance doubly sure that the amount of money set aside for savings and investments are forcefully put into that sector of outflows. Don't compromise it at all. It does not matter; nobody will die except at the leading of the Lord.

It does not matter your level of annual inflows; you can still plan your budget, that is why I did plan for three categories of people, though there is the fourth one, the wealthy class. It may not be necessary here now, but be strict with your budget and maintain it to the letter, and you will observe a significant improvement in your finances and the quality of life you live. God hates waste, and in several places in the Bible, He sounded it to us that we shall be required to give account of everything given to us and this includes: finances, gifts, talents, and wisdom.

Reflection On Chapter 8

Personal Notes:

Guided Action Plan

CHAPTER 9
Personal Financial Management (PFM)

What is Personal Financial Management (PFM)?

Personal Finance Management simply refers to what you want to become, how you want to get there and your tomorrow. (Your physical wellbeing – your visions and dreams).

- It is the process of ensuring that you match your resources with your obligations to achieve your financial objectives for today, without becoming a beggar in future (tomorrow).
- It is a conscious effort aimed at realizing financial security by deliberately and continuously growing your assets' base and watching your expenses.
- It is about a more robust way of looking at your income and expenditure which will make accountability possible both in the now and in future.
- It is to achieve an income stream that is sufficient to take care of your obligations comfortably without further stress.
- It is the process of putting your today's income stream to work, and improve your tomorrow's income stream.

- It is to ensure that we don't indict ourselves in the areas of alteration of our baptismal certificates and birth dates.
- It is to enable you to prepare for retirement and to retire well and healthy.

Why Is PFM A Must Do?

There are lots of reasons why we must practice personal financial management. Discussing these reasons is like discussing the story of creation. Every one of us must realize that the very first day we are employed is the same day our retirement begins. But it is regrettable that many people do not reason along this line. They think or tend to believe that they will remain in office until death. Those who later realize when it is late, resort to forging new birth certificates and other practices to enable them stay on in service because they are not prepared for retirement.

A life story was once told of a clergyman who was born in 1945 but finished his Standard Six Examination in 1931. That is to say; he had completed standard six fourteen (14) years before his birth. I am very sure you know if such a clergyman had done his personal financial management very well, he wouldn't have had any cause for such unchristian act. That only happened because either there was a **negligence of financial management** or **he never considered there would be tomorrow**.

There are such cases everywhere even in the church. We have seen people who have stayed beyond their age of retirement by changing their actual birth dates. Naturally, nobody would want to do this I believe, but when an individual discovers that either he had not planned for retirement or is afraid of what to do afterward, this fear of the unknown can lead even a 'Man of God' to do 'unchurch' things.

The following may be considered as reasons why PFM is a must:

- It will help you to break the siege of financial limitation over your family, both in the present and in the future (tomorrow).

- It will help you to retire comfortably and have peace of mind.

- It will enable you to face sudden occurrences like downsizing, right-sizing, retrenchment, incapacitation, early retirement or even voluntary retirement.

- It will help you to know your financial worth and enable you to refocus your idle assets to areas of high yield.

- Apart from God, it will enable you to have peace of mind and thereby be more productive both to yourself and your immediate environment.

- It will enable you to identify opportunities rather than always see constraints or problems. Challenges or constraints put us off, but they are supposed to stabilize us, if we had planned well in advance. Opportunities abound for those who have planned for their future. They say when you have not planned, that you have successfully planned to fail. Many people today are failures by choice. Again, self-chosen failure is the worst of the regrets of life. When a man refuses to plan for his future from the beginning, he has indirectly chosen to impose on himself self-chosen failure and he is in for a life of regrets without end.

- It will enable you to cope with personal life threats and weakness. These personal life threats and weaknesses come through various avenues. For instance, you can be relocated to a less buoyant territory, or church, or a less viable environment without a reduction in your personal expenditure. You can be asked to withdraw from active service either due to sickness, unproductivity or physical challenge. We have seen the adverse effects on people who were not ready as at when they were asked to withdraw from active service. The list is endless. But if a person had prepared for these things ahead of time, he will be glad to retire without much hazards.

- It will help you to maximize your financial strength and opportunities; to know where to channel your resources for gainfulness, thereby reducing your level of casualty. We have seen people who died two months after retirement and research has proved that, it is usually due to lack of preparation and personal financial management while they were in active service.

- It will enable you to have something to bequeath to your children and family. Proverbs 13:22 says, "A good man leaves an inheritance for his children's children, but a sinner's wealth is stored up for the righteous." Job confirmed this verse when he stated therefore about a weak man, "though he heaps up silver like dust and clothes like piles of clay, what he lays up, the righteous will wear, and the innocent will divide his silver"

(Job 27:16-17). So, when you save for your children and family, you are indirectly obeying the scriptures and proving to your offspring that you are a good man.

- It will help you to be consistently relevant both in your community and the society at large. You are aware that our society abhors poverty naturally and as such poverty makes one irrelevant, not only in the community and society but also in one's very family. Paul stated unequivocally that he who cannot provide for his family is worse than an infidel (I Timothy 5:8). Just imagine it that after working throughout your life and at retirement, you cannot happily go into your own house for rest or provide your immediate needs. Then you are not only a failure to yourself and family but also a disgrace to the society. This is the major reason why most children from Anglican Priests' families hardly believe in their parents' church. Most Anglican Priests retire into uncompleted buildings, and some are laid in state under canopies during their burials because they could not build their own houses. All these are results of lack of personal financial management.

- It will prepare you for an emotional and psychologically balanced life before retirement. Some retirees still parade and wear the garbage of power and authority, without a conscious effort of awareness that authority or influence has changed hands. They still see their successor as their subordinate, hence always quarrelling and complaining of neglect, interference, dissatisfaction, disaffection, hatred, and gossip.

But with personal financial management (PFM), a retiree will know that he has left office, and that will help him to scale his carriage and spare himself or herself the sorrow of agitation, complaining and disaffection.

- It will help you to eliminate debt. The worst thing that can happen to any retiree is to carry a heavy debt burden to the retirement bench. Carrying debt into retirement is a sure way to ruin the retirement. But with personal financial management (PFM), one just needs to work hard to eliminate or payoff all the loans and indebtedness before the actual retirement. More so, you know that income drastically reduces or falls in retirement, hence carrying huge debts will certainly set you up for untold stress.

- It will help you to plan how to manage your retirement and keep you busy during your retirement. It will programme you into profitable and eventful activities and consultancy that can keep you relevant during this period.

Why Do People Overlook Personal Finance?

We will try to consider the major reasons people overlook PFM. If this is an essential aspect of our lives, why do we gloss over it as if it will not come one day? The major reasons include but are not limited to the following:

Lack of adequate knowledge of the implication of not planning for it: If we do not appreciate the full implication of not planning for our lives beyond active service, then we may not be able to prepare for our lives beyond it.

Ignorance of the whole exercise: Many people are ignorant of the workings of the forces of the market and at the same time would not want to ask for help. Especially when one believes he has reached a level in life where he does not need to ask questions over issues he does not understand. Of course, there are many people like that, and we have seen many of such, who are dying in ignorance and would indeed prefer to die in absolute ignorance than ask questions that will betray their self- acclaimed status. Of course, everyone is ignorant in some way, but it is the man who understands this and seeks to correct it, that is a wise man. Even the most ordinary person learns when made aware of his ignorance. Therefore, this book is very important to help you make some corrections in your finances now, so as to help you beyond your active service period. Some who are ready to plan for their future don't even know what to do and where to begin. Remedies are offered here.

Little earnings: Some persons feel that their income or earnings are so small to plan with. There is a saying that "if you cannot plan with one Kobo you cannot plan with one billion", and I believe this saying. Those who do not know how to manage their pennies and Kobos, may not be able to manage their millions because it is the same process. To begin with that low earning, don't despise the little beginning. It is said that little drops of water make the mighty ocean. Those little pennies and Kobos can be turned into a seed instead of food. Little sacrifices today can result in mighty harvests tomorrow. Wisely spend that little coin in your control today, and it will surprise you what the Lord will use it to do or achieve in your life.

Reducing one's spending freedom: Some people believe that this is an indirect way to control their spending habit. Well, if it works that way which is the primary focus, it is all to your advantage. It is still ignorance that makes people think that when you ask them to plan or manage their finances while in active service, that you are controlling their spending habits.

Again, they do not foresee any eventuality, so they expect that things would naturally work out as they used to: It is a poor or untrained brain that thinks in a straight line. Every exposed and right-thinking man with high thinking capacity will always remember that things may not work out the same way all the time. In a Diocese, a certain clergyman collapsed after the Bishop posted him to a new location. This is because he never planned for the posting. He expected that the goodies will continue to flow in as usual and never made plans for any eventuality until the obvious happened that day. When you are in a buoyant church, please do remember that you will not be there for life. One day you will be asked to leave for another person, and that change of location may take you to an unimaginable place where the goodies will not be as sufficient as before. What you ought to do in those areas of abundance is to plan, like Joseph helped Pharaoh to plan for the periods of abundance to cushion the periods of famine. Think and behave wisely before you regret.

They believe another 'manna' will come when the need arises;

The misinterpretation of the Lord's prayer, "Give us this day, our daily bread" (Mathew 6:11): Many persons suppose that we should not labour or work for tomorrow because it is not necessary since we are asking God to give us our daily bread. But when we pray, "Give us this day, our daily bread", we are asking God to supply our financial needs. We are for not only food but also shelter and clothing. We are asking for emotional strength, and clarity of mind, to give us friends and fellowship, to grant us transportation as needed, to equip us for our jobs, careers, and future. To help us get done what we need to get done this very day and to be at our best. To help you in your preparations; for divine providence to further God's plans for our lives. Our daily bread then covers everything that is essential for our wellbeing in life.

Getting Started, How?

Everything in life gets to start somehow. There is nothing too challenging to start. All it requires is to agree to dare the risks and consequences if any. To get started, the following steps may be of help here:

- Articulate all the information about what stimulates you and what you can do very well.
- Take a critical study of your total assets and liabilities.
- Learn the discipline of recording all your expenses in a book or log book daily and place your eyes on your expenses especially the unnecessary ones.

- Curtail your expenditure on the unplanned expenses. Usually, this is hard, but if neglected, it becomes the destroyer of personal financial management.
- Initiate and commence a daily saving plan strategy and plan your financial goals.
- Take a strategic look at your current financial situation and plan to improve on it daily.
- Reactivate and reintroduce your idle assets into the mainstream of eventful investments.
- Cultivate the habit of examining your expenses and income periodically, reduce your unnecessary intakes and demand and look out for wise investments.

Tips On Factors That Hinder Commencement

The following are the character traits of those who would not want to start for various reasons:

- They would not organize their financial affairs.
- They lack the capacity to monitor their money and its whereabouts.
- They do not grow their money by regular savings.
- They think they can do better financially if they had more opportunities.
- They think they can earn more money if they know more people.
- They say, "a few years to retirement, I will start planning."

- They usually say, "you cannot save when you are in dire need."
- They say, "if we earn more, we will begin to save."
- They say "things are so tight now and there are no economic opportunities for me to make it."
- They say, "it is not godly to be very rich, so let me manage what I have."
- They say, "it is not yet God's time for me to begin to make it."
- They say, "all fingers are not equal, after all, the Bible says the poor will always be in your midst."
- They say, "after all; the rich man went to hell while the poor man Lazarus went to heaven."

Take Counsel From Today

- Watch your pennies.
- Develop the savings culture.
- Pay yourself first from every money that comes into your hands and struggle to save a minimum of 10%-20%
- Do not clutter your life with a lot of needless possessions.
- Learn to suffice to buy only the things you need, not the things you desire. The needful is obviously better than the desired.
- Decide to obtain a financial independence strategy and remain focused.
- Climb the tree of financial breakthrough through reduced expenses. More still, discard unnecessary expenses and

refuse to come down.

- Be disciplined with your needs and make them choice needs.
- The wealthiest people on the planet earth today are savers, not spenders.
- The rich is rich because the poor has decided continuously to make them rich. The wealth of the rich always comes from the very poor.

Remember, **without the poor; there will be no rich man on earth because the poor patronize the rich. The rich do not patronize the rich.**

Net Worth Is Assets Minus Liabilities:

If your assets are more than your liabilities, it means that you have a positive net worth, but if your liabilities are more than your assets, it means you have a negative net worth.

What Are My Assets And Liabilities?

Assets are things you own, and they may be in form of the following:

- Cash
- Houses
- Cars
- Investment
- Certificates (education)
- Type One: - Liquid Assets

- Liquid assets are assets you can easily convert into cash and they include:
- Credit account balance in banks
- Travelers cheques
- Treasury bills
- Type Two: Investment Assets
- Deposit Account Certificate
- Bonds
- Real Estate
- Retirement benefits
- Type Three: Personal Assets
- Cars
- Houses
- Personal effects
- Arts and crafts
- Certificates

Liabilities are what you owe to third parties, and they include the following:

- Personal loans
- Mortgage loans
- Accrued rent
- Accrued insurance premium

- Accrued Telecommunication and PHCN Bills
- Type One: Current Liabilities
- Those payable within 1 year
- Installment loans
- Accrued PHCN bills
- Accrued NITEL bills
- Type two: Long-Term Liabilities
- Those payable within 1-5 years
- Long-term loans
- Mortgage loans
- Long term lease
- Balancing your assets and liabilities in a balance sheet form will help you to:
- Highlight and analyze your assets
- Identify your idle assets
- Highlight and analyze your liabilities
- Know your financial condition
- Improve on your financial condition and lifestyle
- Act as a reminder and a check
- Set financial goals

How You Can Increase Your Assets Over Liabilities

(Net Worth)

- Curtail your expenses
- Increase your savings rate
- Make your dominant assets work for you
- Invest wisely and in investible ventures.
- Diversify your investment portfolio
- Exercise your skill and learn new skills
- Take rational financial decisions
- Avoid fashionable things that have short lifespan
- Avoid buying inferior goods because they are cheap. (The bitterness of low-quality drugs remains long after the sweetness of low price is forgotten).

Budget As A Regulator

"Control" is the name of the game. It is one thing we must learn to do. James 3^{3-4} is a typical example of the rudder and the ship.

> *"We put bits in the mouths of horses to make them obey us, and we have control over everything they do. The same thing is true for ships. They are very big and are driven by strong winds. Yet, by using small rudders, pilots steer ships wherever they want them to go" (James 3^{3-4}, GWT).*

Setting up a budget, therefore, entails four (4) simple steps:

- Ascertain your income
- Establish your expenditure limit for each expense
- Stick to your budget by controlling your expenses
- Compose your choices

How Do I Reduce My Expenses?

This is the most challenging area for most people, and if it is controlled, the man will be rich. Necessary steps to take include the following:

- Target unnecessary expenses and neglect them from the onset,
- Learn how to prepare local snacks, e.g., moi-moi, akara, meat-pie, chin chin, fish roll, etc.,
- You can plant vegetables, pepper, and okro, etc.,
- Learn to do some basic household repairs,
- Always avoid unbudgeted and impulsive buying or what is called superfluous buying,
- Locate shops that sells at cheap prices and buy from there,
- Pay off your debts fast and don't save when you are still in debt,
- Don't embark on trips simply because you want to have some good time. Let every of your trips be targeted at something,
- Sew your dresses with allowance to your body fitting, so that peradventure you add weight, they will still be relevant for at least upward of two years,
- Avoid the middleman in your purchases. Always try to buy

directly from the source, and if it is possible, use direct labour for your projects,

- Study your family make-up and if your family is the type that cannot control their desire to eat if the food is at home, then do not buy in bulk at all, or you will end up quarrelling with your wife always,

- Women should be in control of their store and kitchen always,

- Don't allow advertisements to detect your choice or control your desires,

- Become contented; it is the only virtue that can enable you to cut down your expenses.

To Avoid Eventualities, You Must Do The Following:

- Have a vision of the kind of tomorrow you want to enjoy,

- Set your goals: Goals are the vehicles that propel us to new achievements and without well-articulated goals, our life's objectives cannot be achieved.

To Achieve Your Goal, You Must:

- Dream and visualize success
- Be positive about it
- Be focused about it
- Be committed about it
- Review it periodically to check whether you are still in line.

Your goals must be SMART

- S – Specific
- M – Measurable
- A – Achievable
- R – Realistic
- T – Time Bound

Why Must I Have Financial Objectives?

- Protection against personal life's threats
- Premature death
- Disability
- Medical expenses
- Property and liability loses
- Unemployment
- Capital accumulation for:
- Emergencies
- Family
- General investment
- Provision for retirement income
- Planning for one's heir or estate planning
- Property investment and management

Be Deliberate About Saving

Saving is vital to the practice of investment; you cannot become an investor without first and foremost being a saver. This, therefore, confirms that saving is the key to achieving financial independence.

There is a saying, that ***"saving is the first step leading to the temple of wealth and no man may climb who cannot plant his feet on the first step." Another saying goes thus, "I found the road to wealth when I decided that a part of all I earned was mine to keep."***

Saving is the excess of inflows over outflows. If you don't have a saving, you cannot invest, and if you don't invest you don't have a future at all.

The key is to keep your expenses in check and ensure they do not exceed your income:

Identify Your Money Personality. Who Are You:

- Impulsive
- Cautious
- Competitive
- A show-off
- Miserly with money

Identify Your Spending Weakness. Is It?

- Shoes
- Dresses
- Jewelry
- Confectionery
- Dinning out
- Electronics
- Cars
- Cell Phone

Sustainable wealth, like a tree, grows from a tiny seed. The first Naira you save is the seed from which your tree of wealth will grow. The sooner you plant that seed, the sooner the tree will begin to grow. The more faithfully you nourish and water that tree with consistent savings, the sooner you will bask in contentment beneath its shades.

You Must Learn To Invest

What you can set aside as saving is for investment. This differs from one individual to another, and depends a great deal on the following:

- Individual attitude towards future demands
- Individual needs about one's future expectation
- Individual circumstances about where one finds oneself

- Individual discipline about taste and choice
- Individual pattern of life about one's interest areas.

Where And How Do I Invest?

This has been a recurring question each time I handle a seminar on Financial Management and Empowerment. The truth is that there are few areas of investment available to us, or at least few areas we can handle. But there are various areas of investment open to us as well. Some may require vast amounts of money to embark upon by an individual, while others may need enormous capital involvement. Therefore, support from the government and other corporate organizations is necessary.

Areas Of Investment Include:

- Collectibles
- Commodities Trading
- Real Estate

Some of these areas are capital intensive, but we can comfortably invest in capital market and money market.

Capital Market

This is the place where long-term funds are sourced through Equities and Debt instruments. These are subsequently traded openly on a Stock Exchange. There is a primary market, which is the market for New Issues and a secondary market for trading in Existing shares.

Market Players

Regulators: Securities and Exchange Commission (SEC) and The Nigerian Stock Exchange (NSE),

Operators: Stockbrokers who are the most useful market operators to the investor as it is only through them that the investor can buy and sell shares on the Stock Exchange.

Available Instruments

Bonds: These are debt instruments issued by Government and its agencies that carry a fixed rate of interest and are repayable over a definite period.

Industrial Loans/Debentures: Are long-term debt instruments issued by corporate bodies. Like bonds, they also carry fixed rates of interest and are repayable over a definite period.

Unit Trusts: Unit Trust is a professionally managed investment company whose business is to use investors' money to purchase a diversified portfolio or other securities. Annually, the net income of the company is fully distributed to unitholders.

Common Stocks (or shares): This is referred to as Equities. There are over 200 companies quoted on the Nigerian Stock Exchange under Equities.

Benefits Of Investing In Stock

- Dividend Income
- Bonuses

- Capital gains/growth
- Ownership rights, e.g. attendance at AGM
- Borrowing capacity
- Perpetuity
- Board membership

Note These

- Don't buy stocks for buying sake
- Buy reputable shares from reputable companies and industries
- Know when to buy
- Learn to diversify your investment
- Buy stocks in companies with strong dividend payment record
- Buy low and sell high.

Other Areas Of Investment

Fixed deposit (Certificates of Deposit (CDs). They carry a fixed rate of return (interest) and have tenors of 30 days, 60 days, 90 days, 180 days and 1 year.

Nigeria Treasury Bills (NTBs)

These are 90-day tenor Federal Government backed fixed income securities. They are discountable and carry zero risk. Other valuable features of NTBs are:

- Interest income is payable upfront
- Interest can be re-invested
- They are easy to purchase and require no cumbersome documentation.
- Initial outlay of #10,000.00 is low compared to most money market investments
- There are no hidden costs when purchased through a stockbroker.

CBN Certificates: These are 180-day, and 360-day tenor Federal Government-backed fixed income securities. The minimum subscription is #250,000.00 and multiples of #50,000.00 thereafter. They also have the same features as NTBs.

Land Property: You can become a Land Speculator, buying cheap and selling costly.

Conclusion

Make your life an ongoing process of positive visualization, continually imagining and visioneering your ideal goals and your perfect future. This can do more to help you to step on the accelerator of your own potentials than any other exercise you engage in.

Reflection On Chapter 9

Personal Notes:

Guided Action Plan

Continuation

Personal Notes:

Guided Action Plan

CHAPTER 10

God Hates Waste

"Waste is the easiest way to poverty."

Waste of any kind is rejected by God in its entire ramifications. Families should be able to know the quantity of food they can finish at each meal time, whether it is breakfast, lunch or dinner. A well-organized family should be able to know the quantity of food the family should take each time. The idea of preparing meals that are far more than the quantity consumed is unacceptable by God. Go to our dustbins, you will see leftovers. That is the first sign of a careless family and wasteful home. Reading the following scriptures will reveal to us the level of hatred God has for wasteful living and extravagant manner. It is an attitude that when not checked, grows rapidly and leads to laziness. In *Romans 14^{12}*: **"So then, each of us will give an account of himself to God."**

Paul, while writing to the Roman congregation, did tell them that they will give account of how they lived their lives. Paul was very serious about the account giving, and if we will give account of ourselves to God, it then means that everything in our custody would be accounted for.

Hebrews 4[13] says,

> *"Nothing in all creation is hidden from God's sight. Everything is uncovered and laid bare before the eyes of Him to whom we must give account."*

Our actions and attitudes are not hidden from Him, the Bible says; "all creation" including you and your family, are not hidden from God's sight and the most startling of the whole thing is that "everything" including unnecessary expenditure, unaccounted expenses, unbudgeted expenses, are uncovered and laid bare before the eyes of him to whom we 'must give account'. God is not a God of waste, and bear in mind that you are going to give an account of everything entrusted into your care, especially the finances and their usage. You are a channel of distribution.

Luke 16[2] says,

> *"So he called him in and asked him, what is this I hear about you? Give an account of your management, because you cannot be manager any longer."*

Management is the language of the Bible and the vocabulary of God himself, not management science. The Parable of the Shrewd Manager is quite apt to our discussion. The parable discusses a certain rich man whose manager was not giving account of himself with regards to the management of his business. It describes a steward who handled all the business affairs of his boss in such a way that he squandered his masters' possessions. The rich man here is like any of us. You can imagine how painful it was for him to see his enterprise ground through wrong management. The shrewd manager was called to give account of the business under his care. He was shrewd enough to use the means at his disposal to plan for his future well-being but not that of the business, and he was called to give account of the finances given to him to run the business. One day, we will also be called to give account of the finances given or entrusted to us on behalf of God, either by God or BY nature. We must give account.

In Matthew 18$^{10\text{-}14}$, we read the story of the Lost Sheep. In the story, the sheep owner of one hundred sheep lost one of them. We read of how he abandoned the ninety-nine that were safe and went to look for the only one that strayed. Naturally, it is not normal to forget ninety-nine and go after only one. Many people have left their one "stray" business or finance, just because they have enough to cover the absence of the one that got missing. But God in the scripture was simply telling us to be meticulous in the way we handle things and our businesses.

A woman walked into my office only to celebrate how her bad debt was paid back to her. She was amazed that the money could be paid back to her after she had lost hope. Don't count it lost, look for it, you will get it. Giving up on your resources even if it is a bad debt will not improve your finances. Go all out to recover your money. When you do, chances are that you can recover it, or else you lose it for life. Go, you will recover them.

Who would think that this man in the scripture above would find his lost sheep?

> *"What do you think? If a man owns a hundred sheep and one of them wandered away, will he not leave the ninety-nine on the hill and go to look for the one that wandered off?"*

How did he know that one was missing out of the hundred if not that he was conscious of accounting for his sheep daily to make sure they were always complete. How are you accounting for your business, budget, and finances?

In Matthew 25^{14-30}; Jesus gave another parable of Account Giving. The parable of the talents is a parable of accounting. Every business is expected by this parable to yield interest and profit. If your business is not yielding projected returns, the first approach to tackling to challenge is to reexamine the business and understand why it is underperforming. Then come up with new strategies or change to another business. In the scripture, Jesus told us the parable of the talents; how a man who was going on a journey called his three servants and gave them talents for business. The Bible says, he gave the first servant five talents, to the second, he gave two talents, while the third received one talent, according to their abilities. When he came back, he demanded for an account from the businesses of the talents given:

> *"After a long time, the master of those servants returned and settled account with them."*

The first man whom he gave five talents brought five additional talents as profit; the master was happy with him and rewarded him with a corresponding position. The second whom he gave two talents, came with two extra talents as profit from his efforts, and the master welcomed and rewarded him with a benefiting position. The third servant came with the same talent given to him and said:

> *"I knew that you are a hard man, harvesting where you have not sown and gathering where you have not scattered seed. So I was afraid and went out and hid your talent in the ground, see here is what belongs to you."*

How many reasons will you give for your poverty? The servant said: "I was afraid and I went out and hid your talent in the ground." What are you afraid of that has stopped you from prospering? The master replied to the third servant:

> *"You wicked, lazy servant! So you knew that I harvest where I have not sown and gather where I have not scattered seed? Well then, you should have put my money on deposit with the bankers, so that when I returned, I would have received it back with interest."*

From this scripture we saw that, God abhors waste and encourages investment. Any money not invested is wasting away. It is interesting to note that, investment, hard work, and interest yielding savings were preached and taught as a principle of the Kingdom. In the same scripture we saw the dire consequence of idle cash or funds that were not invested. The people with idle cash are called wicked and lazy servants. Again, laziness is associated here with lack of profit and poverty. Remember, we shall all give account of our talents, money, finances, and wealth to him who sees all things and to him that all things are made manifest before.

In Matthew 14$^{13\text{-}21}$, the Bible gives an account of the feeding of five thousand men, besides children and women. This story happened in a remote area of Israel, and these men were with him in that remote place. After he had blessed the five loaves of bread and two fish, he gave them to eat, and they all ate and were satisfied, and the Lord told his disciples to gather the broken pieces which came to twelve baskets-full of fragments of bread. The number they fed were about five thousand men, besides the women and children. The most important message here is the attitude of not allowing the broken pieces of bread to waste. How many baskets of broken pieces of bread have you neglected? Remember that the master did not leave them but picked them up.

Reflection On Chapter 10

Personal Notes: _____

___

Guided Action Plan

Continuation

Personal Notes:

=== Guided Action Plan ===

CHAPTER 11

Types Of Business Organisations

"Whosoever builds with you determines your levels of success; your initial partners determine the lifespan of the organization."

When considering the type of business to establish, I strongly advise you to take note of the following factors. These are practical issues that could either make or mar your business goals:

- Identification of business opportunity
- Environmental psychology of the inhabitants
- Preparing of project
- Selection of business opportunity
- The taste of the dwellers of the community
- Proximity of the viability which includes technical, operational, financial, marketing of the project.
- Deciding the location for production, office outlet and resourcing
- Deciding the size of the project

- Deciding the sources of finance and financing apparatus
- Deciding the availability and accessibility of the market
- Deciding the vision, mission statement and goals of the project is critical to the success of the business
- Deciding the plan, programme, policy, culture, strategy, and norms of the project
- Deciding whether the short term, midterm or long-term perspective will be accepted for the project.

The following six steps will make a good and fine start:

Going Beyond The Business Plan: Careful planning of business before launching it is not restricted to preparing a business plan. It could extend to the following:

The Apprentice Model: This model gives you the opportunity to learn from direct work experience in the industry.

The Fired-Gun Approach: Partnering or sharing with experts who are more knowledgeable and have more experience.

The Ultra-Lean School Of Hard Knocks Tactic: Finding how to frequently test and refine the model at a reasonable cost.

While we approve these suggestions, documenting your business plan is super helpful. The real value is not in having the finished goods in hand, but instead, in the process of researching and thinking in a systematic manner. It assists in thinking things through in depth, to study and research if the facts provided are entirely accurate. Starting a new business or project without a proper understanding and preparation can be a costly set back in the value of planning.

Testing Your Proposed Idea: Researchers has proved that about sixty (60%) percent of new businesses fail within the first six months or one year. This is because of people going into business ventures without first carefully checking out their ideas or intentions and all other aspects to establish their workability.

Knowing The Market: You don't jump into the market to start just because you have money. Instead, you need to study someone who is already a master in the business. I have seen people or organizations get involved in businesses they know nothing about, but simply engage people who have complete knowledge in that area. That is okay but by no means sufficient. Few years ago, I got a bus and engaged a driver without knowing anything about transportation. In fact, that was the greatest mistake of my life. You cannot believe it that each day, the bus either developed a fault or the police impounded it. After several struggles to keep the bus running, I succeeded in spending other investment capital to maintain a business that was not yielding any income. Finally, I decided to sell it off and guess who bought the bus, the same driver. Thereafter, that was the end of frequent repair and police challenge. Few months after he bought the bus from me that was the end of pains of ignorance venturing into a market I do not have cognitive experience. To know your market, question others who are there already, conduct research into the area of chosen business, gain experience by possibly assisting others to learn the details of the market, engage with the leading suppliers, distributors, competitors, and customers.

Understanding Your Potential Customers: Every success or failure of any business is determined by the customers and by the free market manipulators or forces of demand and supply. In most business plans, a critical part of it is entirely neglected, and that is a description of potential customers and how they make purchasing decisions. This usually receives much less attention than operational details such as financing, sourcing, and technology, when in actual sense, customers determine the success or failure of the business. It is crucial to understand the customers' demands and the nature too, what affects their purchase decisions, what can be done to differentiate the offering from that of competitors and how to convince them that the value offer is genuine. In launching a business, acknowledging and understanding and indeed appreciating the needs of the future or potential customers cannot be overemphasized.

It is the potential customers that will really keep you in business. This is where the Church is missing it a great deal. The Church does not buy into the potential customers (worshippers) instead she focuses more on the one who can sustain her now. This also may be the singular reason why the youth who are both present customers (worshippers) and future customers are deserting the Church for fun. In Africa, the issue of desertion of the Church is not critical now it is very critical in the western world.

Establishing Your Cash Resources: You must necessarily put measures and steps in place to frequently capitalize the business and secure ready sources of capital for continuous growth. Some startups rely to a great deal on owners' capital while others look for interested investors. To determine the total amount of cash (liquid and hard) required, develop a cash flow statement that evaluates complete expenses and income of the company. Accurate stages of expenses are marked by researching costs of actual business. Minimizing long-term commitments, like long-term leases, help in limiting the need of cash unless it is important. A noticeable amount of ambiguity can be seen within the initial years, to avoid this, one needs to be conservative in making commitments for utilizing resources that might not be required yet.

Selecting the Right Business Structure: Starting from the initial steps, it is essential to identify the appropriate corporate layout required for the business. This should include tax and legal implementation implication. The chosen layout assures the success of decisions to be made in future, like raising capital or exiting from business. The layout could be the following – liability limitations, startup losses, double taxation and capital raising plans.

There are three major forms of organizations and they are:

- Private enterprises
- Public enterprises
- Cooperatives

You are entitled to venture into any of these kinds of business organizations if you meet the requirements. It is not meant for any particular group of people, but for human beings, of which you are one. People who get into them are not supernatural human beings; they are like you and were given birth to just as you were. You can aspire to own a company of your choice. One young student came to my office to ask for alms; then I asked him what he does for a living, he said nothing. I immediately asked him if he could do anything, he answered in the affirmative. I gave money to him to go and buy a handset and table which he religiously carried out, today he has over three phone booths and has more than seven individuals working for him. You can start somewhere. Don't despise yourself for too long, start something and learn to start there. This chapter provides information on the types of businesses you can get involved in today, without struggle.

Private Enterprises

Private enterprises are those businesses which are run by individuals or group of individuals for private profit. Anybody can start it. It does not require much experience or education. There are three ways private enterprises can be organized:

- Through sole proprietorship
- Through partnership
- Through joint stock companies

Sole proprietorship is the business of one man, partnership may be a general or limited one, and a company may be private or joint stock.

Sole Proprietorship

This is the business of one person. He alone bears the responsibility of running the enterprise, and he also takes the profit made by the business alone. His success is dependent on the level of sacrifice he is ready to make. Why many businesses are not striving is lack of commitment to the call of responsibilities on the side of the sole proprietor. Many sole proprietors have handed over their businesses to other people to manage for them and because they do not have the vision and do not carry the level of burden you have for the business, they cannot effectively represent the business, the vision, the burden, and the expectation (which is the profit) for the formation of the business.

I have a younger one who is in business; he just started and in the same year hired two young girls as his staff and I told him that he was about to crash, that the business was too young to be handed over to somebody who did not have the heartbeat. He became the 'oga' of two staff and meanwhile each day, they were unable to recover their feeding allowance from the profit of the day. He later asked one to leave, while the other continued. A time came when he started asking for money to eat. Listen, don't hand over your future to somebody to manage for you, especially when you are not sure of the ability of the individual.

Even if you know the person's ability, in private enterprise, your success is a personal struggle. You don't need to overlook it for something else. Every other thing should be secondary. It does not matter the number of staff you hire; you must be on ground for it to work and produce result and profit.

Remember if you call it your business, it will respond as your business, but if you have no respect for it, it will disrespect you as well. Whatever a man sows, that he shall reap as well.

Sole proprietorship does not need to be registered except the business name is different from your real name. For instance, if your name is 'Abundance' and your business name is 'Abundance', you don't need to register it. Anybody can start this type of business, it does not require too much protocol but what it requires is conviction, commitment, and dedication. It is easy to organize, and actions and decisions can be without bureaucracy, it is free from any governmental control and is supposed to be free from any form of taxation but for the introduction by the Local Government Council. Sole proprietorship adequately planned, can be inherited by your children.

Partnership

Partnership is an association of two or more persons carrying out a business interest with a common understanding and a view to making profit. Every partner is to act in utmost good faith, and there is usually an agreement that backs up partners in partnership. But, the scripture warns us in several places about who we enter into partnership with. The partner's foundation and disposition are of great importance to the success or failure of the business. Partnership is like marriage. Any partnership you enter is regarded as a marital relationship, and the bond between partners in business is compared to the bond of marriage. See, choosing a partner calls for wisdom and deliberate decision. You don't choose partners because they are well connected, or have the required money or because they have good will. You choose partners because they have the same belief and value system with you. They are honest and dogged as you are and have the same burden and vision with you.

I have seen many people who entered into business partnership with people of different religious backgrounds and belief systems, whom they have nothing in common with. The formation of your team determines whether you will win or lose. Saul's battle team against the Philistines was made up of rejected men, and as such, they could not look at the face of Goliath. For almost forty days, there was no man from the battle team of Saul to challenge Goliath.

Reading 1 Samuel $16^{6-10}; 17^{13-15}$, you will observe a drama and the consequences of partnering with a man, and a group of people God has rejected. In 1 Samuel 16:6-10, God rejected the first seven children of Jesse. These men: Eliab, Abinadab, and Shammah were the three oldest children of Jesse whom God rejected. The same men formed the battle team of Saul; 1 Samuel 17^{13-15}, Jesse's three oldest sons had followed Saul to the war: Eliab was the firstborn, the second Abinadab and the third, Shammah. David was the youngest. Jesse's three eldest sons followed Saul; so what do you expect from such a team if not failure and defeat throughout? Of course, they were all defeated for forty days in the camp until God sent the accepted man, a man anointed and chosen by Him. It was David's presence that brought the victory over the Philistines to the people of Israel. If you partner with rejected men, be well assured that there will be no success your way, it does not matter who you are and how much you have, give it time, and you will see the manifestation.

Abraham, then Abram in Genesis 12:1-3, was asked to do three things so as to separate himself and his entire generation for eternal blessing. The Lord said to him;

- Leave your country
- Leave your people
- Leave your father's household

But in verse 4-5, the Bible did record that Abram had left as the Lord had told him, but Lot went with him. Abram was seventy-five years old when he set out from Haran. He took his wife Sarai, his nephew Lot, all the possessions they had accumulated and the people they had acquired in Haran, and they set out for the land of Canaan and arrived there.

Remember, the mandate for Abram was to leave these people and possessions that he travelled with. Little wonder, soon after they arrived, famine surfaced in the land which drove Abram and his people to Egypt to live there for a while because the famine was severe (v.10). As long as Lot dwelt with Abram, God cut off every source of supply to Abram. The blessing of the Lord ceased, Abram was unnecessarily struggling to survive, though progressing but not happy, though prospering but not by the covenant principle and pattern. This kind of prosperity leads to quarrel. Later on, there was a misunderstanding between Abram and Lot which led to their separation which is the original plan of God.

Genesis 13:8:

> *"So Abram said to Lot, let's not have any quarreling between you and me, or between your herdsmen and mine, for we are brothers."*

Abram tried to manage this misunderstanding without knowing it was from the Lord. Several times, we have been attempting to manage misunderstandings while God was planning to set us free from the Lots hindering our blessings. Lots do hinder blessings, and until they depart from us, our blessings remain hindered. As long as Abram dwelled with Lot, it was problem throughout.

In verses 14-17, we read:

> *"The Lord said to Abram after Lot had departed from him: "Lift your eyes from where you are and look north and south, east and west, all the land that you see I will give to you and your offspring forever... I will make your offspring like the dust of the earth, so that if anyone could count the dust, then your offspring could*

be counted. Go, walk through the length and breadth of the land, for I am giving it to you."

All through the period, Abraham was with Lot; he did not hear anything from God: no directions, no communication, and no blessings until immediately Lot departed from him. You can see why your blessings are hanging; why the Lord has not said anything for some time now; why there is no communication and direction from the Lord. Lot's presence was an abomination, and God detested it. I want you to look around your business, family, and marriage. How many Lots are around you on sympathy ground? God is not an emotional God, but He has a sense of humour.

In your business partnership, make sure you don't partner with Lot; for as long as you allow Lot to be in partnership with you, the survival of that business is in doubt. Inasmuch as you are encouraged to have business partners, Paul while writing to the Corinthian church stated this in 2 Corinthians $6^{14\text{-}16}$,

> *"Do not be yoked together with unbelievers. For what do righteousness and wickedness have in common? Or what fellowship can light have with darkness? What harmony is there between Christ and Belial? What does a believer have in common with an unbeliever? What agreement is there between the temple of God and idols? For we are the temple of the living God. As God has said: "I will live with them and walk among them, and I will be their God, and they will be my people."*

Therein, he asked several questions on relationship, partnership, and union. The questions are as follows:

- What does righteousness and wickedness have in common?
- What harmony is there between Christ and Belial?
- What does a believer have in common with an unbeliever?
- What agreement is there between the temple of God and that of Idols?

These are the questions Paul posed to the church at Corinth. Today, brethren have neglected these questions of Paul to the church in the areas of partnership in business. He was very emphatic about these questions, and I want to ask you, who is your partner in business? Where did he get his money from? Is he a light or darkness, righteous or wicked, Christ or Belial, a believer or an unbeliever, of the temple of the living God or temple of idol?

In your business formation, these are the qualities you must look out for. They determine the livewire of the business. There are lots of scriptures warning us to desist from unholy partnerships. It does not matter the number of reasons you have; your reasons do not empower you to have an unbeliever as a partner. People who risked it have ended with 'had I known.'

Partnership has a lot of advantages, ranging from greater financial resources, diversified managerial talents, and freedom from government control to personal commitments.

Joint Stock Company

It is a form of company or joint venture involving two or more individuals that own shares of stock in the business. Certificates of ownership (shares) are issued by the corporation in return for each financial contribution, and the shareholders are free to relocate their ownership interest at any time by selling their shares to others. It is always associated with incorporation (i.e. possession of authorized personality separate from shareholders) and limited liability (meaning that the shareholders are only liable for the company's debts to the value of the money they invested in the company). Joint stock company is generally known as corporate or limited companies.

Types of Joint Stock Company

- Chartered company
- Statutory company

Registered corporation companies that are formed under prevailing laws of the company are called registered company. It is also a corporation that has filed a registration statement with the SEC prior to releasing a new stock issue.

There are two types of this corporation:

- Unlimited company (the liabilities of the shareholders of this company are unlimited)
- Limited company or limited corporation (the liabilities of the shareholder are limited).

The Limited Corporation is of two types, namely: By **Guarantee** and **Share value**. The company limited by share can be **Private Limited Company** (where the number of shareholders ranges from two to fifty. The shares of these companies cannot be traded in the stock market) and **Public Limited Company** (where the number of shareholders ranges from two to infinity). The share of the public limited company is traded in the stock market.

Advantages Of Joint Stock Company

Huge Financial Resources: The company can collect as much money as it desires from a large number of shareholders. There is no limit to the number of shareholders in a public company. Since its capital is divided into shares of small units, even people of low income can buy into it and contribute to its overall capital by simply purchasing its shares. It facilitates the mobilization of savings of millions for the productive purposes. In addition, a company can borrow from banks to a large extent and also issue debentures to the public.

Limited Liability: The liability of shareholders in a company is limited to the number of shares they have purchased. The limited liability encourages many people to invest in shares of joint stock companies. If the funds of a company are insufficient to satisfy the claims of the creditors, no further demand is made on members to pay anything more than the value of shares held of them.

Perpetual Existence: Due to its separate legal existence, it has perpetual existence. The life of the company is not dependent on the death of a member or such member becoming insolvent. The stability of the company is of great importance both to the society as well as the nation.

Transferability of Shares: The shares of a public company are freely transferable. This transferability of shares brings about liquidity of investment. It encourages many people to invest. If also helps the company in tapping into more resources.

Diffusion of Risk: In sole proprietorship and in partnership business, the risk is shared by few persons. In public companies, all stakeholders share the risk. Since the number of shareholders is large, so many persons share the risk. Therefore, the burden of risk upon an individual is minimal. This attracts many investors. It enables companies to take up new ventures.

Efficient Management: In a company setup, ownership is separated from management. The company has sufficient resources to engage experts and managers who may be highly specialized in different fields of management. It can attract talented people and egg heads by offering them high salaries and better career opportunities and irresistible motivation. The efficient management will help the company to take balanced decisions and can direct the affairs of the company in the best possible manner. It also helps to expand and diversify the activities of the company.

Economies of large-scale production: Large-scale production of our time is because of company form of organization. This results in economies in production, purchase, marketing, and management. These economies will help a company to provide quality goods at lower cost to the consumers.

Democratic Management (Leadership): The Company is managed by the elected representatives of shareholders called the directors. Directors are responsible and accountable to the general body of shareholders. Decisions are taken by majority votes, completely based upon democratic principles and process. This prevents mismanagement of the company.

Public Confidence: The Company enjoys a more significant public confidence and reputation in the market due to legal control, publicity of accounts and perpetual existence. Audit of Joint Stock Company is compulsory. A company's financial reports and statements are published, circulated and are open to public and personal inspection. Therefore, the public has enough faith in it. So, the company can secure loans from different financial institutions.

Social Importance (Vitality): The Company provides opportunity to mobilize the scattered savings of the community. It also creates employment opportunities. Due to large-scale production, consumers get cheaper goods at very low unit prices. The society is supplied with enough quantity of goods, and government gets income in form of taxes.

Limitations Of Joint Stock Company

Difficulty in Formation: The company is not easy to form and establish, due to the number of people required to associate before the company is corporate. It requires a lot of legal formalities to be performed. The shares need to be sold only during the prescribed period. It is both expensive and risky.

Lack of Secrecy: The company must observe all the legal formalities. Most of the business deals are agreed and decided through meetings. Profit and loss accounts and balance sheets are required to be published as at when due; hence trade secrets cannot be maintained.

Delay in Decision: The Company's decision-making process is not only time consuming, but must get the approval of majority of the members. All important decisions are made by either Board of Directors or by General Annual meetings. So many opportunities may be lost while waiting for decisions to be made.

Separation of Ownership and Management: The company is operational by dual ownership and control. It is owned by shareholders but managed by Directors. The owners of the company play little or no role in the management and major decisions of the company. The profit of the company belongs to the shareholders while the Directors are paid commission. There is no relationship between efforts and rewards. At times the management does not take serious personal interest in the workings of company, hence many work against the interest of a clear majority of shareholders.

Speculation in Shares: The joint stock company facilitates speculation in the shares at stock exchanges. It has been found that even the directors and the managers of the company indulge in manipulating the value of shares to their advantages. When they want to purchase the shares, they lower the rate of dividends, and when they want to dispose of the shares, they declare dividends at a higher rate.

Oligarchic Management: The shareholders who are the real owners do not have much voice in the management. A handful of shareholders, which also manage the affairs of the company, can have control over it. Theoretically, the company is democratic, but in practice, it is mostly a case of oligarchy, that is, rule by a few. A few persons hold power and control and try to exploit the majority. It does not promote the interest of the shareholders in general.

Excessive Regulation: The company must observe a lot of excessive and bureaucratic regulations imposed on it by the laws of the land. The excessive regulations are made with a view to protecting the interest of the shareholders and the public, but in practice, they put lots of obstacles and obstructions in their normal and effective workings. This makes it possible that a lot of precious time, resources, efforts and financial resources are wasted, and some get into wrong hands in complying with statutory requirements.

Conflict of Interest: The Company has a lot of parties that make it up, whose interest may differ dangerously. These parties' interests many clash and the result may be conflict of interests. The management, shareholders, employees, creditors and the government may have their own individual interests. These conflicts generally lead to inefficiency in the management and reduce employee morale.

Neglect of Minority: All significant issues in a company are decided by the shareholders who hold majority of the shares. The majority group always dominates over the minority group whose interests are never represented in the management. The Company Act provides measures against oppression of the minority, but the measures are not effective.

Public Enterprises

Public enterprise is a business organization wholly or partly owned by the state and controlled through a public authority. Some public enterprises are placed under public ownership because of social reasons. It is thought that services or products should be provided by a state monopoly. Public enterprises are also autonomous or semi-autonomous corporations and companies established, owned and controlled by the state and engaged in both industrial and commercial activities.

Characteristics Of Public Enterprises

- They are financed by government
- They are managed by government
- They have financial independence
- They offer public services
- They are useful for various sectors
- They are direct channels for using foreign money
- They are helpful in implementing government plans
- They are autonomous or semi-autonomous bodies

Three Types Of Public Enterprise

Departmental Undertaking: It is created by government, is part of the government system and is attached as a department to a government ministry. Department undertaking has no separate legal status. Its activities are business-oriented with a service motive. It follows government rules and regulations; it has flexibility in operations. It is financed, managed and controlled by government. It has public accountability. The ministry is answerable about its affairs. An example of such undertaking is the postal services department.

Public Corporation: Public corporation is created by a special act of the Upper Chamber of the legislative body. It has a separate legal status. Its scope, objectives, powers, duties and operations and procedures are specified by the act. Public corporation is established to achieve the socio-economic objectives of the country. It is guided by a service motive. It enjoys flexibility and autonomy in internal operations and is financed by government and managed by government-appointed Board of Directors. It has public accountability through legislature.

Government Company: Government company is a joint stock company created under the company act. It has separate legislators and can be public or private. The government ownership in shares ranges from 51% to 100%. It can borrow funds, and its activities are business-oriented with a service motive. It also makes profit. The liability of shareholders is limited. It enjoys full flexibility in internal operations. It follows its own rules and regulations and is managed by a Board of Directors. Government nominees are majority in the board.

Cooperatives

The International Cooperative Alliance defines a cooperative as "an autonomous association of persons united voluntarily to meet their common economic, social, and cultural needs and aspirations through a jointly-owned and democratically controlled enterprise."

Businessdictionary.com defines cooperative as a firm owned, controlled, and operated by a group of users for their own benefits. Each member contributes equity capital and shares in the control of the company based on one-member, one-vote principle but not in proportion to his or her equity contribution.

Ivy Wigmore (www.tutorialspot.com) says that 'A cooperative is formed when several people identify an unmet need.' For example, artisans in a downtown area might see the need for a conveniently located market; freelancers might identify the need for a co-working space. Potential members then conduct cost and feasibility studies and explore financial possibilities. A cooperative may or may not incorporate but should draft a document of understanding stating membership requirements, qualifications and responsibilities. The purchase of shares confers membership and members may vote on business issues on a vote-per member basis. Cooperatives are usually run by elected directorial boards.

Principles Of Cooperatives

Voluntary And Open Membership: Because cooperatives are voluntary organizations, membership is open to all persons able to use their services and are willing to accept the responsibilities of membership, without gender, social, racial, political or religious discrimination.

Democratic Member Control: As a voluntary membership organization, members have equal voting rights. It doesn't matter your status, when it comes to electing directors, each member has one vote.

Member Economic Participation: Members contribute equitably to the capital of their cooperative. At least part of that capital is usually the common property of the cooperative.

Autonomy and Independence: Cooperatives are autonomous and self-help organizations. They are usually operated by their members. If they enter into agreements with other organizations, including governments, or raise capital from external sources, they do so in terms that ensure democratic control by their members and maintain their cooperative autonomy.

Education, Training, And Information: New challenges and new technologies affect your cooperative and the entire utility industry. Ensuring continuing effectiveness can only be accomplished by providing information and training to the members and public, employees, staff and directors.

Co-operation Among Cooperatives: Cooperatives serve their members most effectively and strengthen the co-operative movement by participating in local, state, regional, national and international cooperative organizations.

Concern for Community: This principle focuses on members' needs and prompts cooperatives to work for the sustainable development of their communities through policies accepted by their members.

Advantages of Coorporative Society

Easy Formation: Compared to the formation of a company, the formation of a cooperative society is easy. Any ten responsible adult persons can voluntarily form themselves into an association and get it registered with the Registrar of Cooperatives. Formation of a cooperative society also does not involve long and complicated legal formalities. Bureaucratic tendencies are drastically reduced. It does not require any form of strict education to get started.

Limited Liability: Like the company form of ownership, the liability of members is limited to the extent of their capital in the coorperative.

Perpetual Existence: A cooperative society has a separate legal entity. Hence, the death, insolvency, retirement, lunacy, etc., of the members do not affect the perpetual existence of a cooperative society.

Social Service: The underlying philosophy of cooperatives is self-help and mutual help. Thus, cooperatives foster fellow feeling among their members and indicate moral values in them for a better living.

Open Membership: The membership of cooperative societies is open to all irrespective of caste, colour, creed, class, qualification and economic status. There is no limit to maximum number of members.

Tax Advantage: Unlike the other three forms of business ownership, a cooperative society is exempted from income tax and surcharge on its earnings up to a certain limit. Besides, it is also exempted from stamp duty and registration fee.

State Assistance: Government has adopted cooperatives as a useful instrument of socio-economic change. Also, government offers a number of grants, loans, and financial support to the cooperative societies to make their work more efficient.

Democratic Management: The management of a cooperative society is entrusted to the managing committee duly elected by the members based on one-member-one-vote irrespective of the number of shares held by them. The proxy is not allowed in cooperative societies. The management in cooperatives is purely democratic.

Disadvantages of Cooperatives Society

Lack of Secrecy: Since a cooperative society must submit its annual report and accounts to the Registrar of cooperative societies, it becomes quite difficult for it to maintain secrecy of its business affairs.

Lack of Business Acumen and Business Consciousness: The members of cooperative societies generally lack business acumen since it is an all-comers affair. When such members become the members of the board of Directors, the affairs of the society are expectedly not conducted efficiently. They also cannot employ professional managers because it is neither compatible with their avowed ends nor can the limited resources allow for same. This is the major challenge with all church cooperatives. Low capacity people are given targets and tasks far above their required capacity hence, the tendency to fail becomes inevitable. Most churches' businesses have the same challenge as the church believes in using their business to support church members instead of using the money generated from the business to support them. And such businesses most times go into free fall.

Lack of Interest: The paid office bearers of cooperative societies do not take interest in the functioning of societies due to the absence of profit motive. Business success requires sustained efforts over a period which, however, does not exist in many cooperatives. As a result, the cooperatives become inactive and come to a grinding halt.

Corruption: In a way, lack of profit motive breeds fraud and corruption in management. This is reflected in misappropriations of funds by the officials for their personal gain.

Lack of Mutual Interest: The success of a cooperative society depends upon its members' utmost trust on each other. However, all members are not found imbued with a spirit of cooperation. Therefore, absence of such spirit breeds mutual rivalries among the members. Influential members tend to dominate in the society's affairs.

Any group in the church can form cooperatives. Even a few dioceses can come together to float cooperative societies. There are different and many opportunities this can attract to the church and her members. Member organizations can also float a cooperative.

Reflection On Chapter 11

Personal Notes:

===== Guided Action Plan =====

CHAPTER 12
Develop A Speculator's Mentality

"Make your life an ongoing process of positive visualization, continually imagining and visioneering your ideal goals and your perfect future. This can do more to help you to step on the accelerator of your own potential than any other exercise you engage in"
- **Brain Tracy.**

There are people whose job is to speculate the turn of events in the next few years. They are everywhere and in every field of business and profession. I am not talking of gamblers or pool stakers. Speculation works very effectively with people who are involved in Real Estate. They purchase landed property from areas which though are undeveloped, have potentials for development. Some landed properties yield ten times their purchase price after a few years of purchase.

I know a man who purchased almost two hundred plots of land from direct owners at the cost of N10,000. You can imagine as well as I can, the financial position of that man after eight years.

I managed to secure two plots of land in 1997 at N70,000 per plot, and after about eight years, that land went for N1,000,000 per plot. If I had sufficient fund to purchase more of that land, by now I would have been in the billions club.

The ability to develop the speculator's mentality is critical for investors. It affects things we do as individuals. Without this, we cannot take our God-given possessions for our lives. Even politicians are speculators. Speculators are risk takers and result oriented people.

The purchase of common stock also calls for the speculator's mentality. It is the ability to envisage that the price of something will definitely go up with time. Speculators buy as much as they can afford so that any time the price rises, they sell off at that high price. At this time, anything can happen; a poor man who has this mentality can become a wealthy man overnight without much stress or struggle.

A friend had twenty plots of land which he bought at the rate of N3000.00 each. After about fifteen years, he could not feed his family with choice food and could no more take care of his daily expenditure and monthly house rent. He came to me for advice. For him, nobody should tell him to sell off the land, but that was where I started my discussion with him since I knew he had such property. I told him to sell off ten to fifteen plots since the property was located at a strategic junction of the city and use the money to develop the remaining five while the remaining money can be invested to another area of business

Develop A Speculator's Mentality

so that life will start to boom again. At first, he opposed it, but with time he saw reasons. The family then decided to sell only ten plots at N3,000,000 per plot and that came to N30,000,000. He then gave five plots on lease to a bank for twenty years at N1,500,000= per year and this came to N30,000,000.

Now you can see, a man who could not feed his family having in his hands the sum of sixty million Naira (60,000,000). He immediately fixed about N20,000,000 with a bank and used about N30,000,000 to build a two-story shopping plaza that accommodates over sixty stores with an attached office. He further went to underdeveloped areas to purchase about ten plots of land at N3,500,000 and finally created an office for himself with the attached office to the shopping plaza where he and his wife are co-executive directors till today.

Strategic planning coupled with a speculator's mentality is what you need to forge ahead. Just remember that the day of emergency is inevitable, it must surely come. It comes to different people at different times and in different modes. Mine may not be same as yours, but if you prepared for it, you will triumph when it comes.

Permit me to share this testimony from a brother who used to beg before he could feed. According to him, few years ago, precisely seven years ago from the time of writing this, he bought close to N300,000 worth of Mobil Oil shares at a very cheap rate. Last year he decided to sell part of the shares to cushion the effect of hardship on his family, only to discover that he was already a millionaire. You can become one in the next five years if you behave well, and invest wisely now.

If you choose to be careless now, you will regret tomorrow and experience the pains of unpreparedness. Be wise now and save your posterity from perishing in poverty. Spirituality does not and cannot cover this issue. "Principles are not religious, but they obey their rules no matter who is involved."

Those who teach you otherwise, are only cheating on your ignorance. They are enjoying everything life provides; good education for their children, good accommodation for their family members, good vehicles for themselves and family members, good public image globally and domestically and good acceptance. It is not meant for them alone, all of us are stakeholders. God did not create you and decide to close the door of favour. No, God did not plan to hate you and allow you to suffer the way you are experiencing.

One will say, "But Chidi, the Lord says that you will not lack the poor in your midst." I agree entirely with you and it is the truth, but God did not name those that must be poor. He did not call my name nor yours as one of the persons created to be poor. The poor will always be there, but it should not be me or my children, or children's children, or my generation.

This teaching is not godly; it is warming the heart of uneducated Christians. Shun this butter-coated preaching; God did not name you to be the poor in our midst. Anybody who wants to be the poor in our midst, accept my sympathy and gift I will be glad to give you, provided you are the poor in our midst.

The Doctrine of Prosperity

Reflection On Chapter 12

Personal Notes:

Guided Action Plan

CHAPTER 13
Preparing For Retirement

"To achieve all your goals and become everything you are capable of becoming, you must get your time under control. Psychologists generally agree that a 'sense of control' is the key to feelings of happiness, confidence, power, and personal well-being. And a sense of control is only possible when you practice excellent time management skills"- **Brain Tracy.**

Every purposeful life is subdivided into three major parts namely: education life, career life, and retirement life. Each part plays a vital role in the overall well-being of the individual. Once you miss your education life (education here is not only academic but also relates to those who are in business), your career life will be in a severe nervous breakdown. Hence your retirement life will be in high jeopardy and full of regrets. Therefore, the reason for preparation is for retirement.

The retirement process of every one of us starts the day we are born. It baffles me when I hear people say that they have been told to retire and then see them going about complaining and begging to falsify their ages. We have heard of people who were born in '1942', meanwhile, they got their First Leaving School Certificates in 1932. Such people already obtained their Standard Six (6) Certificate even before the marriages that brought them to this world were contracted. You can imagine the embarrassment even among ministers of God. For instance, we had a situation where a Priest voluntarily claimed an age of 60 years, died 3 years later and his children not being aware of his lies, declared his real age as 77 years instead of 63 years, going by what the Priest said. How do you balance this disparity? Nobody would want to tell lies about himself deliberately, but this is caused by lack of preparation. The pleasure of falsifying ages and the new concept of formal age and biological age is only a sign of lack of preparation. To worsen it, the same mistake our parents made is still common today due to lack of adequate information.

The process of retirement is not a few-years affair; it is an entire life matter. From the first day you are employed, it is known to you by **convention**, **experience,** and **practice** that someday you will hand over to younger people to continue from where you stopped, but we have always neglected this.

One man claimed he was born in 1949 while fingers of suspicion were being pointed at him that he was born not later than 1935. He managed to intimidate everybody around him and assumed that age, but he could not intimidate the weakening of the veins; wrinkles on the face; the expected weaknesses associated with old age and the influence of nature on the human frame. Those ones spoke up, and he could no longer hide under the cloak of being young and the dyeing of his hair to deceive people. Again, because of the age he claimed, a duty meant for that age bracket was given to him, and he could not deliver at the expected time. So everything around him began to protest for a change; he decided to bow out voluntarily. You have the power, the hand and influence to rewrite your age to enable you stay in the office longer than your real age, but you don't have the ability and authority to mandate natural associates of old age not to manifest.

You can claim whatever you want to claim as your age to enable you earn a few more coins to keep you going, but your age, I mean your real age, cannot deny itself.

Anybody who starts thinking of retirement from the first day of employment will always retire before the retirement date. In short, I teach in my seminars that people should not work for retirement. Slaves work for retirement; cowards work for retirement; the faithless work for retirement; visionless people work for retirement; purposeless people work for retirement, but men of honour don't work for retirement; men of burden do not work for retirement.

If I had my way, retirement would be abolished, because it has created false hopes in many people who after many years of service hoped to receive their retirement benefits and pension as at when due, but died of heart attacks, heartbreaks, and hunger, because such benefits were not forthcoming.

The government is not helping people, and they don't bother about people who die while waiting for their pension (money which the government took from their salaries to pay them when they will become unproductive). Pension is not free money; it is the pensioner's money which the government ought to pay him when he was in active service, but kept for him as a savings, to aid him when he finally becomes unproductive. Collecting this money is enough headache, and some have died on their way to receive this entitlement while others pay as much as the value of the money they are expected to collect as transportation fare. Even when people are advised to leave this money, since it is less than their expenditure to get it, they insist, that it is their sweat, which is right.

I know of a retiree whose pension value for every month is about N75.00, but he spends well over N250.00 on transportation and food on his trip to collect N75.00 and his children have tried to stop him from taking that risk and wasting his resources by paying him N1000 in lieu of the N75.00 pension, but this man will collect the N1,000 in lieu of the N75,00 and still go for the N75.00 retirement benefit because it is his sweat.

Ageing is not a hidden concept that manifests suddenly to keep us on our toes. It begins at conception, and the process continues throughout the life cycle. The manner in which different individuals age depends on a lot of factors which include the following: heredity, state of mental and physical health, nutrition, belief concept and other variables and factors.

I believe that if people begin to appreciate the fact that we naturally age from the day we were conceived, it would prepare their mentality better. Many people don't think or remember that we are gradually ageing without a deliberate consciousness of it, no wonder it comes to them like the suddenness of death. The truth that all of us know still comes to us as never envisaged.

Retirement?

Every human is made up of three parts namely: **The Spirit, the Soul, and the Body.** The body provides house for the spirit and the spirit as the real person, has a soul. The soul is the storehouse of the emotions, thoughts, and feelings. As a man advances in age, so also does his body. What a man was able to do few years ago may be difficult for the same man to do now. As the body ages, the ability to do these things also begins to decline. Your age affects everything you do, irrespective of what you claim.

Retirement actually means a time to stop active productive work or transition from a life of active work to a life of accomplishment, leisure, and enjoyment. During the time of active service or career period, we are expected to set something aside for this period of which nobody knows how it will be. There is this understanding of people that when they retire, the next thing is death, but I pity you if death refuses to come and you did not plan for a more extended stay. Imagine the mental torture and harrowing experience you would face, meeting your needs.

There is this story in the Bible, of five foolish virgins who did not prepare for a delay in the coming of the bridegroom.

Retirement is like preparing for the arrival of the bridegroom. Many people do not have extra oil; either they believe that they will die immediately after retirement or that little oil (saving or investment) will be enough to cushion the effect of old age. The five foolish virgins never bargained that the bridegroom would be away in such a way that the oil in their lamps would get exhausted, so they did not bother to go with extra oil.

Matthew 25[5-8]:

> *"The bridegroom was a long time in coming, and they all became drowsy and fell asleep. At midnight, the cry rang out: Here comes the bridegroom, come out to meet him. Then all the virgins woke up and trimmed their lamps. The foolish ones said to the wise; Give us some of your oil, our lamps are going out".*

The timing of death should not be attached to retirement. Your oil may go out while you still have many more years to leave. I know of a man who retired at 70 years and afterward lived for 30 years. If this man did not plan or save some oil (savings or investment), how would he have sustained himself and his family for these thirty years after retirement? Don't realize it when it is too late to amend, be careful. The five foolish virgins realized it when it was too impossible and they could not do anything about it. During the years of active work, people usually have been known for the jobs they do. All through their working years, from the morning till evening they are at the same job. In most cases, when they retire, they lose that identity.

Before Retirement

"Before retirement" dates back to the day you were employed. Whenever a man comes to the consciousness of the fact that man cannot be physically strong all the time, his mentality will begin to adjust to do something for the years unseen, for the period of emergency. If the future must be enjoyed, structures need to be put in place now you are strong. I will try to highlight the things you should do while you are strong:

You Must Have A Vision Of The Kind Of Tomorrow You Want To Enjoy: The Bible did say, *"the people perish for lack of vision"* (Hosea 4^6). If you don't think out the kind of old age you want to live, you may not plan for it.

You Must Set Your Goal: Goals are the vehicles that propel us to new achievements, according to one unknown author. He went further to say, without well-articulated goals, our life's objectives cannot be achieved. The issue of setting of goals should not start after retirement, but from the very first day, you get your employment letter. It is the goal that motivates you to action while action creates new prospects which in turn lead to achievements. If your goal is not well-articulated, your objectives for setting the goal cannot be realized.

We have many people whose lives' ambitions were not achieved, not because they were not well connected, educated or exposed, but because they were not focused on their goals which in turn affected their success and expectations from such targets. A well-managed and maintained goal is capable of creating hopes for a man who is about to retire. In achieving financial security before retirement, using the goal-setting weapon, you should be able to determine your personal objectives of the goal. You can break the goals into small units so you can handle them.

Again, set goals that can challenge you, not cheap goals that will not cost you any sweat. Set goals that will crack your ability, that will give you sleepless nights to think on how to achieve them. Not goals achievable with much ease, which are not goals, but mere targets. I encourage you to set goals that are tough to achieve; it is at that point you will task your brain and its ability to bring out what is within you. Cheap goals will only satisfy you temporarily, and the results do not last. Tough goals force innate abilities to manifest. They bring about innovation and speculative creativity. Every tough goal produces a spectacular miracle. *If you set goals within your limits, be sure that you cannot break the limit barrier. But if you set goals beyond your limits, they will stretch you beyond your limits, and destroy the limit barrier, and if your limits barrier is broken, you are liberated from poverty and slavery.* There are lots of people who are under this spell. The stigmatization of poverty is the expression of lack of good goal-setting. Task your brain today by setting tough goals.

You Must Have A Dream: Dreams reveal to us what the future holds for us and if properly managed, will produce the right results and a hopeful end. Dreams are gifts from God, to foretell what is about to happen. Vision is a channel of seeing what is ahead that needs to be accomplished; goals are motivating signs to actualize our vision while dreams verbalize them into reality. Dreams reveal the strategy and pattern on how to achieve the set goals and vision.

When a man sets goals and has visions, without dreaming his visions and goals into realizable positions, such goals and visions may remain unaccomplished in his lifetime. Once you are able to have a vision and set goals, please go into dreaming of how each stage of that vision and goal will be accomplished. Constant reminding of your vision and goals by your dream will always keep you at your feet, and there will be no room for rest and relaxed thinking that you have accomplished anything. It is the burden of the dream that will prompt you to look at every money in your hand as a potential seed that is capable of reproducing other seeds.

When you have a dream, you don't need to stay at home for two years after your retirement without direction, when you are still strong. I was with a family few weeks ago, and it was like a mourning period for the family just because the man of the house and the breadwinner was informed in his office that he should retire by the end of the year. I was surprised because the said man was only forty-eight years. But on second thought, I was happy because he was young both in age and mentally. However, I was baffled by his lamentations about his woes. It was then it dawned on me, that this man, even though aware that he was about to retire, never set goals for himself earlier, for his retirement life. A man at forty-eight years without a continuity agenda for himself and family will end up a drunk.

When I asked him what his next line of action was, he hardly heard me as he was perplexed and helpless. And I could see that if something was not done quickly to save him from his present state of mind, he may die untimely. We have seen people who retire this year die the following year; some have retired and given up the ghost few months later. Some of these deaths are not natural but as a result of lack of dreams. Dreams will enable you to come to the reality of life before you even retire. Retirement is not a sudden thing; it is life-long thing; it is not hidden, and should be known from the first day of employment.

You Must Learn To Invest: It is what you are able to set aside as savings (which should also be invested) that will keep you going after retirement. So if there is anything to do before retirement, it is investing. This differs from one individual to another and depends to a great deal on the following:

- Individual attitude towards future demand
- Individual goals as it affect one's future and upkeep
- Individual needs as regards one's future expectations
- Individual circumstances as regards where one finds oneself
- Individual discipline as regards one's taste and choice
- Individual pattern of life as regards one's interest areas
- Individual lifestyle as regards one's appetite, fashion, and consumption

All these are important when it comes to investment. However, attention is hardly drawn to them. Investment is indispensable when it comes to the issue of retirement because it is what keeps you going after retirement. So if it is not planned for, it will not plan for you. Savings without investment is a waste of resources. Investment is the pathway wherein we utilize our savings. Each money set aside should be invested immediately, except it is inadequate for the investment you have in mind, and then you can keep it on hold in a reasonable bank to make it up. Interest rates do not work anymore so don't put your money in the bank for interest as it does not profit. Instead, the banks use your money for profit and give you about 3% to 4% interest which is nothing compared to the income from your investment.

Where And How Do I Invest?

This has been a significant and reoccurring question, each time I handle a seminar on Financial Management and Empowerment. From my experience, I have discovered that there are few areas of investment available to us, or at least few areas we can handle. But there are various areas of investment open to us, many of which require vast amounts of money to embark upon by an individual, and therefore the need for government or corporate organization's sponsorship. Such areas include:

- Collectibles
- Commodities trading
- Real estate

These areas are capital intensive, but there are areas that are not as capital intensive, and we can invest in, and I will major in those areas in our discussion. This does not mean that you are limited to them. If you have what it takes to invest in the areas mentioned above, go ahead. But here we will try to zero in on Capital and Money Markets which are common and everywhere. In these, you can start with any amount of money.

Capital Market

Even though the subject of capital market was discussed in chapter 9, I consider it relevant enough to expatiate on it in this chapter, and provide practical guidance to those preparing for retirement, and have not decided what investment portfolio to put their money. I also explained how you can participate in the stock market, and possibly buy and sell your shares. You will also know the major players and their functions, to help you make informed decision as a retiree.

Capital Market is a place where long-term funds are sourced through Equities and Debt instruments. It is traded in an open market called Stock Exchange. Under stock exchange, we have the Primary Market and Secondary Market. The Primary Market is the market where New Issues are exchanged while the Secondary Market is the market where existing shares are traded. By this brief definition, you can buy new issues, and you can as well go to the floor of the Stock Exchange to purchase existing shares through your stockbroker. You can buy and sell your existing shares, right there in your house without stepping out, if you have the facility. Major players in this market include:

The Regulators: Securities and Exchange Commission (SEC) and the Nigeria Stock Exchange (NSE).

The Operators: The Stockbroker, who is the most useful operator for the investor since it is only through his services that investors can buy and sell shares on the floor of the Stock Exchange.

Others Include: Registrars/Company Secretaries, Issuing Houses, Investment Advisers, and Trustees.

In the Nigerian Capital Market, the following instruments are also available to anyone who decides to invest:

Common Stocks: They are also referred to as Equities, commonly known as ownership interest in a business. There are over 200 companies listed on the Nigerian Stock Exchange under Equities. You can see this for yourself in our daily newspapers.

What Do I Stand To Gain?

You stand to gain a lot depending on the nature of the investment you may want to engage in. There are three significant areas of trading in common stock. And the gains include, the ownership right you will exercise at the Annual General Meeting, the borrowing ability with the certificates, the opportunity of becoming a board member, the dividend income that accrues to you, the bonus shares you are entitled to each time there are bonus shares for sale and the capital growth of your initial investment. You can still be self-employed by observing the reactions and the behaviour of the stock manipulation.

There are people who have resigned their employment, only to trade in stocks. The three areas of stock business include:

Long-Term Investment: You can invest for long term. That is, you invest an amount of money and allow it to grow through bonus shares and dividends. In that case, you are not in a hurry to sell off your shares, it does not matter if the price rises or not. The essence is for future use.

Another area is investing vast amounts of money in shares and resell them to make profit, immediately the price per share rises. Those investing in this area usually buy from the Primary Market and watch the market behaviour of the Stock Exchange (SE). Most of them are self-employed, and their primary business is to monitor the market forces, and they are making it. It is a great opportunity available, but unknown to many people.

The last area is usually for people who are gainfully employed and don't have all the time. They can enter into partnership with trusted stockbrokers. In that case, the prospective buyer gives the trusted stockbroker an amount of money relatively big, to trade with, on his behalf. The trusted stockbroker is to buy shares at low prices and sell off immediately there is a rise in price and recycles the capital and profit into a low cost stock. The idea here is to buy at a low rate and sell at a high rate. They may agree to share the profit in an agreed proportion. This is working for people, and I know you may not be aware of this provision.

There are warnings also in investing in stocks, and a lot of questions have been asked. Questions like: which stock do I invest in and how do I know right companies whose shares are stable with growth potentials? These are expected fears when it has to do with money. The dominant player here is your stockbroker who should be well experienced. The prospective investor must first establish his investment expectations or objectives which are the purpose of the investment. I did say that there are three major areas of investment objectives or expectations. Again, the investor must also have in mind the level of risk he is willing to take for there are risks as well as gains involved in investing. As the investor expects a rise in price of his stocks, there could also be a decline in their prices. Risk can be reduced but cannot be avoided in any business. Avoiding risks because you don't want to lose your money is not the right stance for a prospective investor. However, you can reduce your risks by trying to diversify your holdings and cash among several portfolios, that is, different companies and industries. For instance, in the Nigerian Stock Exchange, we have over 26 stocks.

Avoid These!

Don't buy stocks for buying sake. Have a target and invest your money wisely and appropriately. We have seen people who buy just any stock just to answer stockholders, without considering the level of relevance of that stock to the value it offers. I made that initial mistake: There are some shares I have today that if I had another opportunity, I would not buy them, even for the least price.

Buy reputable shares from reputable companies and industries: There are companies and industries which have built up their value and reputation over the years; though the shares of such corporations and industries are usually expensive. They pay good dividends, and each of their bonus shares adds value to your total stock and dividend. In my case, there are companies and industries where I have upward of 5000 shares, and somewhere my holding is just about 500. It will interest you to know that the dividend I receive from the holdings of 500 is far more than the dividend I get from the 5000 holdings. Make sure you select promising companies and industries. It does not matter how many holdings you have, what matters is the value they add to your general value at the end of each financial year. Some companies and industries, pay N0.30k as their dividend per share while for some, their dividend per share is about N6.00. If for instance, you are holding only 1000 shares in a company or industry that pays a dividend of N6.00 per share, and another person is holding a total number of 20,000 shares in a company that pays N0.30 per share. At the end of the financial year, the person who is holding 1000 shares with a dividend of N6.00 per share will earn a dividend of N6,000 while the one holding 20,000 shares for N0.30 per share will earn a dividend of N6,000. You can imagine the difference in shareholding.

Know When To Buy

My advice here is that you buy from the Primary Market, that is, new issues, and buy when the price of shares is low. There are periods in the financial year when the price of shares is low, and there are times when it is at the peak. Share prices are usually at their peak when the company or industry wants to pay dividends and give bonus shares. After such periods, the costs of shares are typically low, and this is the right time to buy. Generally, the prices of shares are low at the Primary Market. So each time any company or industry advertises for public offer, you are encouraged to buy as many shares as you want and can afford, provided it is a company or industry that has a promising future. Usually, when the companies or industries come out for public offer, they sell at low prices per share, but at the end of the public offer, the price per share tends to rise. Again stocks can gain significant selling opportunities when their rates are low than when high. Demand and the workings of a typical market policy is that prices tend to be higher when demand is higher than supply. So naturally, the stock whose demand is high will definitely induce high price. This is the rule of buy low; sell high.

Learn To Diversify Your Investment

This implies owning stocks in different industries. It also helps one to avoid the risk of putting all of one's eggs in one basket. Although, over-diversification has its own dangers. Diversification means investing in more than one or two industries. In the case of diversifying, you are encouraged to choose from different sectors. By way of advice, choose between five to fifteen different stocks, with this, you can achieve excellent diversification.

Debenture and Industrial Loan: Debentures are long-term debt instruments usually issued by corporate bodies. They are not for the public but rather, for existing shareholders. Like bonus shares, they carry a fixed rate of interest and are repayable over a definite period. They can be converted into the share value at the time of purchase if the investor so decides. Debenture is a privilege share which is usually higher in rate than the standard share value. For instance; there was a company whose share rate was N50, but at the same period, they issued the right of debenture to their existing shareholders at N1000 per share. It is like asking their shareholders to raise loan for them to meet either the need of expansion or acquisition of new machinery to ensure production efficiency.

Bonds: Bonds are debt instruments issued by government and its agencies. They carry fixed rates of interest and are repayable in full at the agreed period of time.

Unit Trust: Unit trusts are professionally managed investment companies, whose businesses are to use the investors' money to purchase diversified portfolio of stocks, bonds, money market investment and other securities. Annually, the net income of the company or industries is fully distributed to the unitholders.

Money Market

The main players of the money market are bonds and non-bank financial institutions, and the market is regulated by the Central Bank of Nigeria (CBN), with the Money Market Association (MMA) taking active role.

The following are tools of the money market:

- Certificate of Deposit
- Nigeria Treasury Bill
- CBN Certificates

After Retirement

When retirement finally comes, different people have different approaches to it. Some welcome it with pride and even organize thanksgiving services through which they thank God and celebrate with their households, friends, and well-wishers. Once retired, everything around you is minimized naturally. The source of income, as well as salary, is reduced, other allowances that follow the wage every month are no more, benefits and office favours are no more or at least, not as much as before. A good home manager will begin to adjust in every front to finally settle into the retirement life.

Charles Nwankwo, in his book *The Insights for the Elderly*, marshaled out ten ways to reinvent life after retirement and I think it is relevant to help us make informed decision here:

- *Retire the word retirement from your vocabulary.* This word actually means to withdraw or retreat. Spoken words shape reality. Don't you think that 'graduation' better describes your post-career life?
- Realize that retirement is a relatively new concept in human evolution. In the past, elders remained productive members of the society and were relied upon for their wisdom and skills.

- Restructure your priorities. Deepen relationship with family and friends, community service, etc.
- Renew your desire for education.
- Revitalize your energy by finding a group of people who embrace growth and change.
- Rekindle your spirit for risk-taking.
- Respond to new opportunities: Remain open to the numerous opportunities the world has to offer because your full potentials may be ahead.
- Recharge your system – find something you really enjoy doing and make it a part of your life.
- Revisit your childhood dreams – it is never too late to be who you might have been.
- Remember that the power to recognize and act on your true passion is within you.

Phases of Retirement

In the same book, the author *outlines* his ideas for the elderly in phases; he also suggested five phases of retirement as:

- Pre-Retirement
- Transition
- Disenchantment
- Reorientation
- Stability

Pre-retirement: During this period, people realize that retirement is not just something to look forward to in the future but is imminent. At this time, primary tasks involve preparing for retirement and gearing up for separation from work. This time offers the opportunity not only for financial planning but also for emotional and spiritual preparation for a significant change.

Transition: As many that enter this period, consideration must be given to the essential long-term needs of retired life, such as; goals, relationships, and personal meaning. It is important for retirees to prepare themselves and plan during this phase.

Disenchantment: Sometimes, the transition is followed by a period of disenchantment and sometimes depression. The more unrealistic the pre-retirement dreams become, the more likely it is that life after the transition will feel empty. It provides an opportunity to rediscover oneself and redefine the future.

Reorientation: During this phase, there is an active development of ideas and a movement towards a more balanced life and diversified set of interests. It provides a time to think about new avenues of involvement in every area of life, and a time of action and movement towards the life retirees want to live.

Stability: This stage most of all, is retirement. Until now, retirees have been merely gearing up for and moving towards this final period, which does not really have an end. In this period, the retirees are not just thinking about and planning for the retirement; they are living in it. The reality of retirement has become a living experience.

Reflection On Chapter 13

Personal Notes:

=== Guided Action Plan ===

CHAPTER 14
Start There

"Your problem is to bridge the gap between where you are now and the goals you intend to reach"
Earl Nightingale.

You must start from where you are now and today. Don't feel bad about your present condition but resolve to begin there today and now. Always locate yourself in the direction of your vision and intending distinction.

After ministering in a meeting on Financial Empowerment and Management, a young man walked up to me and asked, "Now where do I start since I only have Ten Thousand Naira (N10,000)". I told him, "start there." That is, start with the sum of Ten Thousand Naira. A lot of people think big from the beginning. Think big but start from where you are presently and if you are diligent, you will reach your dream, unfailingly.

I have taken time to study some wealthy personalities. All of them started from humble beginnings, and today they are big and can effectively compete with anybody. Some of them are the world's wealthiest people you can think of. For example;

Bill Gates started as a school dropout who believed that all had ended for him and that schooling was the ultimate. But he did not allow the failure mentality to dominate him for too long before he began to think about what next to do. Today, the whole world cannot operate without Bill Gates. He distributes wealth to the entire global community. The influential, the powerful, the well-connected, the educated, the uneducated, street people, market people, companies, you name it, all bow before Bill Gates' products and he is said to be the wealthiest man on earth at a time. How did he start? He started from nothing! But today, he is something! The school dropout is now the whole world's choice and the friend of everybody. Bill Gates' good morning is a treasure to everybody today.

Indeed it doesn't matter where you are starting from. Only be focused and conscious of the goals set before you. Remember your problem is to bridge the gap between where you are now and the goals you set for yourself before retirement, during retirement, and after retirement. Goals are not mere wishful thinking. They are to be realized with focus, vision, burden, and discipline. As you begin to see the world in its real nature, you will start to adjust your eating habits, thinking ability, your dressing mode, and your competing spirit.

Another person is the late M.K.O Abiola who started from nothing. He was almost a write- off but emerged as the wealthiest man in Nigeria in his time. Yet another is Aliko Dangote, a man we should also understudy. He started from where he was, and today, there is hardly any area of life he has not touched. His investments are in many sectors, namely; the Building sector,

Manufacturing sector, Banking sector, Oil and Gas sector, etc. He is a household name because he 'started there' that is, 'where he was.' Our Former President, Olusegun Obasanjo is another man who had a humble beginning, but today he is the only president who has led his nation through three successful tenures. The day I watched his story on television, of how his mother sold kerosene for the family's upkeep and how schooling was difficult for him because of lack of school fees; I concluded that every one of us must learn to start from wherever we are. If you wait for favourable weather, you may not make it. Don't wait until when it is okay. I assure you, you cannot find such a moment in your lifetime. In fact, there is no such moment or time when the circumstances will be adequately favourable. You need to change your position and appreciate your problems better, so you can find solutions to them.

> *"Whoever watches the wind will not plant, whoever looks at the cloud will not reap" - Ecclesiastes 114.*

A young woman who was retrenched from her job listened to me in one of my seminars. According to her, she could not believe all the things I said during the workshop, so she decided to ask these questions:

- If one is forcefully retired without prior information and what he has is just a month's salary, what would be your advice to such a person on how to start investing?
- If one's salary is less than N20,000 per month and he has over three dependents, can he make ends meet?
- If you want to go into business and you don't have the

- required capital to start the business, how do you go about it?
- You said that all civil servants are slavers, what do you mean by that?

First, let me say that this woman's questions are critical questions that many today ask without getting answers and some don't even have anybody to ask these questions.

These Are Answers I Offered Her:

I started by telling her that she was supposed to have begun planning for retirement or retrenchment from the very day she was employed. And I say it here again; expect anything from your employer any day. You must plan for the worst condition of service so that if it turns out to be good, excellent. Many of us don't think, remember or plan for forceful retirement or retrenchment. The fact that you are not thinking about it does not mean that it cannot happen. Stop deceiving yourself, your mere wishes cannot change the tide of nature, but good planning and goal oriented aspiration can.

As I was saying, I asked her how much she was able to save from her last month's salary, and she said, "nothing," and that it was not even enough, then I asked her, "How about in the last six months." She said, "Pastor, apart from this month's salary I got yesterday, I do not have any other money." Sincerely, I was shocked to my bones that people can collect their salaries and finish them before the new month's salary arrives. Some even buy things on credit. Listen, if you cannot afford anything now, it means that it is not for you now, till you can afford it. Any form of buying without immediate payment is credit. It does not matter how you define it. Credit buying is the first sign of un-satisfaction and discontentment. So, people who buy things on credit are showing lack of contentment. What you don't have money to buy immediately should be discarded and forgotten until you can afford it. Don't plan to buy beyond the amount of money in your hand. Don't expect to take anything you wish to pay for later. Don't imitate anybody.

She had almost (fifty thousand Naira) N50,000, so I told her that she could start from there. Fifty thousand Naira is a big money to start investing with if only you can curtail your appetite and reduce your spending pattern. There are people who think that business will become successful when they start with significant amounts of money. If the amount of money is enormous, it will create the spirit of un-seriousness and limitation in the heart of the businessman, but if the amount of money is small, it will create the sense of thriving and struggling in the heart of the businessman. Drop all excesses, and start from where you are today, you will see a significant change tomorrow. Stop twisting the solution to suit your excuses.

I answered the second question by asking her who those dependents were and what they can or cannot do. Nobody should be a parasite. The days of 'parasitism' and absolute dependency are over. **Anybody who is in your house must be deliberately contributing to the growth of that house.** The time people pack their bags and baggage to people's houses without advanced notice are long gone. Who are the dependents? Are they your friends, your siblings, your relations, your sisters, or children? You are advised to take the number of dependents you can cope with at a time. This is the primary problem with the average African. It is a common knowledge and practice in our culture to accommodate people even when we cannot feed ourselves. We thus paint the picture of caring and trust. Some are squatting with somebody, still when they get home, instead of telling their people the real situation, they paint the picture that all is well and then one dependent who has been planning on how to run away from the village would join them to town (city) to increase the pains of the other occupants. If he says no to that inconvenience, he is capped an unbeliever. Please stop covering evil and wrong planning with spirituality.

I once had the same problem when my uncle's friend pleaded with him to beg me to put up his younger brother. My uncle informed me about it, and since I was living alone, and the young man had just finished school, I decided to oblige him. After three months he brought two of his friends to stay in the house with us in the guise that they were only passing the night. I tell you the truth, from passing the night, they lived with us for not less than four years until we quarreled one fateful day which led to my deliverance and salvation. Stop creating trouble for yourself because you cannot solve all the problems around you. Try to solve the bit you can and leave the rest.

Once, a man was living with over ten dependents, some of whom were his direct brothers and sisters? With time, the house became a bus stop for all his village people. He got married and continued with this spirit, but his wife could not cope with the stress of cooking for over ten persons, coupled with the inconveniences involved. When she started complaining of the stress and inconveniences, everybody around started calling her names. Stop breaking your homes with undefined dependents, some of whom when they succeed, will never remember you. I am not sounding hard but logical and reasonable. Stop being unreasonable and listen to wise counsel, or you will have grey hair early in life.

The third question referred to lack of required capital. As for me, any capital can start any business provided I am interested in the business that my present money can sponsor. I know of a young man who had just N60,000 in his hands but was negotiating for a business deal worth N800,000. That is over-ambition and is capable of leading one astray. If you have, for instance, N60,000.00, start a business of N50,000 and allow the business to grow steadily into a multimillion business. Don't start today and expect the business to grow the next day. It does not matter how long it takes you to get to the multimillion naira business level, all that matters is that you have arrived.

Job 36$^{27-28}$, says,

> *"He draws up the drops of water, which distill as rain to the streams, the clouds pour down their moisture, and abundant showers fall on mankind."*

Start from there, and you will notice a growth of wealth from that little beginning.

Question four queried the assertion "all" civil servants are slaves. Let's begin with the question, who is a slave? A slave has been described as a person who cannot say what he wants to say at the time he wants to say it or a person who cannot do what he wants to do at the time he wants to do it or a person who cannot act on his liberty without referring or seeking permission from a higher authority. If these definitions are true, then every person employed in any firm or business or civil service is a form of slave.

No real civil servant or employee has the liberty to do or act or say what he wants without first obtaining permission from his employer. If you are in doubt of this truth, and you are a civil servant or an employee, try not to go to your office before 7:30am or leave your office before the closing hours tomorrow. Do that consistently for about three to four days and see if you will not be given a query which may be followed by a dismissal threat. But the employer of labour does not need to answer anybody's query. Again, after you have suffered for almost thirty days of the month and have made a profit of about N200,000 for the firm, the owner of the company pays you just five percent (5%) of the total profit. In some cases, one's entire salary is only enough for transportation and lunch. Instead of you to continue being a slave to a fellow man, you can start something today. It does not matter how small; for there is great joy and fulfillment in ownership than in being owned. Masters of slaves determine what to pay them when to pay them, when they will resume the day's duty and when to close for the day. Which aspect of the employment are you controlling?

I was in an office one day, and the Managing Director was talking to an up-and-coming young man in an abusive manner. The young man in question was more educated in every aspect of life than his boss, and all he could reply was, "sorry sir." Finally, the boss said, "You will not receive your salary for last month and this month till further notice." What that meant was that: The employee had not received the previous month's salary when the new month was almost ending. I looked at the young man who was already hopeless in the hands of a man he was better educated, more exposed and accepted than. Then I spoke up to the boss, "you shouldn't do such things, please pay him his salary to enable him cope with the hardship of the time and again avoid the temptation of stealing your money." In reply, he said, "He is very foolish, he does not deserve to be paid. If he wants to resign, let him resign and if he is caught stealing my money his chapter is closed in this state." You can imagine such an inhuman treatment. Is this young man not a slave? Tell me if there is a bigger slave than this man. This is one example out of many. What of people who serve their masters for about seven to eight years, at the end of their service, that is, the year of their settlement for their apprenticeship, the master will come up with a false story in order not to settle the apprentice.

At each of these occasions, the victim is usually helpless and can do nothing than rest in the oasis of regret and 'had I known.' You can start there; it does not matter how you start, what matters is how you finish. Failure is an orphan while success has many siblings and parents.

Reflection On Chapter 14

Personal Notes:

=== Guided Action Plan ===

CHAPTER 15

Develop A Zero Mentality Thinking

"But one thing I do: forgetting what is behind and straining towards what is ahead."

The decision you made in the past can haunt you today, but you must decide to overcome the mistakes of your past decisions. There are decisions you have taken in the past that you wouldn't tolerate now. Push such decisions behind and move forward. Pretend they never existed. There are people who quickly remember their past and dwell on them until they develop high blood pressure and other related sicknesses. Paul while addressing the Philippian church said this,

"Brothers, I do not consider myself yet to have taken hold of it. But one thing I do; forgetting what is behind and straining toward what is ahead" (hi. 3^{13}).

This is what I call zero-mentality-thinking. If you are preoccupied by your former failure, you can never create a new success. The greatest enemy of progress is dwelling your previous shortcomings and allowing them to take hold of your prospects. What is ahead of you is more than your past failures?

Develop a Motif-Mentality

There are many people who have decided to grade themselves as failures in all areas of life. In meetings, they are there as backbenchers. Even when they are called to the front seats, they will shy away from them. In the offices, they are there with all kinds of complex and excuses; in professional lives, it is the same.

The worst thing that can happen to a man is to classify himself as a backbencher. Even if you naturally find yourself in that kind of position, you are expected to wake yourself up from it to the goal of your profession. There is a goal target for every business or profession, and the desire of everyone should be to get to the peak of his business or profession. There is nothing stopping you from becoming the best in that profession. That enviable position is not reserved for anyone in particular, it is meant for the people who aspire and work towards it. Paul again in Philippians 3^{14} did say;

> *"I press up towards the goal to win the prize of which God has called me heavenward in Christ Jesus."*

Pressing on is required on your part while the oriented result expected is from the Lord. As you press on towards the goal of the prize, the giver of the prize is forced by the force of nature to respond towards your direction for a holistic consummation of the success of victory. You must think of becoming the best always for it is not reserved for any specific person. Once you shy away from it, it will shy away from you.

Implication of Idleness

Idleness is a privately acquired system of life. It is not inherited or transferable, but a choice. It is sweet to be idle, but it cripples the future of a man. We have many people who are idle, and they enjoy it very much, but only to regret later in life. There are also people who are working but are idle. This one could be dangerous in the sense that people who ought to help them are deceived that they are employed when in the actual sense, they are not. We have also seen people who are busy doing nothing. Merely looking at them, they are toiling and sweating but with nothing to show for the level of toiling they undergo. Others are idle. They are doing nothing and are acting as one businessman or the other. Some are sharing different categories of complimentary cards without a specific identification, while others are jack of all trades. They are in every business, whether relevant or not. The scripture has warned us in several places to avoid idleness and has as well told us the corresponding implications. We shall look at what a few of these scriptures are saying to us.

> *"Since you ignore all my advice and would not accept my rebuke, I, in turn, will laugh at your disaster, I will mock when calamities overtake you when calamities overtake you like a storm when disaster sweeps over you like a whirlwind when distress and trouble overwhelm you" (Proverbs 1[25-27]).*

If you ignore all advice, don't blame anybody but yourself. When failure comes, people will inevitably laugh at you; when your disaster begins, people must refer to you as somebody who did not listen to advice. When calamity overtakes you, people will make remarks about your stubbornness. So be warned before it will be too late, and you start regretting. There are people today who are in the pit of regrets. Any regret in the pit level is as good as crying over spilled milk.

> *Proverbs 104: "Lazy hands make a man poor, but diligent hands bring wealth."*
>
> *Proverbs 1224,27: "Diligent hands will rule, but laziness ends in slave labour. The lazy man does not roast his game, but the diligent man prizes his possessions."*
>
> *Proverbs 134: "The sluggard craves and gets nothing, but the desires of the diligent are fully satisfied."*
>
> *Proverbs 2125-26: "The sluggard's craving will be the death of him because his hands refuse to work. All day long he craves for more, but the righteous gives without sparing."*
>
> *Proverbs 1423: "All hard work brings a profit, but mere talk leads only to poverty."*
>
> *Proverbs 189: "One who is slack in his work is brother to one who destroys."*
>
> *Proverbs 66-8: "Go to the ant, you sluggard, consider its ways and be wise. It has no commander, no overseer or*

ruler, yet it stores its provisions in summer and gathers its food at harvest. How long will you lie there, you sluggard, when will you get up from you sleep? A little sleep, a little slumber, a little folding of hands to rest and poverty will come on you like a bandit and scarcity like an armed man."

Proverbs 1915: "Laziness brings on deep sleep, and the shiftless man goes hungry."

Proverbs 2430-34: "I went past the field of the sluggard, past the vineyard of the man who lacks judgment; thorns had come up everywhere, the ground was covered with weeds, and the stone wall was in ruins. I applied my heart to what I observed and learned a lesson from what I saw: A little sleep, a little slumber, a little folding of hand to rest and poverty will come to you like a bandit; and scarcity like an armed man."

Proverbs 2819: "He who works, his land will have abundant food, but the one who chases fantasies will have his fill of poverty."

Ecclesiastes 1018, "If a man is lazy, the rafters sag; if his hands are idle, the house leaks."

Ecclesiastes 116: "Sow your seed in the morning, and at evening let not your hands be idle, for you have not known which will succeed whether this or that, or whether both will do equally well."

The Doctrine of Prosperity

Reflection On Chapter 15

Personal Notes:

Guided Action Plan

CHAPTER 16

Total Prosperity

"True freedom is absolute well-being of the total man."

God promised every one of us total prosperity. God does not believe or give lopsided prosperity. Every aspect of how God deals with us is always absolute and complete in nature. Prosperity in itself is not evil, but prosperity becomes evil when it becomes a yardstick for measuring success and providing class stratification. Any prosperity that is not complete, total and absolute has a lot to desire. I tell you, if you are spiritually healthy and other aspects of your life are not in corresponding health, it is not total prosperity but rather spiritual prosperity, and a lot of people are in that position. If you are financially okay but you lack peace, and your health is nothing to write home about, you are not entirely prosperous, but rather financially wealthy and spiritually sick. You may claim that it is well, but you know deep down within you that it is not well. Again, there are people who are physically active, but mentally feeble and poor. They cannot claim that they are prosperous. Most people have lopsided prosperity. Reevaluate the prosperity you cherish, and you will find out that it is just one aspect of prosperity. But it should not be so.

Total prosperity has four (4) major aspects which are as follows:

- Spiritual Prosperity
- Mental Prosperity
- Physical Prosperity
- Financial Prosperity

These are the four aspects of prosperity which make it total. Total prosperity affects our spiritual well-being, our mental plane, our physical health and financial state. Each of these aspects has a significant role to play in our becoming prosperous. Without any one of them, you cannot claim to be entirely prosperous.

Spiritual Prosperity

In the gospel of Saint Matthew 4:4, when the spirit of God led Jesus into the wilderness to be tempted by Satan, the Lord Jesus Christ's reply to Satan was,

> *"It is written: man does not live on bread alone but on every word that comes from the mouth of God."*

In spiritual prosperity, man does not survive by feeding only the flesh; there should be balanced eating of the bread made from yeast and flour (wheat) and the eating of the bread from the Word of God.

There are many people who are physically robust but spiritually thin and feeble. When you push such people physically, they may likely weary you, but when you push them spiritually, they will fall like decaying loaves of bread. In that scripture, Christ Jesus was asking us to balance our eating habit, to match our level of eating physical bread with our level of eating spiritual food. 'Man does not live on bread alone'; you need bread to live as much as you need the word of God to live. Looking at the preposition 'On' that clarifies the bread alone; it will interest us to note the following:

- Bread is needed to continue to live
- Bread was not condemned entirely as evil
- Bread can become a hindrance to living
- Bread alone will automatically introduce spiritual malnutrition.

As we continue to look at that verse, we observe the second part of the balancing: *"but on every word that comes from the mouth of God"* meaning, for a balanced Christian living and well-being, the believer needs to balance up his meal with every word that comes from the mouth of God; not the word of men or circumstances. For your spiritual prosperity, you need the combination of bread and every word that comes from the mouth of God. The question you may want to ask is: why every word that comes from God's mouth? It is a typical lesson to every one of us, that if Jesus, the Author of life and Son of God would rely on His Father for divine provision and not on his own miraculous power, we need that dependence much more in our desires and expectations.

In John 3³,¹¹, Jesus began again to testify to the demand of spiritual prosperity by saying:

> *"I tell you the truth; no one can see the kingdom of God unless he is born again. I tell you the truth, we speak of what we know, and we testify to what we have seen, but still you people do not accept our testimony."*

There was once a case in a law court between two persons. This case had lasted for almost twenty years, and the two parties involved were tired of the endlessness of the case. One day, the judge came to the court and decided to rule the case in favour of one of them. The one who won the case rejoiced home with his people while the other refused to accept the ruling. What surprised me was that the other party's refusal to accept the decision of the judge did not reverse the judgment, it still stood. Friends, not accepting the fact about being born again, does not change anything and in fact, if for anything, it will only bring sorrow to you. In the above scriptures, it does not matter how you want to explain it away; it stands that the only way you can enter into your spiritual prosperity is by accepting the Lord Jesus as your Lord and personal Saviour. Philosophers will fail you at the dying minute. In your resistance to this divine truth, what are your facts? For John, he said, *we speak of what we know and testify to what we have seen.* You blind man, have you seen or known what you are disturbing yourself with? When the chips are down, what will you fall back on? Don't be foolish.

In 2Corinthians 5^{17-21}, Paul continued to discuss spiritual prosperity and said:

> *"Therefore, if any man is in Christ, he is a new creation; the old has gone, the new has come. All this is from God, who reconciled us to himself through Christ and gave us the ministry of reconciliation: that God was reconciling the world to Himself in Christ, not counting men's sins again. And he has committed to us the message of reconciliation. We are therefore Christ's ambassadors, as though God were making his appeal through us. We implore you on Christ's behalf: Be reconciled to God. God made Him who had no sin to be sin for us so that in him we might become the righteousness of God."*

Spiritual prosperity, according to Uncle Paul, is by being in Christ which will bring freshness and newness to our being physically, spiritually, mentally and financially. This freshness and newness will eradicate the old life and whatever it brings; it brings to mind that we don't need to exact any extra energy or power for it is actually from God himself. The reconciliation by his authority has made us to become his ambassadors and his finished products, to continue the appeal of the mystery of reconciliation. Again, he drew our attention that it is not by our works of righteousness but by grace, in that someone who was not a partaker of sin was made sin for us so that we might take up the garment of the righteousness of God which he has exchanged for our garment of unrighteousness. It is indeed a privilege that is never to be abused. Because God cannot take such a step for you to bring a slap to his face and go unpunished; that is not possible!

In Romans 10^{9-10}, Paul showed us how to make it possible, in an easy way and method. As he began in that scripture, he said that the actions involved a personal resolution and decision.

> *"That if you confess with your mouth, Jesus is Lord, and believe in your heart that God raised Him from the dead, you will be saved. For it is with your heart you believe and are justified, and it is with your mouth that you confess and are saved."*

In the pursuit of spiritual prosperity, you must be actively involved. The issue of passiveness is not accepted at all. When we look at the scripture above, we see that the major human parts involved include: the mouth, which we use to confess and the heart which we use to believe. The art of confessing that Jesus is Lord must be done with your mouth; nobody will do it for you. The second aspect of confession has to be done with your heart. I call the heart the 'engine house' which man uses to believe the words our mouth confessed. These two complement each other for total spiritual prosperity to take place. In answer to our hypothetical questions, *verse 10* says that for it is with our hearts that we believe and are justified, and it is with our mouths, we confess. So, if you don't confess with your mouth and believe with your heart, there is no justification and salvation for you.

Mental Prosperity

Mental imprisonment is common among believers. Most Christians are spiritually sound but mentally enslaved. We have seen good Christians who are mentally dominated as they act slavishly and ignorantly. They are imprisoned in their reasoning and do not want to change from that state to a better one. Often times they argue blindly to the extent that one wonders if they have common sense. Though it is called common sense and is expected to be common to everybody, we still find people who don't have it, how much more the ability to task their brains harder. As I go about preaching this gospel, I see people whose mentality is yet to be tapped, and it grieves my heart. Any prosperity without mental liberation is not a complete prosperity.

Paul, while advising his spiritual son Timothy, did point out this mental liberation when in *2 Timothy 1⁷*, he began to denounce the spirit of inferiority complex and warn against the spirit of lack of confidence.

> *"For God did not give us a spirit of timidity, but a spirit of power, of love and of self-discipline."*

Mental prosperity starts when the self in your body which is the garment for the real man in you, is empowered to realize that God did not plan to allow you to be clothed with the spirit of timidity. You are second to nobody, notwithstanding your situation, condition or circumstance, and your mental appreciation of this fact will bring a liberation balm to your soul. There are times when our immediate environment or the problems around want us to believe that we are inferior to others. At such times, just remember that you are second to nobody. Each time you observe the spirit of intimidation at work in you, know that it is a visitor and not from God. He has made the promise in the above scripture to us, and has given us, in the place of intimidation, the spirit of:

- Power
- Love
- Self-discipline

In *Romans 12²*, Paul admonished us not to conform to the strategy and pattern of the world because the pattern of this world is not consistent with the word of God and can lead to mental slavery. The world's system contradicts the system of the word of God. The major problem of the world is its structure and system. In that scripture we referred to above, Paul said;

> *"Do not conform any longer to the pattern of this world but be transformed by the renewing of your mind. Then you will be able to test and approve what God's will is; his good pleasing and perfect will."*

The mentality that brings prosperity must first reject the world's system and structure by not accepting to conform to the pattern of the world. The second step is to transform your mentality by renewing your mind which inevitably will lead to three significant changes: you will be able to test and approve what

God's will is; secondly, when your mentality is transformed by the renewing of your mind, God's will become more evident, and you will begin to appreciate His good and pleasing thoughts to you. Above all, His perfect will, will become clear to you without your guessing or speculating.

In Isaiah 26³; the prophet also exemplified the perfect peace of mind of those who put their trust in God. Prosperity of any sort begins when the mind is at peace, then the brain will think out facts to work with, which will eventually lead to the prosperity of every aspect of an individual's life.

> *"You will keep in perfect peace him whose mind is steadfast because he trusts in you."*

Physical Prosperity

Physical prosperity talks about the well-being of the health of an individual. There are people who are spiritually strong, financially stable and mentally sound, but weak in health. God's gift does not add sorrow at all. Total prosperity is an all-around prosperity, which includes your health. I knew a wealthy man, who was always in the hospital every month, for treatment. People envied the money aspect of his life, but nobody wanted to accept his deteriorating health condition. People admired his spiritual and financial prosperity, but nobody admired his consistent hospitalization. Such a man is wealthy materially but physically poor. We have also seen people who are well to do but are poor in the soul. Such is an incomplete prosperity.

3 John 2, has this to say:

> *"Beloved, I wish above all things that thou mayest prosper and be in health, even as thy soul prospereth."*

The combination of the action words shows their importance and highlights that the prosperity of our souls should be in direct proportion to our general prosperity and the prosperity of our health. From this scripture, it is important to note that your soul's prosperity is not complete without your health prospering. The accepted scriptural prosperity is the holistic prosperity, where; the financial, mental, spiritual and physical prosperity are present and complete. It is at this point that one can talk about total prosperity. In Isaiah 53^{4-5}, Prophet Isaiah calls to mind how the Lord has taken over our infirmities and have loosed us from consistent bad health:

> *"Surely, He took up our infirmities and carried our sorrows, yet we consider Him stricken by God, smitten by Him, and afflicted. But he was pierced for our transgressions, He was cursed for our iniquities, the punishment that brought us peace was upon him, and by his wounds, we are healed."*

If you still carry your sorrows and infirmities, just know that you are on your own. The provision for your good health has been paid for by the divine innocent blood of Jesus to as many that have decided to hand over their infirmities and sorrows to Him. Labour no more, for the price has been paid. Your physical healing is part of your salvation package; change your style and discard your doubts and your present situation will undoubtedly receive a corresponding change. You were not born with sicknesses. Therefore, it is a possibility that you can live without sicknesses. However, you must learn how to relinquish things that are not meant for you over to God.

Financial Prosperity

This is where many people have misunderstood the scripture but sill they need money before they can accomplish almost anything in life, including, even buying the Bible used for preaching the gospel. Though some use the wrong approach to this issue; but money is essential. If there is anybody who needs financial prosperity, it is the child of God. There are lots of reasons why a child of God should be financially prosperous, and there are promises in the Bible to buttress this. Some of these have been pointed out earlier in this book, but I will try to highlight a few scriptures that support financial prosperity. Don't criticize it; if you do, you will only be pretending. For the Bible says, "money answers all things," including the cloth you are wearing now. If you criticize the wrong approach, I don't have any problem with that, but outright condemnation of money or its usefulness is not acceptable.

The following scriptures drive home our point - 3John2;

> *"Beloved, I wish above all things that thou mayest prosper and be in health, even as thy soul prospereth."*

The Doctrine of Prosperity

Malachi 3:10-11;

"Bring ye all the tithes into the storehouse, that there may be meat in my house, and prove me now herewith, saith the Lord of hosts, if I will not open you the windows of heaven, and pour you out a blessing, that there shall not be room enough to receive it. And I will rebuke the devourer for your sakes, and he shall not destroy the fruits of your ground; neither shall your vine cast her fruit before the time in the field, saith the Lord of hosts."

Luke 6:38;

"Give, and it shall be given unto you; good measure, pressed down and shaken together, and running over, shall men give into your bosom. For with the same measure that ye mete withal it shall be measured to you again."

2Corinthians 9:6-10:

"But I say, He who soweth sparingly shall also reap sparingly, and he who soweth bountifully shall also reap bountifully. Every man according as he purposeth in his heart, so let him give: not grudgingly, or of necessity: for God loves a cheerful giver. And God is able to make all grace abound towards you; that ye, always having all sufficiency in all things, may abound to every good work: (As it is written, He hath dispersed abroad: he that given to the poor: his righteousness remaineth forever.

Now, he that ministereth seed both minister bread for your food, and multiply your seed sown, and increase the fruit of your righteousness)".

Deuteronomy 28:1-14;

"And it shalt come to pass, if thou shalt hearken diligently unto the voice of the Lord thy God, to observe and to do all his commandments which I command thee this day, that the Lord thy God will set thee on high above all nations of the earth: And all these blessings shalt come upon thee, and overtake thee, if thou shalt hearken unto the voice of the Lord your God. Blessed shalt thou be in the city, and blessed shalt thou be in the field. Blessed shalt be the fruit of thy body, and the fruit of thy ground, and the fruit of thy cattle, the increase of thy kine, and the flocks of thy sheep. Blessed shalt be thy basket and thy store. Blessed shalt thou be when thou comes in, and blessed shalt thou be when thou goest out. The Lord shall cause thine enemies that rise up against thee to be smitten before thy face: they shall come out against thee one way, and flee before thee seven ways. The Lord shall command the blessings upon thee in thy storehouses, and in all that thou settest thine hand unto: and he shall bless thee in the land which the Lord thy God giveth thee. The Lord shall establish thee an holy people unto himself, as he hath sworn unto thee if thou shall keep the commandments of the Lord thy God, and walk in his

ways. And all people of the earth shall see that thou art called by the name of the Lord; and they shall be afraid of thee. And the Lord shall make thee plenteous in goods, in the fruit of thy body, and in the fruit of thy cattle, and in the fruit of thy ground, in the land which the Lord sware unto thy father to give thee. The Lord shall open unto thee his good treasure, the heaven to give the rain unto thy land in his season, and to bless all the work of thy hand: and thou shall lend unto many nations, and thou shalt not borrow. And the Lord shall make thee the head, and not the tail, and thou shalt be above only, and thou shalt not be beneath; if thou hearken unto the commandments of the Lord thy God, which I command thee this day, to observe and to do them: And thou shalt not go aside from any of the words which I command thee this day, to the right hand, or to the left hand, to go after other gods to observe them.

Total Prosperity

Reflection On Chapter 16

Personal Notes:

===== Guided Action Plan =====

The Doctrine of Prosperity

Continuation

Personal Notes:

Guided Action Plan

References

Abraham M. (1968); *Toward a Psychology of Being* 2nd ed. (New York: Van Nostrand)

Abraham, M. *(1971); The Farther Reaches of Human nature* (New York: Penguin)

Argyris, Chris (2000); *Flawed Advice and the Management Trap: How Managers can know when they are getting good advice and when they are not* (USA: Oxford University Press)

Akpakapan, E. B. (1998), *"Economics beyond Demand and Supply.* (Port Harcourt: Thompson & Thompson Ltd)

Billy, O. (2006). *Multiple Perspectives of Entrepreneurship.* (Cincinnati: Southwestern College Publishing)

Burns, T. & G. Stalker (1961); *The Management of Innovation.* (London: Tavistock)

BusinessDictionary.com

Butter Jr. J.K. (1986). "A Global view of Informal Organization." *Academy of Management Journal*, 51(3), 39-43.

Byine, R.M.J. (2005); *The Rational Imagination: How people create Alternatives to Reality.* (Cambridge: MA MIT Press)

Caine, M.C & F.P Mille (2002); *Strategic Entrepreneurship: Creating a new mindset.* (Oxford: Blackwell Publishers)

Colder, C.C & J.P. Tellis (2005); *Transitions to Competitive government: Speed, Consensus and Performance.* (New York: Albany* State University Press)

Covey, S.R (1999); *First Things first.* (UK: CPL Mackay, Chatham MES STD)

Covin, J.G. & D.P. Slevin (1989); "Strategic Management of Small firms in hostile and benign environments." *Strategic Management Journal, 10(1) 75-87*

Covin, J.G, & D.P. Slevin (1991). "A Conceptual Model of Entrepreneurship as firm behaviour." *Entrepreneurship, Theory and Practice, 16(1) 43-51.*

Crossan, C. (2002); "Strategic Awareness within the Top Management Team." *Strategic Management Journal, 2, 263-279.*

Daft, R. L. & S. Klick (2000); "A dual-Core Model of Organizational Innovation. *Academy of Management Review*, 21, 193-210.

Dale, J. (2002); Differentiate between training, education and development. *Personnel Journal.* 69(10), 44-58

Dayton Jr., H. L. (1979); *Your money: Frustration or freedom?* (Wheaton: Tyndale House Publishers).

Dayton Jr., H. L. (2016); *Your Money Counts.* (Houston, Tx. USA: Tyndale House Publishers, Inc.)

Dorling, K. L. (2002); *Successful-Manager's Handbook.* (New York, NY: DK Publishing Inc). 10014.

Drucker, P.F (2002); "They are not Employees. They are people." *Harvard Business Review*, February, 70-77.

Dutchin, M.S & Oakland (1999); *Making Government work: How entrepreneurial Executives turn bright ideas into real results.* (San Francisco: Jossy – Bass).

References

Earl, M.J & I.A. Scott (1999). "What is a Chief Knowledge officer?" *Sloan Management Review.* 40(2), 29-38.

Exell, Josephs, *Commentary on Proverbs 22:29;* "(New York: The Biblical illustrator, 1905-1909).

Fubara, B.A. (1985), *Business Management: Principles and Strategies.* (Ibadan, Nigeria: University Press Plc)

Gainesville, G.A. (2006); *Crown Financial Ministries,* Biblical Financial Study, *Small Group Student Manual.*

George, S. C. (1988); *The Richest Man in Babylon.* (USA: Penguin Books Ltd)

Grey C, & C. Garsten (2001); *Trust, Control and Post-Bureaucracy.* (Sage Publ).

Goleman, D. (1995); *Working with Emotional Intelligence.* (New York Times, A & C Black Amazon.com).

Heckscher C. & A. Donnellon (Eds.) (1994); *The Post-Bureaucratic Organization: New Perspectives on Organizational Change.* (New York: Sage Publications)

Henri, F. (1966); *Administration Industries Ile et generale* - purveyance organization Commandment, coordination-controle Paris Dunod.

Hoskisson, R. Hitt, M & R.D. Ireland (2004); *Strategic Leadership in Competing for Advantage.* (South Western: Thompson).

House, R. & P. Rodsakoff (1995); "Leadership effectiveness: Past perspectives and future directions for research." In: J. Greenberg, *Behaviour in Organizations* (10th Ed.) (Pearson: Sage Publications)

Jacobides, M.G (2007); "The inherent limits of organizational structure and the unfulfilled role of hierarchy: Lessons from a near war." *Organization Science*, 18(3), 455-477.

Johnson, S.P. (2006). "Measuring organizational effectiveness in institutions of higher education." *Administrative Science Quarterly* 23(4), 604-632.

Kirkpatrick, S. & E. Locke. (1991); "Leadership: Do traits matter?" *Academy of Management.* 5(2).

Larrig, E. J. (2003); "Managerial type determination and its role in the development of an entrepreneurial quotient (EQ) Instrument." *International Journal of value-Based management.* 5, 17-37.

Millane, J. (2002); "The Mission Statement is a Strategic Tool when used properly in management decision." London:, 40(516).

Mohr, L.B (1982); *Explaining organizational Behaviour: The limits and possibilities of Theory and Research.* (New York: Jossey-Base Publishers).

O'keefe, E. J. (2006); *Biblical Economics.* (West Cliff Pres, Amarillo Tx 79105, www.managementguru.net) .

Oparaojiaku, C.C. (2002); *Anointing for Creativity.* (Lagos, Nigeria: Real Value Trust Publishers).

Oparaojiaku, C.C. (2003); *The Mystery and Ministry of Faith.* (Lagos, Nigeria: Rehoboth Publishing)

Oparaojiaku, C.C. (2012); "Post-oil subsidy removal: Principles of National Transformation", Paper presented at the Niger Delta Christian Leaders Forum Schedule Ministers Awareness Conference (Unpublished)

References

Oparaojiaku, C.C. (2013); "Managing and Preparing for Your Future via Your Present Finance", Paper presented at the Clergy and Wives Retreat, Diocese of Mbaise. (Unpublished)

Oparaojiaku, C. C. (2007); "Faithful Steward", Paper presented at the Retreat for Diocesan Clerks Association, Diocese of Niger Delta North (Unpublished)

Oparaojiaku, C. C. (2014); "The Greatest Among You Shall Be Your Servant", Paper presented at the Clergy and Wives Retreat, Dioceses of Awka and Esan. (Unpublished).

Oparaojiaku, C. C. (2013); "GIVING", Paper presented at the Diocesan Synod of Niger Delta (Unpublished)

Oparaojiaku, C. C. (2012); "Who Is a Christian Minister?", Paper presented at the Clergy and Wives Retreat, Diocese on the Niger (Unpublished)

Oparaojiaku, C. C. (2006); "Finance and Budgeting in the Family", Paper presented at the Family Management Outreach, Chapel of Redemption, Rivers State University of Science and technology, Nkpolu, Port Harcourt (Unpublished)

Oparaojiaku, C. C., (2011); "Jesus Cursed the Tree", Paper presented during Holy Week Meditation, Cathedral Church of St. Peter, Umuokanne, Ohaji (Unpublished)

Oparaojiaku, C. C; (2015); "Personal Financial Management", Paper presented at 2015 DIVCCON, at the National Ecumenical Christian Centre, Abuja

Oparaojiaku, C. C, (2015); "Beyond Active Service", Paper presented at the 2015 Clergy Conference, Province of East of Niger.

Pugh, D.S. (Ed.) (1990). *Organization Theory: Selected readings*. (Harmondsworth: Penguin Books)

Quinn, F. (2001); *Entrepreneurial learning.* (Eaglewood Cliffs, N.J: Prentice Hall)

Raymond E. M & C.S. Charles (1992); *Causes of failure in Network Organizations. Management Review*, Summer

Robbins, S.F. & T.A. Judge (2007); *Organizational Behaviour.* (12th Ed.). Pearson Education Inc.

Robbins, S., Judge, T. & T. Campbell (2010); *Organizational behaviour.* Pearson Education Inc.

Robert, J. (2014); *Mind Matters: Applying Emotional Intelligence for personal and professional success.* Create space Independent Publishing Platform.

Rowe, W.G (2001); "Creating wealth in organizations: The role of strategic leadership." *Academy of Management Review*, 15(1).

Simmons, C. (2007). "Falling off the Apple Cart." *Business Strategy Review*, Autumn, 34-38.

Stephen R. C. (1989); *The 7 habits of highly effective people.* (New York: Simon and Schuster).

Steve Elwart, *Biblical Principles of Economics* (**www.tutorialsport.com**)

Teece, D.J, Pisano, G. & A. Shuen (1997); "Dynamic capabilities and strategic management." *Strategic Management Journal*, 18, 509-533.

Teece, D.J (2000); "Strategies for managing knowledge assets: The role of firm structure and industrial context. *Long Range Planning*, 33, 35-54.

References

Thompson, A., Strickland, A. & J. Gamble (2007); *Corporate culture and leadership; Crafting and executing strategy: Concepts and cases* (15th edition). (New York: McGraw Hill).

Tracy, B. (2002); *The 100 absolutely unbreakable laws of business success*. (Benin, Nigeria: Joint Heirs Publications Nigeria Ltd)

Trove.nla.gov.au

Various versions of the Bible,

Walter, A. H. (1977); *Thoughts from the Diary of a Desperate Man*, (Washington Christian Literature Crusade).

Weber, M. (1948); *From Maxber: Essays in Sociology, translated, edited and with an introduction by H.H. Gerth and C. W. Mills* (London: Routledge and Kagan Paul).

Williams, J (n.d); *Every Successful Management Principle is based on Biblical Truths or Principles.* (New York: McGraw Hill).

Wikipedia

www.managementguru.net

www.emeraldinsight.com

www.cpaireland

www.semanticscholar.org

www.shmoop.com

www.sigmundfreud.net

www.researchgate.net

www.amazon.com.interpretaion

www.goodreads.com

www.tutorialsport.com

www.toughnickel.com.business

www.abebooks.com

www.tyndale.com

www.etsy.com

www.sites.google.com

www.affirmativeactionwax.com

www.slideshare.net

www.printerest.com

www.amazon.com

www.linedin.com

www.eig.2.com

www.ingramcontent.com/pod-product-compliance
Lightning Source LLC
Chambersburg PA
CBHW031131160426
43193CB00008B/100